The Orient express

Arthur Moore

Nabu Public Domain Reprints:

You are holding a reproduction of an original work published before 1923 that is in the public domain in the United States of America, and possibly other countries. You may freely copy and distribute this work as no entity (individual or corporate) has a copyright on the body of the work. This book may contain prior copyright references, and library stamps (as most of these works were scanned from library copies). These have been scanned and retained as part of the historical artifact.

This book may have occasional imperfections such as missing or blurred pages, poor pictures, errant marks, etc. that were either part of the original artifact, or were introduced by the scanning process. We believe this work is culturally important, and despite the imperfections, have elected to bring it back into print as part of our continuing commitment to the preservation of printed works worldwide. We appreciate your understanding of the imperfections in the preservation process, and hope you enjoy this valuable book.

THE ORIENT EXPRESS

BY THE SAME AUTHOR (ANTRIM ORIEL)

"THE MIRACLE"

PRESS OPINIONS

". . . Mr. Antrim Oriel is to be warmly congratulated upon a début of a very striking and distinguished order. . . . Mr. Balfour is certainly there ; so, too, is Sir Edward Grey. . . . Its value lies in its vivid and obviously sincere picture of a certain side of modern European politics, and in the suggestion of great and pressing human problems which it presents to the imagination. It is a book of unusual power and earnestness, and it ought to make **a genuine sensation** at the present very timely moment of its publication."—*Daily Telegraph.*

"A shrewd guess at the future. . . . Vigorous battle scenes. . . . He is, in fact, a highly capable writer."—*The Times.*

"Politics, and especially foreign affairs, are handled with a skill and knowledge which contrast favourably with the amateurish methods of the ordinary novelist."—*Manchester Guardian.*

"It is a very brilliant picture of modern political life."—*Daily News.*

"A very up-to-date novel. . . . The girl who plays heroine . . . is a fine creature."—*The Observer.*

". . . Interesting in itself, as a story of enthusiasms and love. It is deeply suggestive as a political and military study."—*Morning Leader.*

"Recalls Disraeli. . . . Some of the author's epigrams are of excellent Disraelian flavour."—*Glasgow Evening Times.*

"A delightfully fresh, witty, and in many respects enlightening book. A perennial fascination attaches to the novel, whose chief characters are the leading statesmen of our time, and in 'The Miracle' they are easily recognisable, drawn with a light, impartial, but assured touch. . . . Mr. Oriel contrives to make his conversations between Ministers and Ambassadors convincing as well as witty. . . . A love affair, delicately handled, supplies an artistic second *motif* to the tale. . . . Mr. Seton Merriman, himself a past-master of the diplomatic story, would have recognised a formidable rival in Mr. Oriel."—*Glasgow Herald.*

"All the glamour of an exciting romance."—*Evening Standard.*

"So brilliantly written that one wishes there was a great deal more."—*Punch.*

PRICE SIX SHILLINGS
at All Libraries and Bookshops, or from
CONSTABLE & CO. LTD., 10 Orange St., Leicester Square, W.C.

THE ORIENT EXPRESS

BY
ARTHUR MOORE, F.R.G.S.

LONDON
CONSTABLE & COMPANY LTD.
1914

TO
LAURENCE CARY SHUTTLEWORTH

PREFACE

Once at Budapest, while I waited for the train, I turned in to a music-hall to pass the time. It was an ordinary music-hall, with the ordinary show that one may see from one end of the world to the other, mixed with the common stock of *cafés chantants* and the other ingredients of mechanical mirth familiar to Leicester Square and Montmartre. It was civilization as it strikes the unbiassed Oriental, for any one who knows his habits will tell you that, whether he be Young Turk or old Chinee, London is for him inseparably bound up with Leicester Square And presently, in the frock-coat that also stands in the East for civilization, there appeared on the stage a rather worse than ordinary imitator He made faces and noises, which he invited a credulous audience to believe resembled other faces and noises, and finally it seemed that he addressed himself to me. For, looking directly at me where I leant from the promenade over the balustrade, he gave an imitation of the arrival of the train, which was creeping to me over the great plain of Hungary through the blackness of the night. Blowing out his cheeks, whistling and rattling, he brought it droning through tunnels and crashing over bridges, till with a final snort it stopped in Budapest. Whereupon he announced: "Orient Express!" and

PREFACE

received his meed of applause, while I paid him the more sincere compliment of looking at my watch to see how much he had shortened the interval before the real coming of the train.

Odd things happen to one in the common way of living, but to me they have the misfortune to appear at the time quite ordinary and natural. Memory adjusts them differently and picks out some for interest to oneself. Others are handed over to oblivion, and some of these one regrets to lose. Others again live in the memory for no apparent reason, being but trifles of no importance. And so it is that the frock-coated entertainer sometimes visits me. I hear the familiar rattle of the Orient Express and see his distended cheeks. I see also the red upholstery of the international sleeping-car, which has carried me eastwards in the past, and will, I trust, carry me in the future.

With the help of my friend in the frock-coat, I can at least in sundry intervals catch the train of memory and, if I have the mind to do so, transport myself without expense to such scenes as are unforgotten. But that is no excuse for asking you to get aboard the car with me and share in my reflections. It is open to you, in a world overcrowded with interesting things to read, to go a thousand journeys of the imagination in more fascinating company. If the East is your fancy, you may board the Orient Express with scores of better guides than I am, and with these in any case I would have you not omit to travel. So, when I reflect on the fact that whereas I and my fancy go free, my publisher will insist on your paying a small sum for your ticket, I am bound to confess that I can feel no surprise if you refuse to journey with me. I

PREFACE

am cursed occasionally with a cross-bench mind, and I cannot help sympathizing with your point of view.

But I shall go further—now that I am in the confessional—and tell you that while it is pain to me to write, because I dislike the effort, it grieves me also for another reason. My adventures are my own, and such impressions as I retain of an experience which has not lacked change, belong to me. To formulate these impressions, to give them away to other people, seems to me not only to expose me to the charge of egotism, but to leave me appreciably the poorer. That is probably an unreasonable feeling, and perhaps it is not a common one, but I am unable to resist it. It is easy to prove verbally that I lose nothing, and that everything is as much mine as it was before; more so, because I may clarify my impressions by recording them. But the fact remains that I feel those impressions weakened and dissipated by sharing them. Something intimate and personal is gone.

This is fine talk, you will say, for a journalist, whose trade is in print and publicity. Has he not already staled all his impressions on paper, and why should he seek to serve us up this sentimental sauce with the cold hash of his forgotten columns? To which my only reply is that a poor man cannot afford to travel for years in the East and keep his impressions to himself. He must find an excuse for his wanderings, and he must find some one benevolent enough to pay his expenses. For me the solution has generally been in journalism, which has the added advantage that it sometimes brings experiences which a millionaire might seek in vain. But the condition of having experiences is that you must be willing to part with

PREFACE

them, and that is what makes me suspect that I am unsuited for my profession. I like the fun, but I hate writing about it.

There are some things here set out, then, of which it has been a small sacrifice to write, even though many of them have been told before. Most of them were witnessed in the service of *The Times* in Persia and in Turkey, and a special acknowledgment must be made to my editor for his kind permission to make use of many articles contributed to its columns. For a similar courtesy I have to thank the editors of *The Contemporary Review* and *The Edinburgh Review*. The editors of *The Daily Chronicle* and *The Manchester Guardian* have also kindly allowed me to use some articles of an earlier date, written in Macedonia.

It is true, therefore, that with some of these pictures I have parted before. But, as we are often told, the public memory is short. If a portion of the public read the articles in its newspapers, it soon forgot them, so that in time I quietly took possession of them again, and was in some degree comforted. But a book, even if nobody reads it, is somehow a more solemn affair, and until the time comes when my publisher assures me that nobody has read it, I shall feel that I have lost my personal property. You will understand that there is much in this book that I part with gladly. There are some imaginary pictures, and the more you like them, the better you will please me. What Cyrus told me when I visited his tomb, and what Alexander talked about at Persepolis—these I do not grudge you. There is also a good deal of Balkan and Persian politics, to which you are welcome. No one has any

PREFACE

pangs at parting with a political impression, and all mine are at your service.

But the other things, the things mine eyes have seen, the Turkey that I knew in the dark days of Abdul Hamid, the unforgettable dawn of the Revolution, the nights and days in the unknown heart of Albania, in the Mat country north of Dibra, where no living European had ever travelled, the Turkey of the Balkan War, the story of the siege of Tabriz, the death of Arshad-ed-Dowleh, the memories of Kashan and Kumisha and of a ride of a thousand miles from Tehran to the Persian Gulf, these are things that in any case I have no art to write so as to make them to you what they have become to me. Just ordinary days most of them seemed at the time, but they have worn well. To me, looking back on nine years of wandering, they seem now, though not at all the things that I pursued, the best things that I gained; the little harvest of a sometimes misspent youth.

There is, however, this consolation open to me when parting with my experiences, that though I shall honestly try to part with my impressions, you cannot get them all. Something one must keep for luck; and some things one can never tell. And there is another reason which consoles me. A right-minded person ought to be more concerned with the future than with the past. So that I await fresh journeys, which I shall take without you. One fine morning very soon I shall dismiss the frock-coated *farceur* of Budapest, walk down Bond Street into Piccadilly, and buy at Cook's a real ticket—for an old road or a new one, but with a coupon for adventures attached. Wonderful things Cook sells across the counter sometimes.

PREFACE

Meantime, I shall with pen and paper make these journeys. They are but loose sallies; sorties by an eastern express from the city of Everyday. There is no great close connection in these pages, nor are they all adventure by any means. There is something of history and something of politics, so be warned in time, for I shall make no later apology for my mixture.

The engine has finished shunting. The fellow in the frock-coat has stopped steaming, and is blowing an ear-piercing whistle. The Orient Express is about to start. But the door is still open, and there is time for you to jump out. There will be no bones broken on the platform, and, though sincerely sorry to lose you, I shall have the carriage to myself.

ARTHUR MOORE.

CONTENTS

CHAP.		PAGE
	PREFACE	v
I	THE SIEGE OF TABRIZ	1
II	THE LAST SORTIE	14
III	THE DEATH OF ARSHAD-ED-DOWLEH	28
IV	PHILOSOPHY IN ADVERSITY	37
V	SOHRAB ON GENIUS	44
VI	SOME MARCHING MEMORIES	52
VII	FROM TEHRAN TO KASHAN	68
VIII	FROM KASHAN TO ISFAHAN	78
IX	BRITISH INTERESTS AT ISFAHAN	86
X	A NIGHT ADVENTURE AT KUMISHA	91
XI	AT THE TOMB OF CYRUS	101
XII	A TALK WITH ALEXANDER THE GREAT	110
XIII	THE PROBLEM OF SHIRAZ	120
XIV	THE TRIBES AND THE ROADS	127
XV	BRITISH INTERESTS IN SOUTHERN PERSIA	133
XVI	THE DECAY OF PERSIA	145
XVII	THE VALUE OF THE MEJLISS	153
XVIII	A LOOK BEFORE AND AFTER	162
XIX	THE DARK AGES IN MACEDONIA	170
XX	THE MILLENNIUM	184
XXI	THE YOUNG TURKS	197

CONTENTS

CHAP.		PAGE
XXII	HILMI PASHA	210
XXIII	THE HEART OF ALBANIA	219
XXIV	THE MIRDITE CLAN	238
XXV	THE SONS OF THE EAGLE	252
XXVI	ATHENS REVISITED	264
XXVII	WHO CAUSED THE TURKISH DISASTERS?	269
XXVIII	SIC VOS NON VOBIS	283
XXIX	A LITTLE MAGIC	291

THE ORIENT EXPRESS

*"The Stars are setting and the Caravan
Starts for the Dawn of Nothing—Oh, make haste!"*
            Omar Khayyam (Fitzgerald).

CHAPTER I

THE SIEGE OF TABRIZ

LET us go first to the Middle East. The Near East was a first love, so let us keep it in its proper place,—as something to which to return.

With the exception of six miles of toy line between Tehran and Shah Abdul Azim, there are no railways in Persia, which is the reason why they are so much discussed at present. But this Orient Express will take you there, for its way is like the definition of the Equator—an imaginary line running round the earth.

"The Dawn of Nothing" is a hard phrase to apply to the beginnings of the Persian Constitution. In the long-run I trust that its cynicism will prove far from the truth, but in the short run of eight years the high hopes that some held have suffered sad shipwreck. The Constitution was like that ill-starred ship—

"Built in the eclipse and rigged with curses dark,"

—which carried Lycidas to his doom. In January 1906 Muzaffar-ed-Din Shah unwillingly granted it to his disloyal subjects. Parliament, known in those parts

THE ORIENT EXPRESS

as the Mejliss, met on October 7 of the same year, and the unhappy author of its being died soon afterwards. He was succeeded by Mohammed Ali, who swore loyalty to the Constitution, but bore it so little love that in June 1908 he bombarded the Parliament House and abolished the Assembly. Tehran was cowed, but insurrection broke out in Tabriz. Throughout the summer there was street fighting between the Royalists and the Nationalists, or Constitutionalists, who held different quarters of the town. Finally, late in autumn, the Royalists were expelled, and the Nationalists held Tabriz against the Shah. Slowly he got his little forces together, and prepared to lay siege to the town where he had spent his youth, and which he had early learned to hate, even as it hated him.

If the siege of Tabriz cannot lay claim to being one of the most terrible in history, it was certainly one of the oddest. I suspect that in this one town in these long-drawn hours of trouble one may see, as in a mirror, the baffling problem of modern Persia, a problem attractive partly because of the Persians, partly also because of its very hopelessness, or seeming hopelessness. The Persians are blest with the happiest and most delightful sense of humour. It is fortunate that there is always laughter in Persia, for if the laughter stopped there would be room for tears.

It was in January 1909, half dead with cold and more than half blind with snow, that I fell into Tabriz a fortnight before the roads were shut. After that I shared the hopes and fortunes of the town; and strange fare it proved. Theoretically the investment may be dated from February 4. The last ordinary European

THE SIEGE OF TABRIZ

post got in by the Julfa road on the 3rd. The Basminch and Sardarut roads were opened again, by the Shah's orders, when he learnt of Russia's intention to open the Julfa road, on April 28, and the town was revictualled. The siege, therefore, lasted eighty-four days on a strict showing. In fact it lasted a hundred, as, though the posts were running till February, the Julfa road was unsafe for caravans some time before, and provisions ceased to enter the town in the middle of January.

After the expulsion of the militant Royalists in the previous autumn, Tabriz was in the hands of the Constitutionalist party. Their resources were considerable. The population is always estimated by Persians as 300,000. There is no census, but there is said to be a register showing 60,000 inhabited houses; and if this be so, the average rough European conjecture of 200,000 may be under the mark. Including their own smuggled arms, the defenders had at their disposal 20,000 rifles, an adequate supply of ammunition, three mountain-guns, and some old muzzle-loading cannon, as well as mortars. The great majority of the rifles and all their bayonets remained undisturbed in the Government arsenal. The nominal fighting force at the disposal of Sattar Khan and Bakir Khan, the two Constitutionalist leaders, was less than 2,000. On one occasion there was a great rally, when a more determined attack than usual was made on the town, and a larger number displayed themselves at the barricades with arms, but to call them a fighting force would be to strain language. They were there *pour encourager les autres*, but they did not intend to get shot, like Admiral Byng, in the performance of this function.

THE ORIENT EXPRESS

The total strength of the three small forces which shut up possibly 250,000 people for three months will never be known, but I do not think it can ever have exceeded 6,000 men. But if the nominal combatants were 2,000 inside and 6,000 outside, the real situation was much more extraordinary. For all purposes except those of noise and the possible damage which may be done by stray bullets, there were not more than 100 men in each of the three besieging camps who mattered; amongst the besieged there were not 250. The warlike resources of the Persian Empire may be gauged from the fact that, while the Shah rightly regarded the subjugation of Tabriz as vital to his own interests, he was only able to send a little over 2,000 so-called regular troops against it. Of these only 400 Cossacks, who owed their training and discipline to Russian officers, were worthy of the name. But the main force consisted, not of soldiers, but of savage tribesmen—Kurds, Karadaghlis, and Makulis—bloodthirsty brigands who, by terrorizing villages and wayfarers from time immemorial, have gained a reputation for fierceness, which should not be mistaken for a reputation for bravery. They possess the common vices of cowards—treachery and cruelty; but of courage they are for the most part totally devoid. They were out for loot, with the minimum of risk. To starve Tabriz and then to pillage it was the dazzling prospect which kept them in their camps.

The people of Azarbeijan, and particularly the Tabrizis, have a great reputation for valour; throughout the rest of Persia and at Tehran a Tabrizi is spoken of with almost bated breath. While this gives one furiously to think what the rest of Persia must be

THE SIEGE OF TABRIZ

like, it is beyond doubt that the townsmen made a better show than their besiegers. They were neither professional soldiers nor belligerent tribesmen accustomed to arms, but just townsfolk, citizens of all grades, who had taken up arms in defence of the Constitution. They repulsed every attack upon the town, and I am quite convinced that it would never have been taken by assault. But it was essentially a contest between two sets of inefficients and incapables, each of which feared the other. The town covers a vast extent, as it is full of rectangular gardens and courtyards. The fighting was therefore always remote from the centre, but the flat roofs of the houses used to be covered with people endeavouring, without any prospect of success, to discover what was happening. Crowds thronged the roads leading to the barricades, but they, too, were dependent on the reports which the combatants brought in, and nowhere does rumour speak more false than in Persia. It was, in fact, impossible for the average citizen, or for the European who was dependent on the gossip of the bazaar, to be sure of the truth of anything. Often, after being present at an action from dawn till sunset, I was greeted on my return with the most astonishing tales of slaughter and adventure, many of which solemnly appeared in European journals. The story of my own end was twice recounted to me with details as picturesque as they were harrowing, and I was welcomed as one returned from the dead. The Royalist camps were on one occasion illuminated in honour of my supposed happy dispatch.

These camps were originally at Basminch, twelve miles south-east of Tabriz, on the road to Tehran; at

THE ORIENT EXPRESS

Sardarut, six miles on the southern road to Maraga; and at Alvar, eight miles from Tabriz, on the Julfa, or Russian, road. Prince Ain-ed-Dowleh remained at Basminch throughout the siege, but in the first week of March the bulk of the Basminch force took up a new position at Barinch, on the outskirts of Tabriz. No preparations had been made to defend any of these positions, and the besiegers were allowed to occupy them without a blow being struck. Of the three Royalist generals Samad Khan alone showed any resolution or any spirit in attack. Only once, and as late as April, did Rahim Khan take the offensive. He held lawless sway on the Julfa road, and lay in wait for such wayfaring men and fools as erred therein. His chief amusement was to strip them naked and to turn them adrift in the snow, which covers the country until mid-March. Two European merchants, who were rash enough to attempt to escape from Tabriz, succeeded indeed, but arrived in Julfa dressed only in their goloshes, their lives having been spared at the intervention of their driver. The Russian merchants in particular suffered heavily from Rahim Khan's raids, but all Europeans felt his hand, and those who had no merchandise lost their letters and their parcels. Even when the officials of the Russian Consulate-General passed with their escort, this worthy Musulman levied toll from them in the shape of bottles of wine and brandy, while to the French nurse of one of the Russian ladies he held out the dazzling prospect that he would cover her with jewels if she would remain and share his fortunes. After the coming of the Russian army, he fled to Karadagh, his native stronghold, with three hundred camel loads of loot. The

THE SIEGE OF TABRIZ

Russians might easily have arrested him, and would have had plenty of justification for doing so, but he was allowed to go free and make trouble at a later day.

Prince Ain-ed-Dowleh remained absolutely inactive until March, when the advance was made to Barinch. From that time desultory bombardments were frequent, but the damage done was insignificant. A new gun, whose approach had been advertised for weeks, arrived from Tehran in April. With this the besiegers succeeded in dropping shells in the centre of the town, and I remember one occasion when, on a peaceful afternoon and out of a clear sky, shells suddenly began to fall right in the middle of the parade-ground where three hundred and fifty men were drilling. It was the only time when I saw any approach to smart range-finding, the distance being more than three miles, and the position of the parade-ground probably judged by a neighbouring turret which caught the sun. But this piece of work had the kind of sequel which is common in Persia, for most of the shells did not burst. The new gun did, however, on other occasions destroy some houses, and wounded, amongst others, Bakir Khan. Not once was the town attacked on all three sides simultaneously, though this would have immensely increased the difficulties of defence. There was, in fact, not the slightest co-operation or co-ordination, and when Samad Khan attacked the guns in Barinch were generally silent. Twice only, on February 25 and March 5, was Tabriz attacked on two sides. These were two of the heaviest engagements, and at both the main attack came from Samad Khan, whose losses were severe. The fight on March 5, when the Kurds got into the Hookmabad quarter and looted it, was the last of a series of what must be called, if we consider the nature of Persian warfare, very determined attacks. The rest of the fighting originated with the defence. Its chief incidents were Sattar Khan's attack on Alvar on February 21; a night sortie on March 21, the Persian New Year; an attack in force upon Barinch on March 24; upon Karamelik on March 28 and 29; and the final attack upon Karamelik on April 20. Sniping at the barricades was, of course, a daily incident throughout the siege.

It will be sufficient to cite two instances of fighting, in different directions, to illustrate the different nature of the ground and the small number of serious combatants in each case. North-west, beyond the bridge over the Aji Chai which guards the entrance to the town, the Julfa road runs through flat and open country, a wide valley at the foot of the low red hills which flank Tabriz upon the north. Eight miles out lie the two villages of Alvar, east and west, the former full upon the road, the latter half-a-mile away from it. With some five hundred horsemen, Sattar Khan rode out on February 21, his men disposed neither right nor left, but straight behind him, all along the narrow road. The Karadaghlis on his approach promptly began to leave East Alvar and to head for the western village away from the road. Seeing this, Sattar Khan rode straight at East Alvar. Rahim Khan from his main position in West Alvar immediately opened fire, and the high embanked road—which was built by the Russians to carry a railway—was swept with bullets. Dropping down to the further side of the embankment, Sattar Khan held on under its

THE SIEGE OF TABRIZ

cover, followed by precisely seventeen men, the rest of the five hundred staying at a safe distance. Three were killed in the last four hundred yards, and there arrived in Alvar just fourteen men, of whom three were wounded. I also reached the village, but at that time I was a non-combatant, as it was not till the end of March that I joined the fighting force. Later, some eighty men, leaving their horses in the rear, approached close up, and posting themselves along the embankmen, which served as a *sangar*, returned the fire of West Alvar. The little force in East Alvar drove out the remaining Royalists, and held the village fourteen hours. The firing ceased, as usual, at nightfall, and in the dark Sattar Khan returned safely to Tabriz. When it was suggested to him that his party might easily be annihilated, and that as his followers had already left the road, he ought certainly to find himself cut off, he replied with a certainty which proved justified, "They will never think of that. It isn't the custom here to fight after sundown."

The general lack of courage made the achievements of a few more noteworthy, and it was at Alvar that I saw one of those unsatisfying things which are so much more common in fighting than the fine successful things; I mean something which came very near being fine and successful, but failed. A horseman undertook to carry the Constitutionalist flag into Alvar, that the little force inside might hoist it, a perhaps unnecessary performance, but one which appeals to the theatrical instinct of the East. With the flag shooting upright from the pommel of his saddle and its folds flying out behind him in the breeze, he galloped at a furious pace full in view of the enemy along the hard highway. A

THE ORIENT EXPRESS

perfect blizzard of bullets flew around him. The flag was riddled, and I looked to see him fall, or plunge to the cover of the bank. Still he held on faster and faster; two, three and four hundred yards were passed, and it seemed as though he might reach Alvar. But at a distance of one hundred and fifty yards from the village, where the most advanced post of those who had failed to come in was firing on the enemy, the cavalier stopped his course and joined them. He had one flesh wound, and had made a fine ride, but not to a finish. The flag never reached Alvar.

The Royalist camp at Barinch lay in a valley before the village, and between it and Tabriz the hills made a horseshoe, the sides of which pointed towards the city. The slopes were open but steep, and often twisted into folds and gullies. Along the range of hills that formed the curve of the shoe the besiegers set their *sangars* and guns. At one time also they ran down the right arm, but they lost so many men in this position that they quickly abandoned it. Bakir Khan, who had entire command of the defence on that side, chiefly because of the accident that his house was situated in the Khiaban quarter, whereas Sattar Khan lived in Amrakiz near the Aji Chai bridge and the Julfa road, thereupon proceeded to turn this right arm into a Constitutionalist *sangar*. Along the top of the steep and narrow ridge a winding trench was dug, which ran for a quarter of a mile and came to an abrupt stop some two hundred yards from a precipitous hill which formed the turning-point of the curve and a principal outpost of the enemy. On March 24, Tabriz mustered something like two thousand men for an attack on Barinch. It was a picturesque and won-

THE SIEGE OF TABRIZ

derful crowd, Seyyids and Mullahs, Mujtehids and venerable members of the Anjuman, with wide flowing robes and turbans, green, blue, or white, according to their holy privilege. Two guns thundered fitfully and ineffectually well in the rear, and were never once advanced during the day. Round these a vast concourse of unarmed citizens and loiterers gathered, and at frequent intervals rent the skies with the piercing cry, "Yah Ali, Yah Ali!" chanted by all in unison, in the twofold hope of frightening the enemy by much noise and convincing them that the besiegers were not Babis, as slanderously reported, but good Musulmans like themselves. Here, as everywhere, the *samovars* were kept going, and tea with Turkish delight and other sweetmeats were peddled to a patient crowd, which was famishing for lack of bread. Once the unexpected happened and a shell fell into the supposed security, killing three non-combatants on the spot, as well as wounding several and producing a hurried change of place. The gun is an extraordinary fetish in Persia. To lose men, or horses, or rifles is bad, but to allow a gun to fall into the enemy's hands is disgrace. Therefore, the gun must be kept well in the rear, so that however hasty the flight of those in front, it shall not be endangered. It must never be advanced on the pretext of any success in front. It must, in fact, be in general a quite useless source of anxiety and pride, comparable only to the "parlour" of the English artisan, a family glory displayed at funerals and feasts.

The centre of the horseshoe was left alone. A handful of about forty men occupied all day a position on the right, that is on the left arm of the shoe, which

THE ORIENT EXPRESS

opened towards the town. Outside the right arm in the deep valley between it and the red hills of the north, Sattar Khan, with three hundred horsemen, was posted to prevent the main force being outflanked. This main force occupied the trenches on the right arm, and from dawn till dark fired rounds innumerable at the barricades along the curve. The trenches were full, but the majority of those in front showed no inclination to move forward, nor was any pressure noticeable from behind. When I reached the end of the trench I found that some sixty had pressed on another hundred yards, and, huddled together in such cover as the hill afforded, were threatening the enemy's strong barricade on top. Further still a party of twenty-one had reached a pit half-way up and were not more than forty yards from the goal. I reached this advance party about noon, and found that it consisted of fourteen Persians and seven Caucasians, while in addition two Persians had already been killed and one wounded and one Caucasian had been wounded. For an hour and a half we remained in this position, losing two more men. Not a man from the large force in the trenches joined us. One by one, a few, perhaps a dozen, ran the gauntlet as far as the second advance party at the foot of the hill, but none came further, nor did this group advance. From a position in the middle of the trench the Armenians fired bombs over our heads, dropping them behind the *sangar* above us. At half-past one, in the middle of a more furious bombardment than usual, the little party rushed the hill, the enemy bolted precipitately to a second line of barricades at a distance of three hundred yards, and amidst ecstatic and ear-

THE SIEGE OF TABRIZ

splitting yells of "Yah Ali!" and a fusillade from everybody that sounded as if nothing ought to be left alive, we found ourselves in possession of the *sangar*. Five more men had been hit, leaving fourteen untouched out of the original twenty-four. Vigorous yells and signals to the party behind now produced some effect, and we were reinforced by some fifty men. There we stuck till sundown. Furious firing lasted all the time, and the bombs flew over our heads. The main body remained far behind in the trenches. Had it only come on, victory was easy and the siege might have been raised. Six more of the advance party were hit. A Georgian just in front of me in the rush to the hill blew his own head to pieces with a hand-grenade as he was about to throw it at the flying enemy, and I narrowly escaped a drenching as all the blood gushed out from his body toppling backwards. These were brave men; but it was odd that even the most cowardly took death and wounds with stoic indifference at the last. They were not ready to die and they took pains to live, but when the bullet came neither the victim nor those around him bemoaned the misfortune; a kind of degenerate fatalism. At sunset everybody retired on both sides. No one stayed to guard the hard-won hill, and next day this strong point of vital importance was quietly reoccupied by the Royalists and doubly fortified.

CHAPTER II

THE LAST SORTIE

By the end of March the town was in the last extremity of starvation. The despair and demoralization were so great that even the duty of manning the barricades seemed in danger of being neglected. It looked as though the Royalists might enter at any moment, and Europeans were in daily expectation of this end. In such a case Ain-ed-Dowleh would have been quite powerless to control either Samad Khan's Kurds or Rahim Khan's Karadaghli tribesmen, who had been repeatedly promised the loot of Tabriz in lieu of pay. A general massacre was only too reasonable a possibility, while the rights and privileges of Europeans stood scant chance of respect.

It was at this stage that Mr. Baskerville—a schoolmaster attached to the American Mission's high school—joined the town's fighting forces along with myself, Mr. Baskerville giving up his position in the school in order to do this. It is, I think, true to say that as a demonstration of sympathy with a town in evil plight on the part of two Europeans—an American is a "European" in Persia—our action produced an undoubted effect. There was an immediate rally to the barricades; the defence was once more put in order; and while the danger from starvation grew inevitably greater every day, with the slow imminence of a grim

THE LAST SORTIE

tragedy gathering force, the danger of capture by assault faded once more into the region of things at which to laugh. But stomach for an attack on Barinch from the right, the obvious place, seemed to be gone after the failure of the efforts in the fourth week of March, and two moonlight excursions of Mr. Baskerville and myself, in which we crawled into the Royalist lines and mapped their positions, went for nothing. It was only when we had definitely given up the possibility of any further attack, and after the Anjuman had invited the Consuls to act as intermediaries in making terms for them, that it was decided to make a final sortie against Karamelik, where food was stored. The Constitutionalist leaders were indeed in an unenviable plight. The famine-struck populace was at length showing its teeth. The bazaars were full of angry mutterings. The riflemen, who were still paid and fed, had long overawed the crowd, but hunger was giving it courage. The women, who had nothing to fear, and in Musulman countries have more than once shown themselves in such crises a terrible and irresistible power—which should be remembered when we talk of the complete subjection of women in the East—were openly rioting in the streets, and spat when they uttered the names of Sattar Khan, Bakir Khan, the Anjuman, and the *Meshruteh* (Constitution).

Negotiations so far had come to nothing. Every hour brought nearer the final rising in which the mob would rush the wealthy houses. A plan was already on foot to attack the Consulates and European houses, in order both to pillage and to bring on some intervention which might yet snatch the town from hunger and the clutches of the ravening tribesmen outside. It was decided, therefore, that an attack was imperative in order to tide over the hours till some result might come from the negotiations. Diplomacy had unfortunately worked too much in the dark, and though we knew that salvation was near at hand and that the British and Russian Legations at Tehran were now at the eleventh hour working furiously to bring the Shah to terms, and could safely be trusted to do more for the town than it could ever do for itself, it was, not unnaturally, impossible for Persians, who had themselves no information and had heard of these Anglo-Russian negotiations, hitherto fruitless, ever since January, to pin any kind of hope on such an unknown quantity. It was, in fact, now as impossible to prevent an attack as a week before it had been to procure one. It was, moreover, held to be necessary to carry out a plan—by way of a night surprise!—which had been attempted a week before, and had then fallen through because none of the promised arrangements had been made. The spy was a flourishing institution, whereas secrecy is in Persia almost unknown and impossible; and it was therefore obvious that the whole of this information must already be known in Samad Khan's camp. The whole strange story as to this last fight is too long to be told; but since Mr. Baskerville lost his life in it, it may be well to put some of the facts on record. He knew that it was unnecessary, and, given the nature of the material, not very hopeful. He took part in it because he was powerless to prevent it, and the authorities represented to him in the strongest possible manner that his absence would discourage everybody, and that the men in the corps actually

THE LAST SORTIE

under his command would probably also absent themselves.

The rendezvous was fixed for midnight. Somewhat to my surprise the whole of my three hundred and fifty men and of Mr. Baskerville's one hundred and fifty turned up at the rendezvous. The rest came more slowly, and hours passed before we moved on. It was arranged that Mr. Baskerville should attack on the right; the handful of Armenians, Georgians, and Caucasian Musulmans, with a Persian force, on the left; while my men took the centre. Sattar Khan was to give support all round with a force which was announced to be one thousand, but proved to be less than two hundred; and in point of fact this never came on at all, or got into action. When my command got close to the enemy's barricades at 4.30 a.m. it had dwindled from three hundred and fifty to twenty-seven. This was entirely to be expected. The system of natural selection worked always with admirable automatic precision, and this residuum of the more resolute cheerfully opened fire at 4.30, and almost immediately rushed the enemy's position. Mr. Baskerville's followers, who had sunk to nine, engaged on the right; while the Caucasians, bereft of their Persian comrades, joined in on the left, numbering some thirty. So little therefore do numbers matter, and such is the engaging inconsequence of war in Persia, that the whole attack on Karamelik, with its garrison of two thousand, was begun by less than seventy men. Mr. Baskerville was shot through the heart before six o'clock, while exposing himself in front in order to try to get the men to advance, and after his death, although later more of his men came up, the right

stuck fast. On the left and in the centre, for the kind of warfare, things went with astonishing and splendid go. Soon after six we rushed the enemy again. They bolted at once, and thus we gained a second garden's length. Some of the recreants plucked up heart, and supports kept dribbling up in daylight till we numbered about one hundred and fifty. Then one of the three promised mountain guns at last arrived, and for the first time in the siege was successively advanced along with each advance of the riflemen. The fear of cannon—considering how little damage is done with them in those parts—is perfectly unreasoning, and the gun also seemed to possess quite extraordinary powers of encouragement for our men. The morning sun was soon burning us with a fierce heat, but the fusillade never slackened on either side. Every one of Samad Khan's two thousand seemed to be blazing away incessantly from somewhere or other, and though they did us very little damage they produced enough noise, along with two twelve-pounders which bellowed away uselessly from Sattar Khan's base, to give the anxious inhabitants of the town the impression of a kind of final Armageddon. Again we tried a rush, and the men came on. A third garden was gained. Another rush—and a fourth garden. Still no more supports came up, and no more guns. The right had remained immovable all the time, and though a gun to help them was often promised and always coming, it never came. By noon hunger, sleeplessness, heat, and toil were telling heavily, and the men were dribbling away. The remnant rose to another rush, and now only one garden's length separated us from the village of

THE LAST SORTIE

Karamelik. It was the enemy's last line. But as had so often happened there were none to claim the final victory which was so easily possible. The stream of supports had long since failed, and the tide was ebbing the other way. Not a man came up to relieve the spent force of the night. It was impossible to get them to advance the last length of garden—some three hundred yards unusually bare of cover. And so, at three in the afternoon, the handful drew off, bringing the gun away safely and unpursued. For the Kurds had lost more heavily than on any previous occasion.

They buried Mr. Baskerville next day. The streets were black with people and his funeral was the greatest demonstration of the siege. The Anjuman, the mullahs, and the foreign consuls all formed part of the procession, and the hard-pressed town, full of divided counsels and sordid intrigues, united in common homage. Takeh Zadeh, the most famous speaker of the Persian Mejliss, after the Christian service in the Protestant Church, delivered an oration over his grave; so did the mullahs; so did the leaders of the Armenians and of the Georgians. Howard Baskerville, who was a very young man, had lived a fine life, and the dearest wish of his heart was to go back to America, become ordained, and return as a Christian missionary. The general verdict was that he had thrown away his life, but the conclusion is perhaps a hasty one. In Tehran they still sell his photograph in the street. His name at least is not forgotten in Persia, and there are many who feel his influence. The Persians have placed a white cross over his grave, and on it is written: "Greater love hath no man than this, that he lay down his life for his friends."

THE ORIENT EXPRESS

Enough has been said to show the nature and the limitations of the fighting on both sides. But it should be remembered that in the previous summer the Tabrizis showed considerable courage in defending their own homes, when the Royalists were in the town. Moreover, there was plenty of courage of quite another sort—the passive resistance and submissive patience of the Oriental. They could not fight, but they could starve. The terrible tortures of hunger were endured with a resignation which compelled admiration. In the last days the people were eating grass, and for weeks before the end the scenes outside the open bakeries, the number of which sank daily, were pitiful to witness. Statistics were impossible to obtain, but numbers died of starvation and in every street lay fearsome figures, all but naked, scarcely recognizable as human beings. The Europeans all possessed large stores, but these were brought very low, and though actual hunger never came to them their situation at the end was critical, as bread had given out. Eggs, milk, and even chickens could still be purchased, though at a price that put them far out of reach of the mass of the population, but the only beef was buffalo. The difficulties of European families were increased by the large number of servants kept in Persia, for whom food had to be found.

Tabriz was ultimately saved by the coming of the Russians. Their entry into the town was the direct cause of the opening of the roads, the dispersal of the disappointed armies of the Shah, the promulgation of the Constitution, and the appointment of a Constitutionalist Ministry. It saved Tabriz from a surrender

THE LAST SORTIE

which could not otherwise have been delayed for three days longer, and thereby it averted the complete collapse of the Constitutional movement.

I confess that I have no belief that, had Tabriz fallen, either Resht or the Bakhtiari at Isfahan would ever have taken the offensive against Tehran. It is much more probable that the Shah would have repeated the triumph won at Tabriz. He would slowly have got the same forces together round Isfahan and starved it into submission, while the country sank daily deeper into anarchy. The English and the Russians robbed him at the eleventh hour of what he naturally considered the legitimate fruits of victory. Tabriz was in his grasp, and it is common knowledge that the feud between himself and Tabriz is deep and old, and dates from the years when he lived in it as Valiahd, or Crown Prince. Prince Ain-ed-Dowleh himself told me that it had been decided to deprive it of all importance and to make Urumiah the capital of Azarbeijan. That the Shah was infuriated at the Russian action is therefore natural; and in the light of former Russian policy it was perhaps not unnatural that he should think that Russia had deserted him. That the town was glad of the coming of the Russians is beyond question. The people wanted not Constitutions but bread, and though they had no love for Russia, they would have accepted bread from any hand.

To give a true picture of the siege of Tabriz, it is unfortunately necessary to make allusion to some less pleasant characteristics of the Persians. The town was theoretically governed by an Anjuman, a miscellaneous collection of mullahs and other notables, who

THE ORIENT EXPRESS

sat on the floor of a large room and spake such wisdom as the spirit prompted them. The *de facto* governors were the two generalissimos, Sattar Khan and Bakir Khan, whose relations with the Anjuman were of the politest and most ceremonious kind. But this smooth exterior was a cloak for an extensive system of blackmail. It was a common thing for the leaders to bring out some of their men to the outskirts of the city, fire off some cartridges in a futile demonstration, and the same evening demand a thousand tomans (about £200) from the Anjuman, for the expenses of a supposed sanguinary battle in the afternoon. Occasionally the smooth surface was abruptly broken, and I was present once at a violent scene when Bakir Khan threatened to hang the dignified members of the Anjuman because they did not accede to his demands for money. The result of this forcible appeal, which Sattar Khan supported, was a "benevolence" of eight thousand tomans, part of which was used to pay the riflemen their daily dole. But it returned to the central chest, for the riflemen had to purchase bread at a high price, and the leaders controlled the corn supply. The balance of the sum was confiscated in a simpler fashion. Bakir Khan, sunning himself in his prosperity, was building a house and had many workmen to pay. After the last fight of all, the leaders, who had not thought it necessary to take part in it, demanded fifteen thousand tomans from the unfortunate Anjuman, of which two thousand five hundred were paid. Sattar Khan gave a bill for the remainder to Kassim Khan, the head of the municipality, as a subscription to the Relief Committee—a magnificent, but chimerical, donation.

THE LAST SORTIE

Saddest of all was the fact that, although the Armenians cared well for their poor, it was impossible until the very end of the siege to organize a relief committee for the general Persian populace, many of whom died of hunger. No members, who could inspire sufficient confidence in any committee or any possible donors, could be found to undertake the duties of treasurer and distributors. Only at the very end of all was a committee formed, yet in spite of the precautions taken in selecting it, some of the funds given by benevolent Europeans for the relief of misery were misappropriated. The subject is not a pleasant one, and I do not propose to deal with it further; but the impression left on the mind by this intimate glimpse of a Persian town in its hour of trial was that almost every one was, in the vulgar phrase, "on the make." Even the mullahs had to be paid for the eloquent addresses with which they stirred the patriotism of the crowd, and discourses could only be bought on strictly cash terms.

In the month of May I left Tabriz. On the Julfa road, by which I had to pass, was Suja-i-Nizam, the young Governor of Marand. His father had been blown up by a bomb, which reached him, oddly enough, by parcel post. When he undid the string which bound the parcel the bomb exploded. After that every parcel which reached careful people for the next six months was put into a bucket of cold water and opened in the garden. The young Suja-i-Nizam, son of the victim, who took his father's title and governed Marand, was so ill-inspired with regard to myself, whose part in the defence had been much exaggerated by the tongues of rumour, as to offer a reward to any one who should succeed in removing me from the earth. Sitting astride the Julfa road, and knowing that I must one day come out of Tabriz and pass along his way, he had a fair chance of catching his supposed enemy himself, and he was believed to derive considerable enjoyment from the prospect. But in the end fate was unkind to him. After the Russian troops had relieved the town and controlled the Julfa road, his position at Marand, with a large mob of followers disappointed in their hope of loot, became daily more difficult. When I set out he was reported to be still there. I drove to Marand and halted to spend the night, feeling confident that, though there were no Russian troops in the town, their presence in the near neighbourhood, on the Julfa road, would ensure my safety. I found on arrival that Suja-i-Nizam, believing that his game was up, had departed the day before with fifteen hundred followers, leaving behind a deputy-governor and about one hundred men.

The deputy-governor thought that affairs had taken the wrong turn, and that politeness was the better part. He came to pay me a visit and to assure me that I should be surrounded by a guard all night. In the course of conversation candour grew upon him. Suja-i-Nizam, he said, had sworn an oath on the Koran that whenever I should try to pass this road I would not reach Julfa alive. "It is perhaps fortunate for your Excellency that he left Marand yesterday." I thanked him for this interesting information, and speculated whether this jovial deputy-governor, who was inquiring so tenderly after my "august health," might not also a week earlier have taken quite a different interest in the aforesaid health. It is a curious

THE LAST SORTIE

sensation to have a feeling of enmity towards a person you do not know, and it is odd to observe the different values one attaches to unknown people. I had no strong feeling of hatred towards any of those who had attacked Tabriz, but I have always felt that I did not much care for Suja-i-Nizam, and I do not think he can really be a nice person. He had irritating tricks. That he should prevent the post running on the Julfa road, from Tabriz to Europe, was eminently reasonable, but a gentleman would not have added insult to injury. I have before me now the fragments of an article which will never be published. Suja-i-Nizam stopped the post which was carrying it, tore it across, and sent it back to me. I tried again, and posted to my editor the fragments that remained. But this time the post fled back to the city under fire. After that there was no further attempt to get a post through.

In an account of the siege which I wrote in the summer of 1909, I find near the conclusion some words which may be recalled—

"Nevertheless, in the atmosphere of inevitable suspicion there is plenty of room for unpleasant incidents at Tabriz, and the cynics have a case when they say that temporary expeditions have a way of turning into permanent occupations, and that Russia will be rather the exception than the rule if she retires. It would also be idle to deny the existence of a powerful party in Russia which is bitterly hostile to the Anglo-Russian agreement, and no friend to a Constitution in Persia. Reaction in Russia and a 'forward' Russian policy in Persia hang together, and should we see the one we should see the recrudescence of the other. . . . In the meantime the friends and lovers of Persia are faced with a bitter problem. They may well take thought. Is a Constitution likely to bring forth fair fruit quickly where it is the gift of two foreign Governments, representing two very dissimilar peoples, to a nation which has failed to win it for itself, where it is guaranteed against violation in each particular article by two foreign Legations, and rests in the last resort on foreign bayonets? It is the experiment to which we are now committed, and whatever its results for Persia, it is clearly better for us than a *condominium*. The danger is that it may lead to something very like a *condominium* in the end of the day."

Four years have followed that first experience, but the Persian scene has retained its character. I remember the performance of Sultan Selim's play at Ijlal-el-Mulk's house in Tabriz, an item in a series of festivities that accompanied my departure. We sat, a dozen spectators, in a great room with rich rugs, and watched the marionettes perform in a booth behind red gauze, with three candles as footlights. We watched merchants, sweepers, soldiers, fireworks, thrones, kings, courtiers, ladies with red silk crinolines—who sang a marriage hymn to a shah—male dancers, acrobats, wrestlers, tumblers, and more ladies. And all the time from a little orchestra came the beating of a drum, and the subdued music of the East rose and fell in our ears. There was a magician, a master of sarcastic humour, who did tricks that you may see in a different form at a Christmas party, but which may have been originally invented by the Magi. The marionettes and the magician make a parable of the ever-changing, irresponsible Persian scene. Its infinite variety is infinitely good. Things that are evil

THE LAST SORTIE

in themselves are often redeemed by some gay gust of brilliance, by some half-revealed touch of inspiration, or by the simpler charm which is found wherever and whenever this old world is still young. But for those to whom the soul and the fate of a nation are a thing of high import, the Persian stage is set for tragedy. The acts are long drawn out. Now, as five years ago, there is a sullen war in an unsettled country. It is hard to foresee the end. And it is best to remember that nothing ever really comes to an end, in Persia least of all.

CHAPTER III

THE DEATH OF ARSHAD-ED-DOWLEH

In the summer of 1909 the Nationalist Party deposed Mohammed Ali Shah and set his son, the present ruler, then a boy of thirteen, upon the throne. Mohammed Ali, at the moment of the capture of Tehran by the Nationalists, fled to the sanctuary of the Russian Legation for refuge. The British and Russian flags were crossed above the quarters allotted to him to show that he was under the protection of the British and Russian Governments, and it was finally arranged that he should live in exile in Russia and receive a pension from Persia. The Russian Government undertook to supervise his movements during his residence in Russia, and to prevent him from conducting intrigues in Persia, the penalty for which would be the loss of his pension.

On July 16, 1912, Mohammed Ali, ignoring his obligations, landed from Russia at Gumesh Tepeh, on the shores of the Caspian, with a few followers, and raised his standard. He gathered an army of Turcomans and, sending Arshad-ed-Dowleh, the confidant of his exile and his principal supporter, with his main force to advance towards Tehran by way of Damghan, Semnan, and Verameen, he himself advanced more slowly through Mazanderan. Arshad-ed-Dowleh had various encounters with Government troops, but his

THE DEATH OF ARSHAD-ED-DOWLEH

advance slowly continued, and by the beginning of September he was in the neighbourhood of Verameen, only a long day's march from Tehran. It was at this point that Yeprem went out against him. Hearing that Yeprem had gone, and believing that now at last there would be a decisive fight, I set forth with two friends some twenty-four hours after him, in the hope of seeing the issue.

There are forty miles of dazzling, dusty road between Tehran and Imam Zadeh Jaffur, or Mirza Jaffur as you will find it marked on most maps. We rode out by the Shah Abdul Azim gate, bright and early, at six o'clock on the morning of September 5, and took our way across the dead level of a weary plain, with hardly ever the shadow of a great rock to ease the broiling heat. A little army had passed the day before, and the dust was chequered with its horses' hoofs and scored with the deeper ruts of gun-carriages. Never a straggler did we meet, nor any messenger returning from the front; only everywhere a trail of water-melon skins, empty mementoes of a thirsty march, taken from the wayside fields.

We came to Imam Zadeh Jaffur an hour before sunset, and found the fight over and the singing troops of jolly Bakhtiari swarming into camp. A special courier was leaving for Tehran, who took with him a telegram for *The Times*, so that the news of the crushing failure of Arshad-ed-Dowleh's attempt to capture Tehran for the ex-Shah might be on the British breakfast-table next morning. It seems that the fight was finished in two hours. Arshad-ed-Dowleh's force of fourteen hundred mounted men and seven hundred foot, with four guns, was in a strong position. The total force

THE ORIENT EXPRESS

on the Government side was about nine hundred, including Amir Mujahid's Bakhtiari. Keri, an Armenian leader, who distinguished himself during the defence of Tabriz, with a handful of men, and Captain Haase, a German artillery instructor in the Persian service, with one Maxim, took the left of the circular range of hills from Verameen. The Maxim was brought up on a spur and at a distance of fifteen hundred yards sprayed on a mass of Turcomans with terrifying effect, doing, as usual, more damage to nerves than anything else. Meantime, Sardar Bahadur's three hundred Bakhtiari and Yeprem's one hundred and fifty men advanced fusillading on the right, and, when the rout began, charged the hill and gained the enemy's camp, Amir Mujahid at the same time occupying their eastern position at Kalinoh.

I was aroused at 11 p.m. with the news that Arshad-ed-Dowleh, the commander-in-chief of the broken army, had been brought into camp. Hastily dressing, I found the prisoner on a rug, drinking tea and smoking a cigarette with his captors. He shook me by the hand and greeted me in French. Somewhere in my rooms in London I had a photograph of him which he had given me more than two years before when he was at Basminch, besieging Tabriz for Mohammed Ali, the master whom he loyally served. The photograph showed him in a gorgeous, much-medalled uniform. Now he wore a red-striped Turcoman shirt and a pair of trousers such as he must have worn in his Vienna days with a frock-coat. One bare foot was bound up, for he had received a slight, and apparently no longer painful, wound.

Queer things happen often if one adventures east

THE DEATH OF ARSHAD-ED-DOWLEH

of Belgrade; but in all the jumble of old memories I remember no experience of such intensely painful dramatic interest as the two hours that followed. I knew that the irrevocable decision had already been taken, not hastily or in anger, but from motives believed to be compelling; and that the prisoner would die in the morning. He, too, knew that he had had a Bakhtiari Khan shot in cold blood the day before, and that, as a rebel and an exile who had come back to raise the standard of Mohammed Ali, he could scarce hope for mercy. But for two hours he and his captors played the game. He was to have no inkling of his fate till morning came, and pride and caution alike prevented him from asking it. So they treated him as one of themselves, and the conversation was carried on in the complimentary language that in Persia even the most intimate friends employ to one another. There he lay, half reclining, at his ease in the flickering circle of the candles, the most eloquent talker of the group, while behind him in the shadow a standing press of silent Bakhtiari leant upon their rifles, straining rapt faces to catch the talk and seized with all the drama of the night. Often there was a witty word, and sometimes a laugh went softly round the talkers, as when they twitted him about his Turcoman shirt. And once we all laughed with sheer relief, as one might laugh at the porter scene in *Macbeth*, when an incautious tribesman, stepping backwards, fell waist deep into a water-tank. Sometimes the channel of the conversation was directed by a pointed question, but there was never an attempt to press the prisoner, for he told his story well, and said that he had nothing to hide. It seemed to me that under the eloquence

THE ORIENT EXPRESS

of his easy speech I detected a tremendous nervous strain, and the sweat came often to his face while he constantly relit his cigarettes. His effort was to make a powerful personal impression, and thus to gain the sympathy of his listeners.

He told us of the day's fight. For two days he himself had had fever. "I was ill, and did not want to advance to-day, so I said that we must wait; that all would be well; that I would arrange matters. But three hundred Turcomans were sent out to make a *shelook*, an uproar, by firing off their guns." These same Turcomans had almost surrounded Amir Mujahid, and, but for the coming of the relief force from Verameen, might have won the day.

"When they heard the sound of the Maxim gun, the Turcomans round me said to me in their own tongue, 'What manner of gun is this?' '*Cheezi nist;* it is nothing,' I answered. But one from the top of the hill rushed in, white to the lips, and cried out that this gun was killing many, and that the fight was lost. So they fled, leaving me, and at the same moment a bullet struck me in the foot. Then I looked up and saw Amir Mujahid's Bakhtiari at the top of the hill. 'Son of a burnt father,' they cried, 'come up and surrender.' 'I am in your hands,' I answered, 'but as for coming up, I have no leg to walk on.' So they cursed me again with evil words, but in the end I was pulled up to the crest; and thus it ended."

"What has made Mohammed Ali Mirza come back to Iran?" asked one presently.

Thereupon, with sometimes a question thrown in by his listeners, he told us that, from the day when he and Mohammed Ali took refuge in the Russian Legation, in the summer of 1909, it was ever their intention

THE DEATH OF ARSHAD-ED-DOWLEH

to return to Persia and raise the flag again. The ex-Shah went to Odessa, and Arshad-ed-Dowleh to Vienna. There he studied military science, and afterwards went to the Tyrol, where he was attached to a corps of *chasseurs des montagnes*. " The colonel gave me a diploma, and said he had never had a better pupil."

Twice he mentioned his diploma. It is of such stuff that we are made. The fallen General was still proud of his European diploma, and in the very shadow of death felt pleasure in its importance. I had a vision of the Tyroler Hof at Innsbruck, and of the rough-shirted, unkempt man,—who now lay by me in a Persian bivouac,—dining with light-hearted Austrian officers. Hard by me was his cabin trunk; it bore the label of the Hôtel Bristol at Meran, where Mohammed Ali paid him a long visit the previous winter.

"I did not go to Odessa," he said. "Salar-ed-Dowleh went there and saw Mohammed Ali. It was arranged that Salar-ed-Dowleh should enter from the Turkish side. Then Mohammed Ali and I met in Vienna. The Russian Minister[1] came to see us, and we asked for help. He told us that Russia could not help us. Russia and England had an agreement with regard to Persia, from which neither would depart. They had resolved not to intervene in any way internally. 'But, on the other hand,' he said, 'the field is clear. If we can do nothing for you, we equally will do nothing against you. It is for you to decide what are your chances of success. If you think you can reach the

[1] The allusion seems to have been not to the Russian Ambassador in Vienna but to the Minister in Belgrade, M. Hartwig, who had been Russian Minister in Tehran during the last critical years of Mohammed Ali's rule.

throne of Persia, then go. Only remember we cannot help you, and if you fail we have no responsibility.' 'Well, there is something you can do for us,' we answered: 'lend us some money.' 'No, it is quite impossible,' he replied. And though we begged much and had a second interview, he rejected our proposal. Only he suggested that, if Mohammed Ali had a receipt for some jewels which were in the keeping of the Russian Bank at Tehran, money could be raised on that receipt. But Mohammed Ali had not got the document, and so nothing came of that.

"We raised 30,000 tomans on the Queen's jewels, and Mohammed Ali had 25,000 tomans for a quarter's pension. Of this 55,000 tomans 50,000 was given to me for the expenses of my expedition. We bought two mitrailleuses in Austria. I brought the guns and ammunition through the Russian Customs labelled 'Mineral water'; they were never opened.

"At Petrovsk we took an oil boat. Mohammed Ali had a Persian passport in the name of Khalil. I do not know what funds Salar-ed-Dowleh has, but he had little. Some money he raised by selling a valuable jewelled cigar-case, and some he was given by a *farangi* woman."

The "*farangi* woman" was said to be the Comtesse de Clérmont Tonnerre, an adventurous French lady, who accompanied the expedition of Salar-ed-Dowleh.

Such was his tale, but as he warmed with the telling of it he forgot caution and launched into an eloquent indictment of the constitutional *régime*. He spoke scathingly of a fine programme and poor achievements. The French Revolution and the history of England were swept in to point his argument. He described the condition of the Persian peasant, and compared

THE DEATH OF ARSHAD-ED-DOWLEH

the Persian landlord system with the landlord systems of Europe. He touched his hearers closely, but one of them took up the answer. He indicted the Kajar family by name, from the first Shah down to Mohammed Ali, as the selfish enemies of Persia. From Nasred-Din's time they were ever "the hired servants of Russia." He went through the departments of State in turn upon his fingers, and admitted that in none had reform yet been established. "And why? Because we are still fighting for our lives. On every hand there is an intrigue. And you, who are, as you say, a lover of your country—is it patriotic to come and promote revolution at the moment when we are straining for reform and the independence of Iran?"

"Aziz-i-man," said Arshad-ed-Dowleh. "The independence of Persia will never march. The Russians are too strong for you, and the people are too foolish. Progress does not lie that way. You call me a *mujtabed*, a friend of despotism. You call yourselves Liberals, Democrats, Socialists. But progress is something apart from all these labels, and I, too, want progress for my country."

It was late when they ended, but he did not wish the sitting to finish. "The talk is good, and why should we sleep yet? I have loved you from afar, and now that we have met it is good to be with you." The hour was late, they said, and the morning start would be early. "But do not leave me alone, for your men used ill words to me when they took me to-day." "They will not do so any more," said Yeprem. "You will sleep here, close by me; and no one will come near you in the night."

Early in the morning he was seated on a chair in the spot where we had talked the night before.

THE ORIENT EXPRESS

Yeprem told him, very gently, that he must die, for the State could not afford to let him live. He looked as though he had slept well, and had no fear. They gave him paper, and with a steady hand he wrote a letter to his wife, a royal princess, the daughter of Nasr-ed-Din Shah. It was read aloud for a testimony. He said that he commended his soul to God, and desired that his body should be delivered to his wife, and that the gold chain which he wore round his neck should be buried with him.

Then he rose and made a speech, declaring that in all he had done he had ever been *vatanparast*, a man who worshipped his country. While he spoke I heard the steady tramp of the firing party. It came up level with his left shoulder, marked time, and halted. He ceased, and turned to them. Between the files, he went with them forty yards away. They put him up at a distance of ten yards. He stood erect, unfettered, without fear. When he heard the command "Ready" he shouted: "*Zindabad Vatan* (Long live my country). Fire." The volley rang out and he fell, but rose again to his knees with no sign of injury, and cried twice, "*Zindabad Mohammed Ali Shah.*" The second section fired, and all was over. I could not watch again, but I heard his gallant cry.

The first section was Musulman, and some say that each man fired wide, trusting to his neighbour's aim. The second section was Armenian. Whatever the truth of that may be, the men of the first section were put in detention in Tehran.

However great be the faults of Mohammed Ali—and they are not few—he found one man who served him well.

CHAPTER IV

PHILOSOPHY IN ADVERSITY

Tehran, March 1912.

TEHRAN is changed in these latter days and has resumed an ancient habit, lately interrupted for a space of years. It has for the moment an intermission of its modern fitful fever of politics; and if it does not, after its fitful fever, sleep either better or worse —the Tehrani has always had a turn for sleeping sound and waking voluble—it now gives back to the philosophical contemplation of existence what politics had stolen. The Mejliss sits no longer, and newspapers are few. The tide of war, which flowed nearly to the city walls in the late tempestuous autumn, has ebbed away to the Caspian gates on the East and the Turkish frontier on the West. Mr. Shuster has gone, and the ex-Shah is going. The exacting patriotism, which rendered life unbearable by a boycott of tea, sugar and tram-rides, is no longer in place. So, with the gentle air of spring and the faint fragrance of violets to charm his garden, the Tehrani has lost interest in politics, and being off with his new love, finds it well to be on with the old. And the old love is all that ever went with philosophy, from metaphysics to the nice conduct of a carven silver walking-stick, which is the Persian fop's equivalent for the clouded cane, the management whereof betrayed so much to the more observant of our ancestors.

THE ORIENT EXPRESS

It was in this mood of revived reflection that Sohrab sat on my verandah and discoursed upon the vanity of human power. For it is not well to plunge abruptly from one absorption to another, and Sohrab, with a nice sense of transition, tinged his mood, not with the contemplation of pure being, but with the philosophical consideration of politics. He has much to say on such subjects that is of interest to me. For I find it a great comfort, and no mean aid to our friendship, that, though he has never travelled further West than Stambul, he has made some studies in the politics and literature of Europe. There is a select company of subcutaneous experts who profess to be able to get into the Oriental skin and to cross the supposed chasm between East and West; but an indolent disposition and some lurking doubts about my own ability ever fully to understand any one else, Oriental or otherwise, have barred me from their number. For I remember a manservant at home to whom I paid a small living wage, and who therefore had, in the opinion of just and reasonable people, no right to allow himself to be in any way a mystery to me, but, nevertheless, daily presented himself as a baffling series of conundrums. Sohrab is more comprehensible than he. For Sohrab takes an occasional and entertaining interest in English politics, and he has even learnt to read *The Times*, as well as the works of Monsieur Anatole France.

Sohrab is a poet, and loves the quatrain. Unlike most of his countrymen, who rather resent our enthusiasm for Omar Khayyam and prefer both Sadi and Hafiz, he admires Omar and imitates him, though somewhat *longo intervallo*. And it was to summarize

PHILOSOPHY IN ADVERSITY

the prevailing mood of Tehran that I quoted him a verse of Omar, and thereby provoked discussion—

> "Iram indeed is gone with all its Rose,
> And Jamshyd's Sev'n-ringed Cup where no one knows;
> But still the Vine her ancient Ruby yields,
> And still a Garden by the Water blows."

"Iram indeed is gone," said Sohrab, "but Iran is not. As for Jamshyd's Seven-ringed Cup, I do not know whether the butler of one or other of the Legations may not have taken it to add to his master's collection, for it is not well to leave things about in Persia. But Iran remains."

"Why, yes," I answered vaguely, "Iran remains." Believing myself to be what Lord Morley has called "a good European," I was somewhat nettled by his innuendo as to the possible fate of Jamshyd's Cup.

"I do not mean," he continued, "that there are still remains for the picking. Nor am I speaking in the geographical sense, that Persia remains only because, unlike the Cup, it is not portable, and so cannot be carried away. What I mean is that Persia as a nation has still something of its own, which is its contribution to the general stock of human value. It is true that we have just left a glorious future behind us. Two years ago we talked in that glorious future, the era of liberty and independence. But we have been like the thieves who found themselves in heaven—we have looted Paradise instead of living in it, so that we may say of the Constitution and of the country that it is a poor thing and not our own."

"If that be so," said I, "what have you left?"

"You," he answered, "judge a nation by its material power and riches. If a country is so great that, when its Ambassador speaks, every one is seated on the carpet either of hope or fear, expecting either war or peace, or at least a loan or a railway, to come out of his mouth, so that there is general disappointment when he only asks for another glass of tea, you consider the citizens of that nation blessed. We, too, have pursued that shadow, and the Mejliss has wasted much time in giving orders that there were none to execute. We sent great Governors and Princes to pacify disordered provinces, and Sardars to crush rebellious tribes. And the Governors and the Sardars salaamed and said, '*Chashm!* by our eyes, we will go at once.' And six months later I have found those Governors and Sardars still smoking the opium of content in their houses in Tehran, or cheating the city of its wheat supply at great profit to themselves, and in general giving to the interpretation of the era of liberty and independence a personal and joyous application. But had the breath of the Mejliss been able to create fleets and armies—in which case I make no doubt that we should have been in the front rank of nations both by land and sea—so that we should have been a cause of fear to other nations, what profit would that have brought to the souls of our citizens? Or wherein is a man happier working at the bottom of a great ship than singing on the top of a high camel? You will say that he is sustained in his toil, and compensated for the blackness of his face, by the thought that the ship, though for the most part he sees only the bottom of it, is one of the largest warships in the world. But, for my part, I think that he is sustained by the thought that he will receive sufficient money for his needs, which is, perhaps, what makes the camel driver sing, or perhaps it is not. Moreover, the camel may be the

PHILOSOPHY IN ADVERSITY

largest of his kind also; and in any case it is not given to every country to have such large animals, whereon one may sit with a clean face and see the sun."

It seemed to me that several fallacies floated on this sea of illustration, but my admiration of this instance of Persian adaptability, in one who had lately been amongst the most thoroughgoing constitutionalists, overcame any instinct of combativeness. Here indeed was the εὐτραπελία which of old was the hallmark of the best Periclean Athenian. Sohrab had risen superior to political circumstance, and discovered anew the true greatness of his country. But he had not as yet revealed wherein it lay, and my curiosity was unsatisfied.

"I understand you to mean, Sohrab, that in the possession of the elements of happiness the modern Persian is at least no worse off than the citizen of a great Empire; but that every great country possesses a distinctive quality of its own, and that in this sense Persia is still an independent nation."

"I am not speaking of Literature or Art," he said. "I might contend that a country which has excelled in these has perpetuated itself for ever, and that, for this reason, my country need take no notice either of armies or of ultimatums. But I speak only of a still existent contribution to the art of life, an art wherein nations may learn much from one another. For example, the essential contribution of the English seems to me to be comfort. The English are held to be hard workers, but in my judgment they toil only in order to make themselves comfortable; and they have made of comfort a fine art, so that every country learns from them in the production of comfort. With the Germans I am, by circumstance, less well acquainted. Were I to judge from the newspapers, I should say that they excelled in the production of discomfort, and that other nations were recognizing a master in this art. But I am more disposed to judge them from their philosophy, and to believe that their special attribute is calm. The Russians excel in hospitality, and the French in gaiety and cookery—though in this latter we rival them in the matter of rice; and it seems to me that the Italians, having conquered the world by macaroni, might have left Tripoli to the Turks without loss of glory. As for the Turks, they also have an art of pleasing by their innocent stupidity, which is somewhat difficult for Persians to acquire, but nevertheless repays cultivation."

"But I take it that it was not of your acknowledged and unique position in the matter of rice that you spoke," said I. "I am seated on the carpet of expectation."

"The carpet was made in Persia," retorted Sohrab. "But it is not of excellence in carpets that I would speak, were it for me to mention the qualities of my own countrymen."

"But this is the abode of friendship and the court of frankness."

"No, it is for you to say what is the proper virtue of the Persian, and if, in my opinion, you are right, I shall surrender the citadel of modesty, not as concerning myself but for my countrymen."

"Dignity," I answered, without hesitation.

"You have hit the mark. I speak not of national dignity, so much as of personal dignity. For is it not the test of dignity that it survives even when bereft of resources and in humiliating conditions? And this

PHILOSOPHY IN ADVERSITY

is in the nature of the Persian, so that even the servility of your servants is dignified, and the friendly greeting of cabmen—I speak not of their quarrels, wherein the difference is perhaps less—is a ceremonious form of words; whereas I understand that in your countries it is of a ribald and barbarous character. It is true that, in these latter days, it has often pleased God to deprive us as a nation of the resources wherewith we should like to comport ourselves in a dignified manner; as, for instance, when last week we wished to give the Turkish Ambassador a salute, but, owing to a misunderstanding between our officials and those of our Northern neighbour, the guns were missing at the appointed hour. Yet I am assured that, even in the lamentable absence of the guns, all things were conducted in a proper and worthy manner, and everything humanly possible was done to comfort the heart of the afflicted Ambassador, who naturally resented an entry without either the smell of powder or the sound of shot."

The contemplation of the calamity of this silent and inodorous arrival produced a long pause. The stillness was at length broken by Sohrab reciting one of his own quatrains, which may be rendered thus—

> "The Kingdom, Pow'r, and Glory, since we must,
> We leave beneath Time's Key to Moth and Rust;
> But let the Flow'r of Dignity and Pride
> Blossom for ever in Dishonour's Dust."

Sohrab left me revolving in my mind an Oriental compliment, which, being unspoken, was perhaps more sincere than most. For I thought that he was justified in his optimism, and that the nation which produced him could never die.

CHAPTER V

SOHRAB ON GENIUS

CASTING his mind back, in a mood of cheerful melancholy, upon the sorrows of his country in recent years, Sohrab enunciated one evening on my verandah the very tenable theory that Persia's principal misfortune was that she had produced a series of crises without producing any one capable of finding a solution for them. An inveterate but, in this instance, misplaced turn for originality had made her prove the rule that the occasion finds the man by herself providing the exception.

"Or rather a series of exceptions," he added; "for we have had enough Ministers in two years to have lined the road to Paradise, but they have unfortunately led us to quite another destination."

"But," said I, "genius is so rare in all countries, and crises are so common, that it seems to me that mankind must be content to apply to their solution, not genius, but common sense."

"Political genius," Sohrab replied, "is in a community only a highly cultivated common sense in politics. When this has been practised by a number of people for some generations an atmosphere is created in which it is possible for an individual political genius to be born."

"Genius is not, then, a pure accident?" I asked.

"The flowering of genius is a subject which I have

SOHRAB ON GENIUS

submitted to some examination. For instance, in a nation which has for a time decayed it cannot be said that the quality of common sense in the conduct of ordinary affairs has decayed in any comparable manner. A Persian peasant is perhaps not inferior in mother wit or in native shrewdness to a European peasant, and I have even heard Europeans say, with a certain bitterness, that the merchants of Tehran were possessed of great ability in the art of bargaining, which is the art of the merchant. I have indeed observed that certain Europeans, of defective education, regard with amusement the fact that Persians prefer to sit upon the floor rather than upon chairs, and to eat with their fingers rather than with knives and forks; and they speak as if this were contrary to common sense. But you, my friend, will agree with me that these artificial arrangements for sitting and eating do not really forward the business in hand; and, though in your company I adopt them by habit with some comfort and a pleasant sense of European diversion, it is yet possible for the Persian in turn to regard them with a secret amusement, as being the uncomfortable devices of people with stiff joints who have not the cleanly habit of washing their hands after their meals."

"But would it not be common sense to make a more general use of machinery?"

"In the first place, the general diffusion of machinery depends upon railways, and you are aware that in Persia that is not a question for the individual, but pertains to political common sense and high politics, so that indeed it is not all our fault that we are still without railways. In the second place, if we consider the difficulties of transport, the number of machines, as, for instance, sewing machines, in Persia is very large. And, thirdly, it seems to me that the people for whom it is a matter of individual common sense to employ machinery may be divided into four classes. First, there are those who elect to edit newspapers, and Tehran has a sufficiency of printing presses. Secondly, there are those who elect to live by selling machinery; of these we have few who have chosen this trade by preference, and all can earn a living without it. Thirdly, there are those who elect to live by exploiting the labour of others; it is to the interest of these to employ a large number of workmen to produce goods quickly and cheaply by machinery. But in Persia the workman sells for himself and employs only the labour of one or two apprentices. The articles which he produces by his handicraft are durable, and their price is in proportion to the cost of living; moreover, I have heard Europeans admire them for their beauty and declare them preferable to those made by machines. Fourthly, there is the farmer, who beyond doubt would reap a greater reward for his toil by the use of agricultural machinery. But I am not aware that the farmer in any country shows any readiness to adopt machinery until it is forced upon him, either by those who have machines to sell or by the political common sense of the community, which sends missionaries to convert him. The Persian farmer would be no more unwilling to adopt machinery were it within his reach; but he has neither seen it nor heard of it, and its acquisition at the present time, when there are no means of transport, would be entirely beyond the power of his purse."

"So that, given the kind of life to which he is

SOHRAB ON GENIUS

accustomed, the Persian conducts it with ordinary common sense?"

"Most assuredly, as far as his own needs are concerned. It is the sense of common organization, and of serving the general need, the spirit of social, not of religious, self-sacrifice, which is lacking; and this is a political sense. Hence there is no atmosphere into which a political genius can be born, or wherein he could thrive. Where many study machinery a mechanical genius arrives, and where art is worshipped an artist may be born. Thus in Persia there is perhaps no pure passion except for religious and philosophical subjects; and though I myself am not an admirer either of the Bab or of Bahai'ullah, there are many who believe that Persia has in modern times produced two religious geniuses."

"It seems to me to follow from your theory, Sohrab, that before a new kind of genius can be born a new movement must first be born. This movement, also, must suffer from its uncongenial atmosphere, so that its beginnings may appear abortive. And in general the genius, instead of arriving with the movement, is likely to arrive a long time after, so that every genius has many puny and unacknowledged predecessors."

"That also is true, and the question of movements is of great interest. It is always important to discover whether a movement which suddenly flames forth is really new, in which case it is likely to die down and to pass through many stages before gaining strength. And this may perhaps be true of the Persian Constitutional movement. Or it may already, almost unobserved, have passed through its earlier stages, in which case it is likely to produce capable leaders and to attain a measure of success. This may be so with your movement for women's suffrage."

Supporters of women's suffrage should be gratified that even in the midst of Persia's sorest trials, when the ex-Shah had raised his standard and civil war was loose, a champion of the woman's cause was found in the Persian Mejliss. This was none other than Hadji Vakil el Rooy, Deputy for Hamadan, who in August 1911 astonished the Mejliss by an impassioned defence of women's rights. The House was quietly discussing the electoral law and had reached the clause declaring that no woman shall vote. Discussion on a proposition so obvious seemed unnecessary, and the House shivered when the Vakil el Rooy mounted the tribune, and declared roundly that women possessed souls and rights, and should possess votes.

Now Vakil el Rooy had hitherto been a serious politician, and the House listened to his harangue in dead silence, unable to decide whether it was an ill-timed joke or a serious statement. The orator called upon the Ulema to support him, but support failed him. The Mujtehid whom he invoked by name rose in his place, and solemnly declared that he had never in a life of misfortune had his ears assailed by such an impious utterance. Nervously and excitedly he denied to women either souls or rights, and declared that such doctrine would mean the downfall of Islam. To hear it uttered in the Parliament of the nation had made his hair stand on end. The cleric sat down, and the Mejliss shifted uncomfortably in its seats. The President put the clause in its original form, and asked the official reporters to make no record in the journals of the House of this unfortunate incident. The

SOHRAB ON GENIUS

Mejliss applauded his suggestion, and turned with relief to the discussion of subjects less disturbing than the contemplation of the possibility that women had souls. Yet perhaps some members had their doubts, occasionally privately expressed, whether, after all, woman may not somewhere have a soul.

"In England, I understand," said Sohrab, "you have many 'suffragettes' who clamour to vote on equal terms with men. In Persia such a demand has the air of outrageous novelty, and when a Deputy in the Mejliss so far forgot his surroundings as to advocate something of the kind the Assembly was naturally shocked and distressed. But in England, where your women have for centuries meddled in the course of politics, it is possible that the movement has been long fostered before making such a noise in the world, and, if this be so, it is possible that a woman who is a political genius may be produced."

"The genius of the suffragette at the present time," I suggested in English, "might be defined as an infinite capacity for breaking panes."

Considering this remark obscure, and probably irrelevant, Sohrab ignored it and launched a much wider speculation.

"If," said he, "one could contemplate the genesis of, and the stages reached by, all the movements that are going on in the world at the present or any given time, one would be in a position to make some reasonable conjecture as to the meaning of existence, and as to whither we are going."

"The hypothesis is too colossal," I answered, "but at any rate you hold that there is a meaning?"

Sohrab replied by one of his own quatrains—

THE ORIENT EXPRESS

"For all the Toil of all the aged Past,
For all the Bread upon the Waters cast,
For all the Prayers that Men have prayed in Vain,
Shall come a subtle Answer at the Last."

"The satisfactory nature of an answer," I objected, "is generally in inverse ratio to its subtlety."

"For starving men, yes; but for philosophers, no."

"But for me, for example, who do not starve, and am an indifferent philosopher?"

"The plain man will always invent his own answer, and sometimes he may even be satisfied with it. But perhaps also, although the Prophet of the Gospels forbade this practice for men, the diverting spectacle of swine contemplating a pearl cast before them was in the scheme of the framer of the subtle Answer. You have seen the *dallals* when they bring you an antique *aba*, or a beautiful old tile, stare at it, turn it over as though they knew its secret, and assert loudly its beauty and great value. Of its beauty they know nothing, for we Persians despise our own art, but of its value they are very solicitous, that being precisely what they can persuade a *farangi* to pay for it. Is it not so also in your country that some men make much money by the manufacture of soap and other necessary articles; or by lending money at much interest; or by selling to a limited company of more ignorant persons something to which they have no title, or which is situated at such a vast distance, as for instance a diamond mine in Persia, that its worthlessness is not immediately discoverable? And these people, having become millionaires, collect beautiful pictures and statues, which are selected by those who are experts in such matters. But they themselves know only that

SOHRAB ON GENIUS

these pictures and curios are valuable, and the secret of their beauty escapes them; for the vast sale of necessary, or unnecessary, articles to the world is not the garden wherein this kind of knowledge is cultivated. With such men one may compare the well-informed swine who nose the pearl of the subtle Answer. The well-informed swine have learnt that here is some mysterious value, though the subtlety escapes them. And just as your millionaires eagerly collect works of art, so the well-informed swine are often very strong either in theology or in philosophy or in the ceremonies of religion, thinking thereby to demonstrate their possession of the pearl, and their understanding of the subtle Answer."

"In general," said I, as Sohrab prepared to say good-night, "I am disposed to agree with you. Yet, though I have no objection to being called a plain man, it seems to me that you are developing your argument and analogies in a way that will ultimately cease to flatter. Moreover, the epithet 'well-informed' appears to me singularly unsuitable for swine, inasmuch as in my country it is by tradition almost exclusively reserved for the correspondents of *The Times*."

CHAPTER VI

SOME MARCHING MEMORIES

WHEN the *Titanic* went down I told the news to Sohrab, whose philosophy runs in a shady stream with a light windy ripple over it, where a man may sometimes get a surprising rise if he throw a fly in season. Sohrab was not startled as Europe and America were startled by the news of the colossal disaster, for, in truth, American millionaires were nothing to him. But his imagination grasped the fact that people of vast importance had suddenly been swallowed up, and that two continents were unable to think of anything else. He was impressed by this; but the moral which he drew was, as usual, comforting. Persia might be behind the times, but at least there were some evils which she was spared.

"After all, it is better to travel on the lame donkey as we do," said Sohrab. "The sea is a cold and unwholesome place, and a hole in a ship's bottom leads to more unpleasantness than a sore on a donkey's back."

For my part, the lame donkey with a sore back, a too common sight in Persia, affects me more unpleasantly than the *Titanic* disaster, which, though none of us admit it, produced in all of us an agreeable sensation of excitement. But on the main point Sohrab was right. Western civilization has advantages if you

SOME MARCHING MEMORIES

are in a hurry, or if you want to kill people on a large scale. But you are for ever skating over thin ice, and a slip of the foot when crossing Piccadilly Circus, a slip of the tongue to the man at the wheel, a second's loss of somebody's nerve on motor, locomotive engine, ship, or aeroplane, will cook your goose. If you are not in a hurry and prefer to die quietly of disease or old age, or if you like to see a good deal of strange and exciting fighting with a fair prospect of living to fight another day, the unregenerated portions of the East are the safest place.

It is not an easy or perhaps a possible task for a European to give an impression of what it is like to be born a little Hassan or Hussein in modern Persia. It is an odd thing to be born into a country which, though it has behind it a long tradition in war, in literature and in art, that makes its name ring magical in our ears, is to-day a fallen empire, slumbering in the sun, forgotten by the busy West, remote from its ways and its works, unthreaded by its railways, known but as a name, remembered only by troubled statesmen, who see in it a source of present worry and the sure promise of evil to come.

You may be the illiterate child of a peasant inhabiting some small green oasis in the wilderness, in which case your life to-day will probably differ in very little from that of your fathers for many generations. Camels, mules, and donkeys, the local *kanat*, or watercourse, and the wrestlings with the crops, will bulk largest in your life, as in theirs; the name of Allah will be for ever on your lips, though perhaps little in your thoughts; the raids of robbers, the exactions of tribal chieftains, and the occasional violence of real

THE ORIENT EXPRESS

war, will trouble your existence in the old familiar way. Or you may be a town-bred schoolchild and imbibe the classical education of the *madresseh* of Tehran or Isfahan, Arabic and Turkish, the Koran and the Thousand-and-One Nights, the funny stories that for ever make the East hold both its sides with laughter, the sweet songs and sayings of Sadi, Hafiz, Omar Khayyam, and many another, the daring speculations of innumerable poets and philosophers, whose acute brains have never hesitated to criticize this sorry scheme of things, and have even had the temerity of the German philosopher who detected errors in God as well. Or you may be a moss-raiding, cattle-lifting, free-fighting tribesman, living for loot like your ancestors, but possibly investing your military exploits with the new glamour and dignity of political aims, constitutional or anti-constitutional. Yet again, you may be educated in the West, and speak one or other of the tongues of Europe, in which case the bitter irony of the past and the present will have seized hold of your spirit and you will be an ardent "nationalist," dreaming, in the intervals of the old careless Persian life, dreams of a strenuous future, of a Persian revival, of revolution, equality, republics, socialism, all that ever went with modern progress. These things are too hard for my imagination and for yours. It is perhaps a simpler and a better way to give you some broken fragments of my own experiences, with which you may piece together in your own imagination a necessarily imperfect picture of life in modern Persia.

Wars show no sign of ceasing, but the trade of the war correspondent is a decaying industry. It is some consolation for those of us who were rash enough to

SOME MARCHING MEMORIES

drift into it that, though the first-class fields are no longer open to it, some countries remain where the trade may flourish. It is not first-class fighting, but in the minor revolutions and expeditions which rarely fail in Persia a man may see to his heart's content all the fighting that there is. If he chooses to head the charges, no one will object, and no one worries much about secrecy. The comradeship of war is perhaps the best there is, and it was during the siege of Tabriz, in the course of various expeditions against the ex-Shah and Salar-ed-Dowleh, and on long marches day after day through troubled southern country, that I made more Persian friends than in the pleasant idleness of many months in Tehran. Sir Valentine Chirol, in *The Middle Eastern Question*, has told us that never in his wanderings in many countries has he experienced any charm like that of Persian travel. Nothing but the recollection of never-to-be-forgotten days in Albania prevents me from agreeing whole-heartedly with this learned judgment. Memory swings to a nine days' ride over the old road by Nobaran to Hamadan, at the end of September 1911, when Yeprem and the Bakhtiari sallied forth against the often beaten but still uncaptured Salar-ed-Dowleh. The latter is the most turbulent of the brothers of the ex-Shah, and his tattered flag of rebellion has been waving intermittently in Persia for the last three years. Day after day we rode for hot and dusty but cheerful hours, till we reached the village which was the day's halting-place. They are rich villages in that fertile district. Most of them had already been occupied by the enemy and had suffered much. I fear they had no great reason to welcome us, for though Yeprem kept his men in hand, the Bakhtiari swept up what loot was left, even to the samovars, and day by day the burden of the mules in our baggage train grew. My plan was to ride as near the top of the column as possible, get into the village early, make for the best house I saw, and commandeer it. The owner, on hearing my unexpected announcement that I proposed to pay for everything with which he supplied me, and that I would also keep the Bakhtiari out, instantly became my grateful host. Sometimes, however, I was beaten by guile. There was the occasion when Hassan, best of servants, had shot a chicken in the courtyard for his master's supper, and carefully left it on the verandah, believing that my presence in the adjoining room would secure its safety, while he went to water the horses. There was a smiling Bakhtiari on a verandah across the narrow street, who held up a large bunch of grapes from his store, and offered them to me. Still unfed and parched with thirst, I gratefully accepted. He came across with his present, sat down, and entertained me with light-hearted conversation. He left me overcome with gratitude, subsequently modified when Hassan returned and burst into uncontrollable wrath against an unknown thief, none other than my Bakhtiari friend, who had removed the chicken.

My quarters were shared by Sohrab Khan—not the philosopher, but a young doctor, who was one of the best and most extraordinary men I have ever known in Persia. He had received his medical training at Lyons, and was very skilful in his profession, but his heart and soul were in the reform movement in his country. He knew no fear, and no European could have displayed more ceaseless energy. He accom-

SOME MARCHING MEMORIES

panied every expedition in the double capacity of soldier and doctor. He was with Yeprem when the Nationalists took Tehran in 1910; he was with him again in the wars of Ardebil, at the death of Arshad-ed-Dowleh, and in the wars against Salar-ed-Dowleh. Finally, he was killed more than a year ago by Yeprem's side, when the latter was shot in another battle at Hamadan. Day by day he took his share with the army, with a rifle and double belt of cartridges, and when he arrived at our quarters ran up the Red Crescent, got out his camp-beds and bandages, and with the assistance of a very small staff installed his hospital. Queer things we did on that journey. For days we had with us, sleeping in a small adjacent room with an open door between, a patient whose diphtheria was so bad that it sounded as if his throat would burst. How he survived the daily ride was a mystery. Even Sohrab said he would die, but he did not do so, and the hard and healthy life saved the rest of us from infection.

In the evenings we would all gather in the quarters either of the Bakhtiari or of Yeprem for a council of war. Tall Bakhtiari warders, with long silver staves, stood outside in the courtyard to show that the great Khans sat within, but access was denied to no one of any importance, and it was a large council that sat on the floor, grouped round the greater gods. The chief event of the evening was always the examination of the spies, who returned from a supposed hard day in the enemy's country. Pleasant and wonderful liars they were, and could always be counted on to delight the company with an interesting tale of their own achievements, their clever disguises, and their hairbreadth escapes. They did not belong to the army,

THE ORIENT EXPRESS

but were local villagers well acquainted with the country. To me their tales frequently sounded too good to be true, so that I suspected that they had done little more than ride out of sight. I think the whole of the company often thought the same, but no one breathed such an unkind suspicion, and at every witticism of the spy, at the smart repartees which he had made to the enemy who had captured and cross-examined him, at his brilliant improvisations of having come to look for a brother who was reported to be in their village, or to do a deal about a mule, or to visit a sacred Imam Zadeh, there would be a roar of mirth and cries of "*Barak Allah! Barak Allah!*" from the crowd of black-eyed listeners. Thus encouraged, the spy would proceed to higher and finer flights, above a deep gurgling obligato from the water pipes which his audience smoked.

It was on this journey that an American gendarmerie officer, who had come out with me as a spectator of the expedition, fell ill at a critical moment. The little army swept forward and I was left behind to take charge of my companion, who had been but a short time in the country and could not yet speak the language. After a terrible twelve hours in which he fought with an old Philippine fever, we struggled forward. We made a day's march and hoped to reach camp at nightfall, but when the sun set it became clear that we had lost our way. My friend could hardly sit his horse and had to take frequent rests, but for three hours more we struggled on in the dark, climbing hills and searching vainly for the lights of the camp. My servant, Hassan, stuck close to us with the mules and baggage; and by ten o'clock, when we struck some

SOME MARCHING MEMORIES

fresh water and green grass, much as I feared for my unfortunate friend, I decided that there was nothing for it but to bivouac, as we had seen no human habitation for hours and were completely lost. Fortunately we had a bed for my friend, who was in high fever. I dosed him with quinine, and ate supper alone with a shamefully good appetite. It was a perfect night of stars, and I shall long remember my odd sensation of complete physical comfort, as I lay warm and comfortably tired upon the ground, drinking in all the enchantment of the night, yet nipped by a strong twinge of remorse at the contrast between my own content and my companion's misfortune. A glorious dawn found him somewhat better, but the wonderful sunrise threw little light on our situation. We were in a high dingle surrounded by great hills. Armed with a pair of field-glasses and a Mauser pistol, I climbed the highest to scan the surrounding country. When I reached the topmost point, some miles away in the clear blue I saw two great eagles come sailing towards me. They were at first but distant specks, coming out of the north, but they had seen the intruder and flew towards me. Larger and larger they grew, till finally they poised above me and glared down upon me from a height of perhaps eighty to one hundred yards, tremendous objects with outspread wings, almost motionless, one to the right and one to the left. I raised the Mauser pistol, and foolishly fired at the one between me and the sun, missed it, and disturbed it no more than to make it slightly swerve; but I turned round and fired at the other, which dropped stone dead with a tremendous whirl of wings, while its companion sailed away. The dead bird was a great, clean-fed eagle, with a head and breast of glittering gold, and a spread of wing 8 ft. 2 in. from tip to tip. More than half sorry at having shot it, I hauled it down the hillside to the bivouac, where Hassan gutted it and salted it. From the top of the hill I had spied a village, almost hidden among thick trees, not more than two miles away. We made straight for it, and by great good luck we had found the army. We had been stumbling in the dark around the very spot for which we were looking, and had gone to sleep almost within sight of the camp. There I got some alcohol for the eagle, but it was many days before it reached Tehran, a sorry and, in spite of my poor precautions, a none too sweet-smelling sight. The taxidermist made something of it, but the short golden feathers on the crest and throat had suffered badly.

The village we had stumbled into was Bagh-i-shah, where Yeprem fought his great engagement with some six thousand of Salar-ed-Dowleh's men. It was a sharp four hours' fight, in which Yeprem's quick-firing guns did heavy work. Twenty-four hours later I rode over the battlefield and counted as many as seventy blackened corpses, before giving up in disgust a task which I had by no means half accomplished. Horrors make a recital which one would prefer to avoid, but it is always worth while to discredit "glorious" war. Worse than the shattered bodies of the dead men and horses were the still untended, yet still alive, wounded. There was one man who lay with face black and with his body swollen up to enormous proportions. He looked dead beyond all hope, but as I watched him I saw every few moments a bubble form at the hard congealed mass of his wounded mouth. At first the

SOME MARCHING MEMORIES

awful thought that there could still be the breath of life in this terrible object came to me, but Sohrab Khan quickly reassured me. It was only, he said, the foul gas from the swollen corpse. There was a wounded soldier from Kirmanshah, no tribesman, but just a poor *topje*, one of the ragged town artillerymen who had been swept up into Salar-ed-Dowleh's miscellaneous horde. His ankle-bone had been shattered by a bullet, and was already rotten. He had dragged himself to some brackish water, and had a store of bread in his waistcloth. We gave him cigarettes, which he smoked with famished eagerness, and then we set about the gruesome job of dressing his wounds. There was another correspondent there, who did the real work. He cut away the boot with a clasp-knife, cleaned out the swarming maggots from the hole, fixed it with clean cotton-wool and antiseptic bandage. My part was only to hold tight the poor wretch's hands, and help him to control his appalling agony. He did not shout, but his teeth sawed together and his eyes rolled in a way terrible to see, while his nails dug deep into my flesh. Then in the midst of the most excruciating pain he raised his head, wrenched both my hands down towards him and covered them with kisses. But presently his pain was over. We gave him more cigarettes, and told him a mule would be sent out to pick him up.

Then came an incident characteristic of the country. Yeprem's braves were a miscellaneous lot, as I have already indicated. Just as Sohrab Khan was half a doctor and half a fighter, so did others ply a double trade. One of his stoutest followers, an Armenian from the Caucasus, is in normal times a professional

THE ORIENT EXPRESS

photographer at Tehran, and whenever he goes to the wars his great professional camera goes with him. The picturesque photo is a great institution in the East, and no Persian hero omits to be photographed on any possible occasion. The photographer was making the round of the battlefield with a group of friends, and had paused to watch the dressing of the Kirmanshah gunner's wound. For some reason it does not appear to have occurred to him to photograph the group at a moment when we were intent on attending to the soldier and would not have observed him; yet, as though it were the most natural thing in the world, when we had made the poor wretch comfortable, he solemnly proposed that we should pose for him and reproduce the tableau of my companion cleaning the wound while the soldier kissed my hands. His astonishment was great when we rejected the offer, and I suppose there are still moments when he wonders why it did not seem to us an appropriate thing to do. The cinematograph man has little to teach the Persians.

The photographer did not show a fine taste on this occasion; but no picture of Persia in these later days would be a fair one if it omitted to take account of the Armenian element. There is a prejudice in many quarters against Armenians, which I have at times shared, but my personal experience of the Armenian irregular fighter has greatly raised him in my estimation. The ordinary Armenian of the towns has frequently the worst characteristics of a subject race, and it is by him, unfortunately and inevitably, that the whole of his people are generally judged. But there is an Armenian peasant, a true mountaineer, who has qualities of bravery that merit comparison with the grit of Bulgar peasants, and has in addition an

SOME MARCHING MEMORIES

element of poetry and passion which a Serb cannot eclipse. It is worthy of note, too, that he takes on some of the characteristics of the country in which he lives. The Armenian of Constantinople is perhaps little better than the Armenian of a Persian town, but the country-bred Turkish Armenian is infinitely braver than any Persian Armenian, and the Armenian from the Caucasus is perhaps better still. Amongst all the heroes of Tabriz and Tehran, I doubt if there was a single Persian Armenian. Several had learnt the language, but the native tongues of all were Armenian and Turkish, and they came either from Turkey or from Russia. Some of them were men in every sense, and their memory will not easily leave me. The greatest of all was Yeprem, a man who would have been remarkable in any company. He had the great head and lustrous eyes of a poet, and a low-toned, musical voice, as gentle as a woman's. Yet he was a born leader, swift in surprises, and a terrible martinet when occasion demanded. His origin, like that of all his brotherhood, was mysterious, and he had been known by many names. Rumour said that he was the son of a bricklayer, and it was certain that the Russian Government had sent him to Siberia, whence he had escaped to Persian soil, and at Resht thrown in his lot with the constitutional movement. He fought innumerable fights with mere handfuls of men, always against tremendous numerical odds, and was never once defeated, so that his name rapidly became legendary, and the mere announcement of his presence would strike terror into a Persian host. He was a prey to an internal disease, but he once told me that he knew that he would never die in his bed; and his words came true at Hamadan, when he and Sohrab

THE ORIENT EXPRESS

Khan fell together. Others there were, of that terrible brotherhood of the Dashnakzutiun, who used to sing the "Marseillaise" in memorable evenings at Tabriz, with a contagious rolling swing that might have lit the fires of revolution in the soul of a usurer. Swarthy, deep-chested, merry fellows, with the inevitable bandoliers and Mauser pistols on them even at their feasts, they made a curious company. In truth, only dimly and slowly did I begin to guess what an unusually curious company they were. Most of them had wandered far. Some of them had addressed national socialist congresses, of one variety or another, in Fleet Street or its neighbourhood. One of them told me in a moment of confidence that he had been concerned in the Peckham murders. There was another, still more terrible, whose identity was only revealed to me long afterwards. It was he, I was told, who attempted to assassinate a viceroy of the Caucasus, and he was the chief executioner of the Dashnakzutiun Society. His victims were all fellow-members of the society, who were condemned to death for breach of confidence, and I was told that he himself admitted having committed over two hundred murders in fulfilment of the society's decrees. He passes under many names, and when I last heard of him he was said to be in India on a mission which I do not attempt to guess. The Armenian who revealed his identity to me had concealed him on his southern journey from Tehran to India, and gave me an interesting account of his conversation. The executioner had expressed himself as weary of his work. He told his friend that all his life he had acted from devotion to the revolutionary cause, and had carried out the society's terrible decrees without the slightest

SOME MARCHING MEMORIES

doubt that he was doing right, and in fulfilment of a sense of duty. But with the advance of age doubts had begun to creep upon him, and self-disgust was seizing hold of him. He professed an intention of finding a quiet haven in a foreign country, and devoting his declining years to making his peace with God.

Then there was Rustum, keenest but not most successful of bomb-makers. He had a little laboratory where he spent many hours preparing hand-grenades for the besieging force to throw at the enemy, but I always remember him with one or other of his arms bound up, as the result of premature explosions in working hours. There was an evening when Rustum, Keri, and I rode round Tabriz, making a reconnaissance together, and in old doorways Rustum would place experimental bombs, that I might view his results. I showed what sympathy I could, but poor Rustum was disappointed. The doors always withstood assault, and were only spattered over with small marks. Rustum could speak French well, and I have seen him hold a whole room enthralled while he recited passages from Byron and from Scott's *Lady of the Lake* in Armenian and Russian. I have a letter before me now which he wrote to me some time afterwards from Constantinople. It is on the notepaper of the Dashnakzutiun Society, headed with a dagger crossed by a pen, and begins, "Cher compagnon d'armes."

It was early in the siege of Tabriz that I first got to know Zoarabian. Well I remember him, brushing the snow from his rough fur cap one morning in Sattar Khan's house at Amrakiz, whither he had come to join in counsel. Vartanian came with him too—Vartanian, who had seen much war and whose fiddle ravished all hearts.

THE ORIENT EXPRESS

Zoarabian was an Armenian from the Caucasus, and a tiger to fight. But he was not one of the soldiers of fortune who had swept into the fighting city with the autumn storms along the Julfa road. He was a Russian exile of old standing, and had for some years lived in Tabriz a sober, upright and respected life. His wife and family were with him, and he lived in a large and comfortable house. His children married in Tabriz, and Zoarabian had become a leading member of the great Armenian community of the city. Remembering that his head was forfeit in Russia, he eschewed politics, and lived in peace. The Russian Consulate molested him not at all, and may well have been in ignorance of his honest mercantile existence.

Then the troubles came, and last of all the siege, and Zoarabian did not hesitate. He defended the town.

After that first meeting I saw him often, and we became friends. He would come and sit for long in the rooms that I had rented behind the Consulate for the special reception of " politicals," the Anjuman and their friends. Sometimes—as at Easter, " for the sake of Holy Religion "—he would pay me a ceremonious visit, but his informal calls and confidences were frequent.

Once he asked me to a party, still a rueful and comic memory. The message came to me through Haji Khan, my Persian secretary, and whether the description of the entertainment was due to an error on Zoarabian's part or on Haji's, it reached me as an invitation to dinner. Accordingly, at eight o'clock, the appointed hour, I betook myself to Zoarabian's house, and found a large company sitting ranged in a row on hard bentwood chairs, all round a room. There was no Persian there except Haji Khan; the

SOME MARCHING MEMORIES

remainder of the company consisted of the Armenian and Georgian Fedai, the backbone of the defence, and a number of Armenian ladies, their relatives, all dressed in their holiday best. Sweet biscuits and glasses of hot tea circulated freely, and presently the company became gay. Vartanian played the violin, and country dances started. For an hour or two no suspicion of the truth dawned on me, for in those parts of the world one may dine at any hour, and eat and drink anything as a preliminary to dinner. But as the evening wore on and songs and dances alternated, it became clear to me that the unfortunate Haji Khan and myself were the only two of the company who had not already dined, and that this was an evening party. It was a merry party enough, but perhaps the person who was most amused was Mr. Consul-General Wratislaw, with whom I was staying. I returned to him towards midnight, and made him produce from his larder a large ham—a thing of great value in those days of siege.

When the Russian troops came, and the siege was over, Zoarabian returned to his peaceful way of life. He became once more a plain, useful citizen of Tabriz. For a time no one molested him, but some six months later his account came. What his old political offence was I do not know, but the Russians had not forgotten. The following winter he was arrested and hanged. Others suffered a like fate. Two years later Ijlal-el Mulk, who had been Governor of the town during the siege, visited Tehran and came to dine with me. I asked after old friends, but was soon discouraged. The first four for whom I made inquiry had been hanged.

CHAPTER VII

FROM TEHRAN TO KASHAN

On August 26, 1912, I left Tehran with the intention of finding my way to the Persian Gulf. South of Isfahan, the alternative routes through the Bakhtiari country to Mohammerah and through Shiraz to Bushire were both declared closed to travellers, and were in the hands of plundering tribesmen. I hoped, however, by one way or the other, to reach the Gulf in a few weeks, and, after a short tour in India, to see the lights of London town again by the following November. It was a sorry reckoning. It was November before I reached the Gulf, and by January 1, 1913, after a visit to India and a brief halt in Egypt, I found myself in Salonika. There was little left of February when, after a tour through Macedonia and a glimpse of the second bombardment of Adrianople, the Orient Express brought me back to London.

But of these things I had no inkling when I set forth from Tehran on a warm August day.

It was in the cool dark of the tunnelled archway that spans the road at Shah Abdul Azim, as I watched the mules being loaded in the sun for their first long march, that a Musulman woman whispered in my ear—

"Sahib, how long will your journey to the Persian Gulf take?"

FROM TEHRAN TO KASHAN

"If it be God's will, not more than six weeks," I answered, showing none of the surprise which I felt at being addressed by a woman, whose neat dress made plain that she was no beggar, in the sacred and somewhat fanatical village of Shah Abdul Azim. It was also strange that she appeared to know my destination.

She lifted her veil a little, showing a childish pretty face with eyes full of tears.

"When, then, will Hassan come back to me?" she asked.

Hassan was my servant, and the tiny mystery thus disappeared. His family had come to Shah Abdul Azim to see him off. This was his wife, and hard by stood her mother holding his infant in her arms. I answered her questions as well as I could, whereupon she disappeared with a sudden shy movement and the words—

"*Hassan bi shuma supurdam* (I have entrusted Hassan to you)."

Two hours later, when I started alone to overtake my caravan in the cool of the evening, an unknown man held my stirrup.

"I have entrusted Hassan to you," said he, and proved to be a brother of that much-related person.

Inasmuch as Hassan had been with me for two years, and twice to the wars, the idea that I was in charge of him, when for so many purposes I daily expected him to take charge of me, came with the force of novelty, and incidentally shed a light on the evil reputation of the southern roads. I devolved responsibility with the easy pious phrases of Islam—

"I have entrusted him to God. May He be his keeper!"

THE ORIENT EXPRESS

After that for one week the word *supurdan* (entrust) fell frequently on my ears. In the dusk of the same evening, as I followed the iron poles of the Indo-European telegraphs in a short cut across the desert, a shadowy horseman suddenly appeared upon the curving road that I had left, and, seeing me, galloped towards me with a rifle on his saddlebow, shouting a challenge. When we met I discerned the uniform of a gendarmerie officer, and he explained that he merely wished to satisfy himself that I was not a robber.

"But the road from here to Kum is quite safe. As far as Aliabad it is entrusted to me, and nothing could be safer."

"That is good news. For I was not quite certain that you yourself were not a robber." And I showed him the revolver that I had cautiously got ready on his approach.

He laughed away its necessity with pleasant vanity. "I am the revolver on this road, and better than any six-chamber. But after Kum you will need it. There are no gendarmes there. This road is entrusted to me."

I thanked him for his very interesting information, and after profound bows we lost each other in the dark. But his boast was true enough. The road to Kum is well policed by the Swedish gendarmerie, and at each post one finds a small squad of men whose desire to do all in their power to assist the traveller does credit to their European instructors. This disposition is the more welcome as in several cases the caravanserais which they have taken for their use are now the only rest-houses available for the traveller. The post-houses are closed, for the post-carriage

FROM TEHRAN TO KASHAN

service to Isfahan no longer exists. It was never a brilliant affair, and one grumbles still at its counterpart on the Resht road, the crazy carriages and the scrawny horses. Yet it was a miracle of speed, with its relays night and day, in comparison with present means of progression. And in truth it did always wear the air of a miracle of Persian efficiency to find at each successive stage four horses, not fresh indeed, but at least different, to take one on one's journey. It was a gigantic conception, and when the *entrepreneur* for the Isfahan road died in the spring, there was apparently no remaining brain capable of grappling with it. So the post-houses were shut and the carriages disappeared. The Tehran mail goes on donkeys now, and takes seventeen days to reach Isfahan.

It is conceivable that there are a number of people in England who have never heard of Nayib Hussein. Yet he has frequently been "in the papers," and in Tehran his name is a household word. Household words are frequently bad words, and Nayib Hussein is one of the worst, a bogey to frighten children. He is a robber chief, an old barbarian steeped in crime, who holds sway for many miles round Kashan. He has frequently occupied the town itself, and in the last two years has defeated every expedition sent against him. Two years ago he caused the resignation of the Foreign Minister, because in the street fighting at Kashan an over-zealous police officer entered the house of a Persian under Russian protection. Ten months ago the Indo-European telegraph office was bombarded by Cossacks in an endeavour to assert the majesty of law against some of Nayib Hussein's followers who had taken uninvited possession of the

THE ORIENT EXPRESS

roof. Six times his violent end has been joyfully announced in the official *Gazette* of Tehran, and reported to me, with indignation at the scepticism which forbade my telegraphing it to an unexpectant world. The old brigand seems likely to equal the cat in the number of his lives, and may die in his bed at the last. He is now building himself a huge fortified castle on his " estate " near Kashan, where, supported by his sons, apt heirs of his villainies, he levies blackmail in the bazaars of the town. But he has lately appeared in a new *rôle*. The Government, having utterly failed to bring him to the gallows, has invited him to assume responsibility for the safety of the roads from Kashan to Kum and Yezd, and for several stages from Kashan to Isfahan, these being the roads on which no caravan was safe from his depredations. Nayib Hussein has been pleased to accept, and this should be the classic rendering of the part of the poacher turned gamekeeper. So jealous is he of his new responsibility that he did not desire that the two hundred men escorting the new Governor of Shiraz should even pass down his road. A message reached the Governor of Shiraz saying, " The road is entrusted to me. You must not travel on it with an armed force." The hint was taken. The expedition, which left Kum the morning I arrived, took a westward route and avoided Kashan.

It was on the second night's journey from Kum to Kashan that I first met the new protectors of the peace. In Persia it is better to rest during the hot day, and to strike camp at night when the moon is up. Even the hot desert wind, that blows almost incessantly by the salt lake of Kum, flags to coolness in the midnight

FROM TEHRAN TO KASHAN

hours, and simulates with half success the coolness of a zephyr. Thus it was that at three in the morning under a bright moon a turning of the road brought two advancing horsemen into sudden view, at a distance of a hundred yards. Instantly they shouted me a rough challenge to halt, and the moonlight flashed on the barrels as they unslung their rifles. "*Ashna*," I shouted back, which means an acquaintance, and is the customary lie which one flings to agitated sentries in the small hours of the morning at Tehran. "*Salamun aleikum* (may peace be upon you)," I added in an effort at propitiation, as I continued to approach until we met and halted.

"Where are you going?" they asked.

"To Kashan. Who are you?"

"We are the men of Nayib Hussein. The road is entrusted to us."

"In that case I may reasonably hope to arrive there safely."

They were as abrupt and rough a pair of policemen as any road could have, and I trusted to the softening moon to conceal both anxiety and irony. But I think the latter did not quite escape them, for one of them gave a rude chuckle.

"Yes," he said, "the road is quite safe." His tone regretted the good old days.

They asked minutely as to the number of mules and servants I had in the rear, on all which points I gave correct answers. I hoped they meant no harm; for I remembered that, if the road was entrusted to them, Hassan was entrusted to me. But I feared the confidence trick.

However, my camp arrived all right with no worse

incident than the levy of a little blackmail from the muleteer by these bravos for protecting him. My next meeting with one of Nayib Hussein's men was later in the same day at Sinsin, when I found him outside my tent, engaged in the wholly praiseworthy occupation of prodding with the butt of his rifle one of the famous scorpions of Kashan, and quite the largest I ever wish to see. The rifle was an old Martini and bore a Muscat mark, so that it would appear that the guns run in by the Persian Gulf do not all go to Afghanistan and Bakhtiariland. He was very young and friendly, and altogether less alarming than his colleagues of the night. He informed me that he was helping to take care of the road, which is "entrusted to us."

"And what did Nayib Hussein do before he found this occupation?" I asked.

"*Chapou mikard* (he used to plunder)."

"And what did you do?"

"I did the same."

"But, of course, it is better to be a road guard?"

He grinned with simple charm, and answered honestly—

"No, I like robbery better."

The proverb's dogmatic assertion that honesty is the best policy was to him mere self-evident nonsense.

"Then why," I asked, "has Nayib Hussein given up robbery on the road?"

"I do not know. Many of his men are leaving him, and going to plunder elsewhere. We do not get enough money now."

He seemed to think that the old man was becoming somewhat unaccountable, and that only his eighty

FROM TEHRAN TO KASHAN

years of age could excuse his incursion into partial honesty. But there is perhaps another explanation of Nayib Hussein's action. For, while his abstinence from road robbery gains him the favour of the Government and immunity from the vexation of occasional expeditions against him, he has by no means ceased to terrorize the neighbourhood. There is neither a horse nor a rifle in Kashan safe from him, and both merchants and peasants feel his hand. Landowners also have to sell to him at his own price, so the market is very cheap.

"You have a very good horse," remarked the smiling youth.

"Where?" I asked.

"In the caravanserai stable."

"It is not bad," I said, deprecatingly. "It was kind of you to go and look at it."

"If you wish to sell it, Nayib Hussein would like to buy it. It is just the sort of horse he likes."

"I cannot sell it, for I am on a long journey. But I am glad that Nayib Hussein's well-known taste in horses agrees with mine."

"It is a pity that you will not sell it."

His tone was disappointed, bashful, suggestive. It implied that wisdom and true nobility alike dictated that I should present the horse to him for Nayib Hussein.

During the day several other bandits arrived, all of whom examined my horse and broached the subject of his "sale." As evening approached it was even asserted that Nayib Hussein had heard of the horse, and had himself sent word that he desired to purchase it, but this I did not credit, as his headquarters were a long day's march distant. The brigands spent a merry evening in the vain but inexhaustibly amusing attempt to teach my dwarf-like Malabari cook some words of Persian. When the moon rose and my horse was led out a dozen armed men gathered round in mute demonstration while I mounted. They did not wish to press the matter further with a foreigner, but they hoped that at the last I might yield. A Persian would have taken the hint and recognized that Nayib Hussein's word was law. But *farangis* are obtuse, and I rode away, leaving them disconsolate.

All through that night the desert road rang with the sweet music of camel bells. The Eastern world was awake, and long processions of pilgrims, come from far, filed slowly on their way to Kum. Another march would take them within sight of the flashing dome of the golden mosque of Fatima the Immaculate, and into the sacred city on the 21st of Ramazan, the day of the death of Ali. Up long single files of hundreds of slow-paced, soft-footed camels I rode, and it seemed that they would never end. Sometimes the full chorus of the bells, filling all the air, would die away, but no sooner was it lost than the first faint tinkle of another caravan approaching made itself heard, until once more the night was ringing with the melody, and the swaying, shadowy shapes drew near. Some had bales of tobacco from Isfahan for the hubble-bubbles of Stambul, and some bore bales of silk from Yezd, but the more part carried pilgrims. Men and many women, slung in panniers on either side of camels, rocked with slow monotony to the dipping stride of the beasts. So had they done for many days, and so would they do for many more.

FROM TEHRAN TO KASHAN

From Kum they would go to Kerbela, and thence to Nedjef. This is religion in the East; and, if the Shiah seem in many ways to have fallen from their faith, there is still a power left that draws men and women to face the long discomforts of a pilgrimage in a country with neither inns nor railways, little water, and much sand.

But the pilgrim and the camel are eternal, and they are the magic of Persian travel. To sit in camp on a still, starlit night and hear the faint enchantment of the bells, as they die away upon the desert road, is the best of all rewards for weariness and thirsty days.

And here and there beside the camel files rode the men of Nayib Hussein, "protecting" the pilgrims. The Persian Government has entrusted the road to them. For it and all that fare thereon I can only repeat my pious wish for Hassan, "May God be their keeper!"

CHAPTER VIII

FROM KASHAN TO ISFAHAN

Happy is the owner of the horse that has no history. I had hoped that the admiration of Nayib Hussein's men for mine would have no further consequence, but at Kashan excited servants brought me news that the tale was not yet ended. Nayib Hussein's men had come into the town, and had by hap or design put up at the same caravanserai as housed my coveted horse and the mules of my caravan. All day they had laid ineffectual siege to my servants in the matter of the horse, but finally it appeared that they had despaired of compassing its acquisition from a Sahib, and had consoled themselves by taking possession of two *yaboos*, or pack ponies. The ponies were not part of my caravan, but they belonged to my muleteer's brother and partner, who was carrying goods to Isfahan for the Lynch Company, and had sociably attached his caravan to mine. It seemed from the conversation of my servants that in some mysterious way I was deeply implicated. The muleteer was a poor man, and he had established a kind of relationship. There was a clear hint of opinion that while the loss of the ponies would mean ruin for him, it would also leave an indelible stain upon my honour. What was I going to do about it?

What indeed? To appeal to the Governor against Nayib Hussein was, from all I had heard, worse than

FROM KASHAN TO ISFAHAN

useless. He is a Bakhtiari with a small body of tribesmen, and by studiously avoiding any interference with Nayib Hussein he is contriving to acquire some wealth for himself in the familiar fashion. Moreover, time pressed. The sun was setting with the inconvenient rapidity of the East. My caravan was already being led out, and my horse was saddled for the night ride of twenty-eight miles to the next stage. The stolen ponies had been taken to the *Bagh-i-Fin*, a distance of six miles in the opposite direction, the headquarters of Mashallah Khan, most powerful of Nayib Hussein's sons, who styles himself Sardar, and, now that his father has reached his eightieth year, has become the chief of this family of robbers.

Clearly there was nothing to be done but to sacrifice the ponies and accept the supposed slur upon my name, or else to prefix a twelve-mile ride to my horse's long night march, take the matter into my own hands, and seek an interview with Mashallah Khan, who was reputed to be not insensible to the influence of Europeans. The mention of the *Bagh-i-Fin* offered me some compensation for deciding on the latter course. For it came to my mind that this, which is now the home of a robber chieftain, must be none other than the royal garden of Fin, where Sir John Malcom was entertained during his stay at Kashan, on his famous embassy to the Court of Fath Ali Shah above one hundred years ago. Malcom found beauty in most things Persian, but Kashan he damned in one comprehensive sentence; it is "on the verge of a desert, and no city can present a more uninviting aspect." But in the excellent garden of Fin he found a clear stream and a small but delightful royal residence, and held learned discourse with his Persian friends as to whether there was truth in the legend that the venomous scorpions of Kashan, partaking of the Persian spirit of hospitality, refrain from stinging strangers!

There was a sudden difficulty about finding a guide, though Fin must be as well known in Kashan as Hampton Court in London. It seemed that the horses of those who knew the way were lame and that their relatives were ill; but at last a guide was found, with whom I went to the *Bagh-i-Fin*. A man with a lantern immediately emerged from the crowd of retainers at the entrance lodge and conducted me to Mashallah Khan. Through the long garden we went, and even in the dim light I could see that it is still " excellent," and that the cool stream still runs over blue tiles. How it has fallen into the hands of Mashallah Khan I do not know, but doubtless by no honest means. I found him on a rich rug in the verandah, transacting a mixture of business and merriment with his "khans" and secretary, and smoking an after-dinner water pipe. He is a man of less than middle age, with a striking face, which indicates the possession of far more than average Persian initiative and energy. Strong, curly black hair, powerful eyes, and a short curving nose add zest to the theatrical air of brigandage that many weapons and doubled cartridge belts on waist and shoulder give to all these ruffians of the road. But, as Shelley says, in Peter Bell, "sometimes the Devil is a gentleman," and it would be unbecoming to say more in criticism of Mashallah Khan, for to me he was the very flower of gallant courtesy. We exchanged compliments and cigarettes, and I got quickly to the business in hand. Then it appeared that it was all an unfortunate mistake. In the first place, he had not known that the muleteer was poor. In the second place, he had not realized that the muleteer was connected with my caravan, and that the removal of the ponies would in any way inconvenience me. Thirdly, he had desired to buy the ponies, and had merely had them removed for examination. To-morrow he proposed to send the money for them; and in proof of this a large bag, heavy with silver krans, was produced and handed to me, that I might realize what a good price would have been paid. This very bag was to have been sent to the muleteer, and was it not enough? Such ocular demonstration must have convinced the most sceptical. I agreed that it was indeed a weighty price, and regretted that circumstances prevented the muleteer from selling at so handsome a profit. Well, then, the ponies were mine and should be brought round at once, and an escort of four cavaliers should accompany me back to Kashan. So within a quarter of an hour of my arrival I took the road again, and with my muleteer's ponies and a protecting force of banditti clattered back triumphantly to Kashan.

It was eleven o'clock when I started under a bright moon to overtake my caravan on the long road to Kohrud. But it arrived before me, and in the chilly dawn I found my tent being pitched in a green, delightful mountain valley, nearly nine thousand feet above the level of the sea. The caravan had spread the news of the stolen ponies, which aroused intense curiosity, and the villagers came round to question me as to the issue. Elsewhere I have never seen Persian villagers so spontaneous and outspoken in their conversation. Their remarks were to me more interesting than they knew, and seem worth recording just as they were spoken. When I had satisfied their curiosity as to the ponies, I asked them whether they had any news of the expedition accompanying the Governor-General of Shiraz which had passed to the westward. They told me what they knew, and one asked—

"Who sent this Governorship to Shiraz; the English or the Russians?"

"Neither," I answered. "The Persian Government in Tehran has sent it."

"That cannot be. There is nothing in Tehran. *Iran kharab, Iran raft* (Persia is a ruin, it is gone)." He blew with his lips and swept the palms of his hands across one another. It was the third time within a week that a peasant had used this very gesture in addressing to me words of precisely the same import.

"The expedition must be bound up either with the Russians or the English," said another.

"The Persian Government is sending a new Governor to Shiraz," I insisted. "There is disorder there, and the Government thinks it needs a Governor."

"Of course it needs a Governorship. But is the English Government doing nothing?"

"Well, the English Government said it was time to send a Governor."

"Of course it is. We need a Governorship, too. When will they do something here? Here in Kohrud; is it English soil or Russian?"

"Neither. It is Persian."

"But will the English not come here?"

"Never."

"The Russians, then?"

FROM KASHAN TO ISFAHAN

"Perhaps, some day. I do not know. Would you like that?"

"English, or Russian, or Persian, we do not care. We want quiet. Which has the better police system, the English or the Russian? Let us have that one. Which is better?"

"I am English, so I think the English better. But if you ask a Russian, he will think the Russian better."

"The Sahib speaks the truth," said an old man. "Each for his own. But the Persian raiat knows what he wants."

"What does he want?"

"Plenty of money, plenty of bread, peace and quiet, and safe roads. Here there is good water and fine cultivation. But we have no rifles and we do not fight. We are always pillaged."

I was soon to have another instance of the prevalent alarms. Next morning early I reached Soh and sat down to wait for my caravan, which I expected in two hours. Four hours passed and it did not come. Then news came in that at a distance of only five miles from its destination it had turned back to Kohrud. The Governor of Murtchehar had sent out a courier with news that fifty mounted robbers, variously described as Kashgais, Turks, and Lurs, were in the neighbourhood, and that no caravans should proceed towards Isfahan—advice which my muleteer had promptly followed. Here was more delay. With difficulty I got some messengers who set off on foot to Kohrud, to spur on my caravan with the information that I had come safely through and seen no robbers. They promised to return by noon on the following day, bringing the muleteer with them, and I resigned my-

THE ORIENT EXPRESS

self to a campless night of waiting at Soh. Noon came on the morrow, but no caravan; only lurid tales of robbers in its stead. At four o'clock there was nothing for it but to go back and fetch the caravan myself, and the sun was sinking on the Kohrud Pass, sheer behind it in a blaze of glory, as I climbed and crossed it for the second time. I got to Kohrud village in the dark, where I found my muleteer smoking the opium of content, and with no intention, save for my arrival, of facing the perils of a road which he affected to believe was infested with cut-throats. The block of caravans was growing, for several had come in from Kashan and were likewise halted. Kohrud is the pleasantest village on the road, and the muleteers were perhaps not averse to an enforced stay, provided their daily pay continued. But for me there was no such inducement, and after I had had some hours' sleep my caravan was loaded up. Such is the force of example that the others followed suit, and by half-past three in a moonlit morning the bells of five hundred mules went ringing up the pass. The top was set in the pink flushes of the false dawn when I crossed it for the third time, my horse's head looking south-east to Isfahan. No robber nor any other molestation visited us, and two more marches brought us to the ruined greatness of Shah Abbas. *Isfahan nisf-i-jehan* was once the proud saying of its citizens. If Isfahan be in any sense to-day the half of the world, it can only be because the other half does not know how it lives. It has fallen far from its old-time majesty, and with no single caravan moving towards it from the sea, it is losing the links with the trade of East and West which

FROM KASHAN TO ISFAHAN

have made its bazaars among the most famous for merchandise in all Asia.

One more incident of the road is worth telling for its simple significance. At Kum I made my stay at the hospitable Indo-European Telegraph office, and as I rode to its door I rubbed my eyes. For there, if I saw aright, in the middle of a city was a low black tent of hair, which could belong to none but nomads. It is a familiar sight in the upland pastures of the East, where the wandering tribesmen pitch it, but what was it doing in Kum? The tale was soon told. A tribe of nomads which had the immemorial right of pasturage on certain lands had lately been dispossessed by a covetous local landowner, in connivance with the Governor. The tribesmen could get no redress, and, having tried every other form of protest, had come into Kum and taken *bast*, or sanctuary, at the Indo-European Telegraph office. For forty days the heads of the little tribe had been there, addressing vain protests to Tehran. The Prime Minister, the Treasurer-General, the Ministers of Interior and Finance, these and other officials had all been petitioned, but Tehran had no ear to lend to the grievance of poor tribesmen and had no authority to wield. So no answer came, and nothing had been done. It is little wonder that the telegraph clerks tell one tales of how Persians from outlying districts come in and visit them secretly by night, begging them to transmit requests to the British Legation to accept the applicants as British subjects. Naturally nothing comes of such entreaties. Many also turn to Russia, who makes no difficulties about dispensing her protection to petitioners.

CHAPTER IX

BRITISH INTERESTS AT ISFAHAN

In an old London geography, dated 1765, which I found in Isfahan, I read that the city "contains one hundred and sixty mosques, eighteen hundred caravanserais, two hundred and sixty public baths, a prodigious number of fine squares, streets, and palaces, in which are canals and trees planted to shade and better accommodate the people." The spacious days of Isfahan came earlier, when Elizabeth ruled in England and Akbar the Great in Delhi, and both these powerful monarchs sent missions to the splendid Court of Shah Abbas. To speak more precisely, the English mission of Sir Anthony and Sir Robert Shirley was self-appointed, but it obtained a great success, and the two brothers won the munificent favour of the Shah. On the outer walls of either side of the hall of the Chehil Sitoon, or Forty Columns, I found a fresco of an English gentleman in the costume of the early Jacobean period, and it seems not impossible that these two frescoes represent the brothers Shirley. Sardar-i-Zaffer, the present Bakhtiari Governor of Isfahan, tells me that they have been only recently uncovered, and they do not appear to have been known at the time of Lord Curzon's visit, though their records existed, for he writes that " smaller cabinets originally opened out at either end, and were adorned with portraits of European ladies and gentlemen of the day

BRITISH INTERESTS AT ISFAHAN

of Shah Abbas." Lord Curzon, who found the famous *talar* suffering from sore neglect, may be interested to learn that it has temporarily fallen on better days. The long tank before it is no longer empty, nor is the building abandoned, for it is the Governor's favourite spot, and there on the loggia he daily holds his Court and transacts all his business. It must be counted for righteousness to the Bakhtiari that they have shown a little more interest in the historical and artistic treasures of Isfahan than is customary amongst Persians. Sardar-i-Zaffer has carried out some much-needed restoration to the ceiling of the Chehil Sitoon, and himself took me out upon the roof to examine the condition of the gigantic trunks and beams. The famous wall-paintings are still in almost perfect condition. Before I left Tehran Sardar Assad showed me a set of full-sized reproductions, which had been made for him by an Isfahan artist, and had just arrived to be installed in his house in Tehran.

But Isfahan is the mouldering shrine of a vanished past. On the world-famous bridge of Ali Verdi Khan alone, of all the glories of Shah Abbas the Great, has the hand of Time fallen lightly. The dome of the beautiful *madresseh* is half denuded of its tiles, and the garden of the Eight Paradises bears the witness of decay. Even since the time of the eighteenth-century geographer, who in his figures seems to have been following Chardin, Isfahan must have fallen far, though in his day it can have been no more than the shadow of its former greatness, inasmuch as it never recovered from its savage sack by the Afghans in 1722.

In 1890, Lord Curzon relates, the commercial

THE ORIENT EXPRESS

situation was a source of legitimate pride and satisfaction to an Englishman. Though Isfahan stands midway between the Caspian and the Gulf, four-fifths of her foreign trade was British, and British commercial ascendancy was in his opinion so firmly established as to defy all assaults. Were the roads open British trade would still easily outstrip its rivals, but one can no longer say that it is safe from assault. Cotton piece goods are the largest import. In 1890 Manchester was, in Lord Curzon's words, "the universal clothier of Isfahan." In the year ended March 1911 the tale was still satisfactory enough. In spite of the block on the Shiraz road, the Ahwaz route was still open and British goods continued to come in. The import of cotton piece goods amounted to £357,000, and of the 23,000 bales 22,000 were British and 1000 were Russian. The Consular report for the year ending March 1913, which will appear in 1914, will tell a very different story. The representative of a Moscow firm has recently visited Isfahan, and, as not a bale of goods had come in from the south since the Ahwaz road was closed, four months before my visit, he had no difficulty in booking large orders for Russian cotton goods, and caravans containing them were coming in. Equally significant are the figures for sugar, the import of which is worth £160,000. In normal times 65 per cent. of this was French sugar imported by British firms by way of the south, and 35 per cent. was Russian. The last Consular report printed points out that in 1910–11 this proportion was precisely reversed. Since then the southern figure has fallen heavily, and the import in the summer of 1912 was simply *nil*. The shifting

BRITISH INTERESTS AT ISFAHAN

balance of trade has naturally caused the opening of a Russian bank, for which a few years ago no necessity could have been found, and so, after previous failures, the Russian Banque d'Escompte was definitely established in Isfahan at the end of 1910.

But the familiar trend of foreign trade is British, and if only the roads were reopened it would thrive once more. Nevertheless it is no longer unchallenged, and it is probable that the Isfahan market is one in which in the end British merchants must resign themselves to seeing their supremacy pass away. Insecurity on the roads has already sadly constricted it, and Isfahan no longer serves as a distributing centre for Western Persia and for Tehran and the Caspian provinces. But, apart from any question of security, British merchants must learn to realize that by agreement Isfahan is in the Russian sphere, and that Russian influence, hitherto unfelt, must be expected to increase and English influence to wane. The truth is that in modern conditions the prevalence of English commerce and the English language in Northern Persia is something of an anomaly. In former times Russia was content with a military and political predominance. Business was not for her, and unless an English concession appeared to assume too large dimensions, as in the case of Reuter, internal exploitation was left to Englishmen. Thus it came about that England covered Persia with telegraph poles, and that England became the principal banker and trader in Tehran as well as in Isfahan and Southern Persia. She attained, in fact, a position in the north which she had no military or diplomatic strength to maintain. The capital is close to the Russian frontier, and is by many weeks removed from the Gulf. Russia therefore must in the nature of things always control Tehran, and now that she is no longer indifferent to commerce she has the means of making her power felt. This it is that the English trading community in Northern Persia are slow to realize. They complain of a diminution of English influence, and of a lack of support from the Foreign Office. They overlook the fact that in the last resort there are few means of supporting Englishmen in Northern Persia, and that English banks and telegraphs are relics of an easier-going past. Their foundation to-day would be impossible. Isfahan is the central point between north and south, but by agreement it is in the Russian sphere. Its mercantile character is English, but in time it will be otherwise. No Englishman, perhaps, can see the change without a pang. But it has been so decided, and it is idle to regret it now. Some words of the eighteenth-century philosopher have a certain aptness to the present situation, even if we hope that some fortunate issue may yet appear. He wrote: "The great scheme of the English in trading with the Persians through Russia promised great advantages to both nations, but it has hitherto answered the expectations of neither. But nothing can be said with certainty on that head till the government of Persia is in a more settled condition than it is at present."

CHAPTER X

A NIGHT ADVENTURE AT KUMISHA

FROM Isfahan south to the Gulf there was no road for the ordinary traveller. Both the Bakhtiari road to Mohammerah and the Shiraz route to Bushire were at the mercy of bands of well-armed tribesmen, who delight in loot and suffer no caravan to escape them. Having reached Isfahan I had therefore a choice of evils before me. The authorities informed me that it was merely a question whether I preferred to be robbed by Bakhtiaris or Kashgais, and that I was free to choose. If, however, I could wait a few days I might hope to reach Shiraz in safety by accompanying the new Governor-General of Fars, who had already reached Isfahan with two hundred men, two Swedish officers, and four Creusot guns. From Isfahan he would move south with a still larger force, as a squadron of gendarmerie, with two Swedish officers, had come from Shiraz to meet him, and a "regiment" was to be raised in Isfahan.

But the Governor-General, though he had arrived four days before me, showed no sign of moving, and declared that he was waiting for the Isfahan regiment to be collected. As his preparations in Tehran had occupied seven months, the fear of spending Christmas in Isfahan rose before my eyes. It seemed possible that the anticipation of the Governor's march

THE ORIENT EXPRESS

might in itself tend to clear the road of robbers, and that, with good luck, I might get through. So after nine days in Isfahan I set forth alone, leaving a shower of gloomy prophecies behind me. At nightfall I reached the first caravanserai, and found it barricaded, with a local caravan, travelling to Kumisha, bottled up inside it in a state of panic. I had the greatest difficulty in persuading the inhabitants that I and my servants were not robbers, and that it was quite unnecessary to discharge rifles at us in the dark. The firing was fortunately wild, and presently it ceased, and there was an excited rally to the great main gate, which, with infinite caution and repeated demands for assurances as to my harmless character, was opened by a babbling crowd of muleteers. They explained that at a pass four miles further on there were two hundred robbers, and that they had already spent three terror-stricken days in the caravanserai, waiting for these to depart. They had that day sent out a series of scouts, none of whom had returned. Therefore their nerves were somewhat strained, and hearing the sound of horsemen they had feared that the tribesmen, grown weary of waiting for the caravan, had come to attack it in the caravanserai.

A scout came in before the dawn with news that the road was clear; so we all moved out and travelled for two days without seeing any enemy, to Kumisha, the caravan's destination. At Kumisha there is a telegraph office, and by this I received information that the Governor-General would really leave Isfahan that day, and urgent Consular instructions that on no account should I proceed further alone, as a large body of Kuhgelui tribesmen was reported to be on the

A NIGHT ADVENTURE AT KUMISHA

move at a distance of two stages. There was nothing for it but to wait, and the good portion of the news proved somewhat illusory; for when, two days later, the Governor-General arrived he was still without the Isfahan regiment, and was determined to wait for it in Kumisha. So for seven days more we sat in Kumisha, till Isfahan collected its men, and sent them on, three hundred strong.

The resources of Kumisha are limited, but there was the pleasant company of four Swedish officers, and after five days the hand of time flung an adventure into our laps as a reward for our delay.

The truth of the matter we only learnt later. A certain Ali Khan, with a band of seventy robbers, had for years terrorized the district, and successive Governors of Isfahan had sent expeditions against him in vain. Of late, finding the arm of government weak, he had come into Kumisha itself, and occupied a quarter close to the Government house, holding the local Governor under his thumb. The advent of gendarmerie under European officers with the promise that presently the road would be made safe and vengeance meted out to robbers was highly displeasing to this brigand. The petty Governor was therefore induced to write a series of vexatious letters to Count Lewenhaupt, the Swedish commanding officer, bringing charges against the gendarmerie of obtaining goods in the bazaar without payment, all of which proved, on examination, to be false. Finally, there came a midnight letter which stated that some gendarmes in a house close to the Governor's were at that moment guilty of the crime of singing. Dancing men were also present, and the whole quarter was

THE ORIENT EXPRESS

being kept awake. The Governor announced that he could not be answerable for the consequences which might flow from these enormities.

The gendarmes concerned were two officers, and two men of good family who were passing through the ranks in order to obtain a commission, this being the only method allowed by the Swedish officers. All four had been granted special leave to dine with a friend in Kumisha whom they had known in Tehran. Count Lewenhaupt therefore proposed that we should abandon our game of bridge, and accompany him to the scene of revelry by night in order to stop any proceedings which might shock the Governor. So we threaded our way through the silent, dim bazaar, and out into a maze of moonlit alleys. Suddenly we heard the sound of rifle shots in quick succession, and, hurrying on, we came upon the four gendarmes, chattering in a state of wild excitement. They declared that one of them had been taken to the Governor's house and beaten. He had made his escape by shouting that he had a bomb and by producing something which threw his assailants into such a state of terror that he had been able to rush out, whereupon all had been fired upon from the roofs of the adjacent quarter and of the Governor's house. This seemed true enough, for in the middle of the tale the fusillade recommenced and the bullets began to patter round us, burying themselves with a quick succession of thuds in the mud walls.

Count Lewenhaupt sent for fifty gendarmes, and we approached the Governor's door. It appeared that the Governor slept soundly, for not the most thunderous knocks and shouts could elicit any

A NIGHT ADVENTURE AT KUMISHA

response. Save for our noise, the silence of the grave reigned once more throughout the quarter. At last a servant shuffled behind the door and, on being informed that Count Lewenhaupt had come in answer to the Governor's letter, declared that the Governor had run away. Nothing would induce him to open the door, so we withdrew to await the gendarmes. Fifty came up at the double, and some more shots rang out, whereupon the gendarmes returned the fire, and some one must have seen his man. The Governor's house was quickly surrounded, and we mounted the adjoining roofs The firing ceased, and Count Lewenhaupt announced that if the house were opened to him in order that he might speak with the Governor, no further steps would be taken that night. If, however, this were not done the doors would be forced. A gendarme with a stentorian voice was selected to make this mild announcement, which I duly translated to him. But the excitement of this giant was too much for him, and the message which he bellowed down into the silent courtyard was this—

"Open the door, you sons of burnt fathers The major himself has come with four thousand men. He has cannon, he has bombs, he has everything. He will kill you all; so open the door at once."

"Laughter holding both his sides" is a dangerous companion on a roof, and I was endeavouring to recover my equilibrium, disturbed by this unexpected version of the major's message, when I was overwhelmed in a rush for the ground. With no bones broken, but with eyes full of dust, the commanding officer and I, in each other's arms, found ourselves at the bottom of a wall from which one would not willingly jump in daylight. Some one had shouted that a back door had been forced open, and a rush carried us thither. We checked in the doorway, where a wounded man lay in a pool of blood. A bullet had passed right through his body. The courtyard was empty, and so were the main rooms. Huddled in a corner of the kitchen we found a corpulent cook, who simulated with astonishing art the aggrieved air of a newly awakened man. By the Prophet, he swore, he neither knew nor had heard anything, either of shots or of thunderous batterings on the doors. Another servant was unearthed and told the same tale, till some one unkindly nudged him into the courtyard tank by which he stood. When he floundered out from this unexpected bath the chorus of laughter seemed to reassure him, for he summoned up the semblance of a grin, and confessed that he kept the door but had been afraid to open it.

His Excellency the Governor was still to seek, and a curious search it was. The building at one end of the courtyard proved to be a prison, wherein were nine old men without a gaoler, their feet locked in wooden stocks and heavy chains round their necks and wrists. No doubt their crimes were many, but the sinners were old and battered, scarcely recognizable human wrecks, and Count Lewenhaupt released them all. This produced an unexpected scene, for the old men indulged both in whimsical antics and in pathetic demonstrations of the most vehement kind, to show their gratitude for such a miraculous deliverance. The stable was the most productive place, for there, one by one, seven of the Governor's trembling bodyguard were found. Two were hidden in mangers and the rest

A NIGHT ADVENTURE AT KUMISHA

were buried in the hay. All were detained for examination on the morrow, and nine rifles were seized. The Governor himself was found later in a neighbouring house. But, in the street outside, one of the Swedish officers made the biggest capture of all. For, seeing a man creeping along under the shadow of a wall, he seized and held him. It was none other than Ali Khan himself, with a Mauser pistol, the magazine of which was half empty, six of its cartridges having been fired at us earlier in the night.

There was a Court-martial upon Ali Khan next morning, over which Count Lewenhaupt presided; and the whole strange tale was then revealed, proving that the prisoner had planned an attack upon the gendarmes. It was a curious hotch-potch of tragedy and comedy. The witnesses were kept apart and examined separately; and, though the life of a man was at stake, it was impossible for the Court to maintain its gravity when some of the evidence was given. Each of the Governor's retainers who had been unearthed from the hay presented a more comic appearance than his predecessor, and each told the same convincing tale of the epidemic of fear that had spread inside the Governor's quarters when the clever gendarme whom they were beating had asserted that he had a bomb and, pulling something from his wallet, had jerked it in the air. The Governor himself, who had been urging on the beaters, bolted up the chimney. The other witnesses described how they had dashed for any available hole or corner, and avowed their fear without shame. The examination at this point in every case was something like this—

"Have you ever seen a bomb?"

THE ORIENT EXPRESS

"No."

"What is a bomb?"

"I do not know. Something terrible, that bursts and destroys everything."

"Is this what the gendarme had?" the President asked, holding up the tin case found in the gendarme's wallet.

"Yes," the witness replied, obviously uneasy at seeing it so carelessly handled.

"And here is the bomb," the President blandly added, drawing the gendarme's spectacles out of their case and showing them to the shamefaced witness.

The climax of absurdity appeared to be reached with the last "soldier," who declared that his name was Haji Baba, and who, with a fat, crimson face, long hair, a huge hat, a smocklike overall, and a capacity for comic folly in his answers, presented the picture of a rustic butt as played in Shakespeare. But Haji Baba was surpassed by an ancient coal-black negro gaoler, with a hairless face and a squinting eye, who, on being asked what information he possessed, pushed outwards the palms of his hands, threw back his head, sent a roll of smiling wrinkles rippling from his chin up to the top of his skull, like a Venetian blind being drawn up, and replied in a long-drawn, high falsetto, "*He-e-e-e-eech* (nothing)." He had heard a shot, and promptly left his prisoners and hid in the straw. He knew no more till a gendarme had come and pulled him out; but he expressed great satisfaction at the release of the prisoners, which promised him a temporary holiday.

The robber's tale was as simple as it was unconvincing. Yet, though he lied throughout, he held his

A NIGHT ADVENTURE AT KUMISHA

head high, showed no fear, and with his gentle, handsome face inevitably produced the impression that he was a better man than all the quaint figures who were swearing his life away. Though all the population was prepared to testify to his misdeeds and to recount how he had killed an enemy by placing him head downwards in a caldron of boiling water, Ali Khan maintained that he was only a poor and inoffensive shepherd. The Mauser pistol he had purchased to protect his flocks against robbers, and the fact that it was richly ornamented with silver bands was due to an expensive caprice when he had had a little money. He had not fired it for two months, and the four cartridges found in it must have remained from that occasion. The state of the barrel was due to the fact that it had not been cleaned. He had an aged father, who lived in another quarter of the town. Returning from his father's house in the small hours, he had heard firing and, in alarm, was endeavouring to reach his home unobserved when he was unjustly arrested. As for the Governor, he had never met him personally.

The Governor also denied personal acquaintance with the robber, but there was a host of witnesses to prove extensive intercourse, and the Governor's servants separately testified to the fact that Ali Khan had been with their master the previous afternoon. Finally the two men were brought face to face, when the Governor admitted that he knew the robber. All the witnesses testified that the latter had a mother living in another quarter of the town, but that his father was dead. Nevertheless he stoutly maintained the existence of his aged father.

For seven hours the Court listened to witnesses,

after which it condemned the prisoner to death. The President informed him of this decision, and, after reminding him of the crimes proved against him, asked him whether he had any requests to make or desired to see his relatives before his death.

"I have committed no fault," he answered. "But let the will of God be done. I should like my mother to be summoned to see me."

"You have no other request?"

"No."

"Very well. It shall be done. But you have an aged father. If you will tell us where to find him, we shall send for him also."

For the first time the colour left his face. He bowed his head and put his hands on his breast, in silent admission that he had lied.

Half an hour before sunset he was shot.

Two days later the regiment swung in from Isfahan, and four days' marching brought us to Abadeh.

CHAPTER XI

AT THE TOMB OF CYRUS

You may usually be sure of finding yourself alone if you visit a ruin, however famous, at midnight. All the world since Byron seems to have been to the Coliseum by moonlight, yet when once I wandered into it under the Roman stars I found myself in a solitude that seemed complete. Perhaps, as befell Lothair in the same enchanted spot, some unseen watcher followed me, or it may be that the policemen were changing their beat; but, however it happened, there was no footfall but my own to break the silence of the dungeons. If this could be the case in the Coliseum, to which, spurred by the sentimental fumes of poets, mild-eyed, melancholy tourists might more especially be expected to resort by night, were it not that they so strongly prefer the garish day, how much more may the chance traveller count on solitude if he visit the tomb of Cyrus by night? Pasargardæ is set in the Persian wilderness, hard by a road on which at present no one dares to travel. The local inhabitant of the oasis takes no interest in a building which he ignorantly believes to be the grave of Solomon's mother. The Governor-General of Fars had pitched his camp five miles away, and therefore, after an afternoon spent in examining the ruins, when night fell and the fancy seized me to visit the tomb once more, I had little doubt that I should find it as deserted by night as it is by day.

Great, then, was my surprise when I found seated at the entrance a man clad in a long, flowing robe. Evidently no common peasant this, for the majesty of his bearing and the force written in his face were such as you will nowhere find in modern Persia. He greeted me, without rising, in a slow, pleasant voice; and when I had returned his greeting he said—

"I am Cyrus, son of Cambyses, the King, the Achæmenian, the King of Kings; whose tomb you have come to see."

There was no boasting in his tone as he uttered his titles; rather was there the gentle irony of one who stated an amusing fact. It was as if he had said, "How fine it used to sound, and how little it all means now!"

There was nothing for it but to respond to this unexpected introduction, and to explain that I was but a wandering correspondent.

"I trust that I do not disturb you," I added. "Your Majesty has clearly a right to your own tomb, but I did not expect to find you here."

"Nay," he answered. "I am even glad to converse with you. But since I am but the shade of that I was, call me not 'Majesty.' Yet where else should I be found, if not in my tomb?"

By starlight the logic of this seemed unanswerable. To a shade who took himself for granted it was difficult to explain that neither there nor anywhere else did one expect to find him at all.

"But I know," he added with a smile, as though solving the problem. "You have a professor in

AT THE TOMB OF CYRUS

England who even denies that this is my tomb, and has buried me elsewhere in a Pasargardæ of his own."

Confusion covered me. I regretted the professor and inwardly anathematized his theory. Hastily I endeavoured to apologize for my country.

"It is true that some, both in France and England, have denied the tomb. But the great majority of our learned men make no doubt that it is yours."

"Wonderful discernment! I am he who overthrew Astyages the Mede, and Crœsus, King of Lydia. The world rang with my deeds. Did I not release the children of Israel, of whose records you are so curious, from their captivity in Babylon? The Greek colonies fell before me, and my satraps governed Asia to the western sea,—all but those stubborn islands that have ever been to conquerors more trouble than they are worth. But with Polycrates and his Samians, too, I should have dealt, had I lived; and not by treachery as did Oroetes, satrap of Sardis, after my death. The Greeks themselves, who by their art in writing have made the world believe what they willed, wrote generously of my greatness. They have written history to suit themselves, so magnifying their own deeds as to cause laughter amongst us shades at the tales they have fobbed off upon mankind for evermore. But Xenophon, who was a plain soldier, did me justice, and I must even confess that I was not all he painted me. My deeds, then, are what the world calls remembered; that is to say, they are set, though not accurately, in the volume of history, and here and there a scholar reads them; and so shall it be for ever. But I, Cyrus, am forgotten, so that men learn with difficulty where my body was laid. And who knows or cares what manner of man I was when I was not making war?"

"And yet," said I, "it seems to me that mankind in peace is curious of its history. It is you warriors who make history and at the same time destroy it. How many records of Astyages the Mede did your soldiers deface in Ecbatana? And, in turn, how much more of you and of the empire that you founded might we not know had not Alexander burnt the city of Darius? As for your tomb, had your posterity been left to worship at their fire-altars in peace I doubt not that all men would know your burial-place. But Musulman conquerors came in, the flames upon the altars of Zoroaster were quenched, and with them the memory of the kings who worshipped Ormuzd. Has history any guarantee of its existence while wars continue? Even now, when records are so plentiful that we despair of reading them, men say that our civilization is not safe, and that it might be submerged in some furious wave of conquest from the East."

"Have no fear. For even if the millionth part alone of what is written now survive, the historians will have a prodigious deal to write of your generation. But what you say is true; for it was the Persians who forgot my tomb. And none of them now believe your learned men. For they all hold that Solomon's mother lies here, and fond women come often with shreds of cloth for offerings, thinking to gain the lady's favours in their loves or in their labours. Yet Bathsheba's bones were laid in the dust of Palestine hundreds of years before I was on earth, and at no time did she pass this way. Nor was there any memory of her when I defeated Astyages in this very place, and built

AT THE TOMB OF CYRUS

thereon my royal city of Pasargardæ, naming it after my tribe. Thus strange are the legends of history. The grave on which my loving wife lavished all her care, and which even Alexander respected and restored, passes for the tomb of an adulterous woman of another country and an earlier day."

Curiosity here overcame me, and, perceiving that the shade of Cyrus seemed already fully informed as to the deplorable gaps in our information, I had the less shame in betraying my ignorance.

"Who, then, was your wife? For it grieves me to say that this also is a matter of dispute, as is the origin of the tomb."

"My wife was Nitetis, daughter of Apres, King of Egypt. Better than war and better than wine I loved her. Of all the glories of my time and state she is the least remembered, and yet to me she was the greatest. They called me the King of Kings, but in truth I was the slave of Nitetis. And now, out of all that vanished greatness, her wisdom and her beauty alone seem desirable. To me, as to you, the empire that I founded is but dust and vanity; but so that I might hold Nitetis in my arms I would live in the body once again. Of all the gods and goddesses whom we ignorantly worshipped there was none like Anahita, whom the Greeks called golden Aphrodite. Nitetis and I were fast bound in the chain of love, so that she was well content. Only she could never forget her own country, and her talk was always of Egypt: how that the Egyptians were more lettered and more polished than all other nations, and the women more beautiful and more elegantly clothed. So that I was fain to humour her by ordering my Court in the

THE ORIENT EXPRESS

Egyptian mode, and by endeavouring to soften our rude Persian customs to the tone of Egypt. She herself was ever dressed in the Egyptian fashion, and her earrings and other golden ornaments were so wrought. Architects and masons also I brought from Egypt, and in this way Egypt set the fashion in my kingdom; until the time of Darius, son of Hystaspes, when the Greeks began to assert their supremacy in the arts.

"In truth, Nitetis so stirred the imagination of our son, Cambyses, with her tales of Egypt, that after my death he must needs go thither, pretexting that he was the grandson of Apres, King of Egypt, and seeking the throne for himself. This my tomb was built by the care of Nitetis in our paradise, and hence it is that it differs from those of the other Achæmenian kings which you will see near Parsa, the city of Darius burnt by Alexander, whose shade you may find there. For this is built in the Egyptian fashion, and on yonder statue you can see the Egyptian crown."

He pointed in the direction of the monolith with the statue of Cyrus crowned, where till recently might be read the cuneiform inscription *Adam Kurush Khshayathiya Khakhamanishiya* ("I am Cyrus, the King, the Achæmenian").

"When I died here—for I was not slain, as some have fabled, by Tomyris, Queen of the Massagetæ—Nitetis caused my body to be embalmed in the Egyptian manner, and placed it not in stone, but in a gilded wooden coffin, which she set within, here, upon a couch the feet whereof were of beaten gold. On it was a coverlet of Babylonian tapestry, with purple cloaks and rich Median garments. Near by was a

AT THE TOMB OF CYRUS

table with offerings which Nitetis gave for me, according to the custom in Egypt: swords, necklets, and earrings, cunningly inlaid with precious stones by Egyptian craftsmen. Yonder where the wall ran was a house for the Magi whose duty was to guard my sepulchre, to whom and their descendants an allowance was made of a sheep daily, with corn and wine in fixed measure, and once a month a horse for sacrifice. Such was this tomb when Nitetis wrought it of her love for me. And here above the doorway ran the inscription, 'I am Cyrus, son of Cambyses, who founded the Empire of Persia and was King of Asia. Grudge me not therefore this monument.'

"But the descendants of the Magi were drunken, thieving fellows, fitter to serve Ahriman than Ahuramazda. So they stole the treasure from the couch and table, and even wrenched the golden lid from my coffin. Nor did they reverence my body at all, but cast it on the ground. And in this wise Alexander found it when he came to Pasargardæ on his homeward march from India. For the Magi had concealed their theft, and the fame of the tomb was spread abroad, so that Alexander desired to visit it. But when he found my sepulchre rifled and my embalmed body in fragments, his heart was touched. Some said that he who had burnt the palace of Darius at Parsa, and had taken the treasure of Pasargardæ six years earlier, had come back to plunder my tomb, which he had then forgotten; and that, finding himself forestalled, he covered his chagrin by an act of generosity. But I know that it was not so. For when the inscription had been read to him his heart was very full, and he said to Aristobulus, 'So, then, his own people have grudged his tomb to Cyrus, King of Asia, of whom the world stood in awe. Shall I, who have conquered Asia, fare better?' Then he called the Magi and questioned them as to who had done this deed, and when they all denied he caused them to be tortured. But none confessed; which was, in truth, natural, for it was not they but their fathers who had robbed my coffin. At the last he entrusted Aristobulus with the task of restoring all exactly as it was in old times. And this Aristobulus did, enclosing my body in the coffin, restoring the couch, and reproducing the offerings and ornaments as before. The door he sealed with Alexander's royal signet, and the fear of this preserved the tomb inviolate a little space. But tidings of Alexander's death did not long delay, and the Magi once more despoiled it."

"This second outrage must have been peculiarly exasperating," I murmured, much at a loss for comment.

"Nay," answered the shade of Cyrus. "It was a matter of indifference to me. Alexander might have spared himself both trouble and expense, except in so far as I took pleasure in his desire to respect the dead. But the love of Nitetis in life was all to me, and the tomb by which she strove to manifest it in death was nought. As the delusion is still prevalent amongst men, it may be of interest if you give them an assurance from me that the dead derive no satisfaction from the magnificence of their graves."

"Who will believe my report? It were better that I say nothing, lest men say that I do not speak the truth."

"But I think that newspapers desire strange tales,

AT THE TOMB OF CYRUS

and that my name is still so spoken amongst men that they would rejoice to read of this our interview."

"Newspapers do, indeed, desire strange tales, but my newspaper is very exacting that the tales be true. And this is beyond belief."

"There is an incredulity which is simply folly," said Cyrus. "It compels men to falsehood, lest they be thought liars."

In his tone I detected a shade of disappointment that he was not to figure in *The Times*. One does not like to quarrel with a ghost, and there is a Persian proverb which says "Beware of kings, poets and women."

"I might try to tell the tale," I answered, "but I cannot guarantee its publication. In any case I shall have to say that it was a dream. There is a spirit of scepticism in London, which would otherwise manifest itself in blue pencil."

"It is even as I said. You must lie to be believed. Call it a dream then, but there is one who will believe in its truth."

"And who is that?"

"A satrap whom your great Queen sent to govern the Empire of India. Twenty-three years ago he came here and examined my tomb. Afterwards he wrote learnedly in a large book to prove that it was indeed mine. He will believe your report, and will rejoice that you have heard from me that Nitetis built it."

But would he believe? I doubted. And while I looked at the stars in doubt, the shade of Cyrus vanished.

CHAPTER XII

A TALK WITH ALEXANDER THE GREAT

AT Persepolis the Governor-General of Fars and his staff camped in the very city of Darius. The white tents of the army dotted the plain below, but we were above on the gigantic terrace covered with ruined columns and broken walls, carved with the figures of gods, and kings, and bulls. My horse verified the boast of the ancients, for he carried me easily up the broad flights of shallow steps that lead to the halls of Darius and Xerxes. All the afternoon the dead palaces hummed with the life of a camp. In every hall and by every carving were curious groups of Persians, standing to gaze at the mammoth relics of a past which they have totally forgotten, and fondly ascribing to Jemshyd and to Rustum the marvels of the Achæmenian age. Here are to be seen all sorts of inscriptions. There is cuneiform for the palæologist; there is early Arabic, and modern Persian; and here, too, you will find the names of many modern travellers, carved in schoolboy mood. There are the records of Malcom and his staff on his two embassies from India to the Court of Fath Ali Shah; Captain John Malcom in 1800, Brigadier-General Malcom in 1810; sure proof of quick promotion. Hard by one sees the words "Stanley, *New York Herald*, 1870," cut boldly by the great explorer before his search for

TALK WITH ALEXANDER THE GREAT

Livingstone; and on another wall "G. N. Curzon, 1889." *Dulce est desipere in loco.*

It was after nightfall, when the camp had sunk to sleep, save for the pacing of a rare sentry in the shadows of the ruins, that I left my tent and, entering the Hall of the Hundred Columns, came upon Alexander the Great. He rose from the shadow of a broken column and greeted me. Here was a man of the world who, of whatever violence and brutality he might himself be capable, knew what civilization meant, and was not to be overtaken by any boorish surprise. He led me to a couch on the further side of the column. Beside it was a table whereon were wine and fruit, and he filled two golden cups from a flagon.

"You will like this Persian wine," he said, handing me a cup. "It is the same that I drank here at a famous feast, the night I burnt this palace to the ground." He laughed, not as one ashamed of a deed supposed to foul the pages of history, but like an undergraduate recalling a "rag."

"Cyrus told me that that tale was true. The wine must be strong, then," said I, tasting it. It was old Shiraz wine, still the most famous in Persia, gold in colour and like sherry to the palate.

"Yes, it is an insidious drink. And I remember that on the morning after that feast and fire my head ached much."

I remembered the tale of the revel; how the Athenian courtesan, Thais, had spurred him on in the drunken riot, and had herself held a torch to fire the building. In spite of his frankness and apparent indifference to the judgment of history on these deeds,

THE ORIENT EXPRESS

I hesitated to press inquiries on a subject that he might, perhaps, have been expected to avoid. But curiosity overcame my hesitation, and urged me to question him.

"And you were sorry in the morning?"

"For the headache? Naturally." He laughed.

"And have you not regretted that you burnt the city of Darius?"

"Why, no." Alexander answered. "Repentance: that is something that I do not understand. There were times in my life that were great or gay; there were others that were sad. I was gay when I burnt the palace, and that was good. I was sad when I had the headache, and that was bad. But whatever has been, has been; just as whatever is, is. Repentance I have never known. It is true that had I not drunk the wine and burnt the palace, I should not have had the headache. But I regret neither the one nor the other. Even a headache is enjoyable after it is over."

Often as I had of late reflected on the regrettable consequences of the burning of Persepolis, this was one which had not occurred to me. Endeavouring to appreciate the importance of an Alexandrian headache, I submitted that the affair had other aspects also.

"But," I suggested, "not only would you have escaped the headache, but we might now have a colossal historical monument by which we might learn many things of the past. Even from these ruins we can see that Persepolis must have been one of the most wonderful cities in the ancient world."

"I understand your argument, but your reasoning makes no appeal to me. In another mood I might have spared Persepolis, and, had I done so, I should

TALK WITH ALEXANDER THE GREAT

not have regretted it. Neither do I regret that I destroyed it."

"Then we, who are posterity, have made no appeal to you?"

"Not so. You yourselves had a man who, when told to pause and think of posterity, asked, 'Pray, what has posterity done for us?' In a sense that is a just question. I have watched the course of the ages since my death, and my interest has never failed. Hannibal, Cæsar, Trajan, Charlemagne, Jenghiz Khan, Timur Lang, Frederick, Clive, Napoleon; all the warriors have I marked, and all the scroll of history also. Posterity, too, has, I readily admit, done something for me, for it has not forgotten me; something which perhaps it could not help, for my mark went deep and shaped its history to this day. But posterity's regrets over its ancestors' deeds are not only vain; they are also misplaced. What right have you to say that the world has lost anything by the destruction of Persepolis? Is not this to claim a power to reconstruct the course of history which you do not possess?"

"That is a pleasure of the imagination which is at least harmless."

"Then I have given you the possibility of indulging it. Here among these huge ruins you have a stimulus to set the most sluggish historic fancy working, whereas, did Persepolis exist, it would be a poorer thing. Believe me, who saw it, the Persian Empire which I overthrew had nothing much to give the world. Neither art nor literature has suffered great loss. Still you can see, as you have done to-day, the gigantic tombs that Darius the son of Hystaspes,

THE ORIENT EXPRESS

Xerxes, and Artaxerxes had hewed for themselves. And here you can still see the gigantic masonry of which these palaces were built. Gigantic masonry—and that is all; the astonishing product of the muscular effort of many slaves. What grace there was was borrowed from Egypt and from Greece. And, think you, had I spared Persepolis, would it not have suffered in the wars of the Sassanian kings? Or could it have survived the Islamic conquerors? You have seen the Sassanian monuments carved yonder long after my death, the pictures of Sapor enslaving the Emperor Valerian. There you see the vestiges of a later and a finer art than that which built Persepolis, but the Arabs destroyed it. And as for Persepolis itself, the Persians have forgotten the name of Darius and call it the Throne of Jamshyd."

"Yes," said I, remembering Omar's couplet on these very ruins of Persepolis—

> "They say the Lion and the Lizard keep
> The Courts where Jamshyd gloried and drank deep."

"Omar ought to have known," observed Alexander with a smile, "that it was I who drank deep here."

"He himself has said that he 'was never deep in anything but wine.' But modern scholarship has restored your credit on the point. It is now generally agreed that this was the scene of your carouse."

"What a carouse! I remember how Thais strung vine-leaves round the brow of dear old Hephæstion, who was the first to get drunk, told him that he was Dionysus, and made him lead a Bacchic dance. But he would have it that he was Aristotle, who used to be our tutor, and stopped the dance to give a lecture on the necessity of preserving the golden mean in all

TALK WITH ALEXANDER THE GREAT

things. He had a great success with that, and then Aristobulus carried him to bed, discoursing learnedly on birds, and asserting in particular the superiority of the ostrich. Sometimes, on a warm moonlit night, the shade of Thais will come and quaff a cup of wine with me, where you sit now. A pretty wench she was, with a pretty wit; but ever one to brew trouble at a dinner-party. To-night she is at Athens, where the shades have revived one of Menander's plays in which she has a part. Let us return to our discussion. You regret the destruction of Persepolis, and I understand you to say that you would regret the destruction of the Pyramids, both of which were but the cruel follies of tyrants and not the product of loving artists; but you feel no pang that they should ever have been created by the blood and tears of slaves."

"That is true," I replied; "I am no retrospective humanitarian. It seems to me folly for mankind to bear the pains of previous generations, and that it is better employed in trying to lessen those of its own day. When a man is dead his bodily ills are over. It is only for the living that we need care. I have felt pain for many wounded men, but once they were dead the pain they had suffered was nothing to me, even though I regretted their loss."

"You have answered honestly," said Alexander. "But just as no one truly feels sorrow for the slaves who built the Pyramids, so no one, save a very sickly scholar with a particularly pale cast of thought, need regret the destruction of Persepolis more than twenty-two hundred years ago. For in exaggerated imaginings of what you have lost you may forget what you have gained."

THE ORIENT EXPRESS

"And what is that?"

"A tale; a poem; better meat and drink for the ages than they would have were the roof still standing on these columns. Is not the story of my revel at Persepolis immortal, and beyond the destructive power of any future conqueror? Has not one of your own poets sung of Thais and myself?"

And, standing up, Alexander declaimed in Dryden's verse how his minstrel had wrestled with his melancholy, singing first of his victories, but in phrases all too sad—

> "He sung Darius great and good,
> By too severe a fate,
> Fallen, fallen, fallen, fallen,
> Fallen from his high estate."

Then from war the minstrel's theme changed to love, and Alexander's heart grew warm within him—

> "Lovely Thais sits beside thee,
> Take the good the gods provide thee"

So his sadness passed, as the bright notes raced on, and his courtiers saw his cares fall from him and the hour of revelry begin—

> "The many rend the skies with loud applause.
> So Love was crowned,—but Music won the cause."

There was a silence as the English lines died away in the ruined halls of Darius. Then Alexander spoke again—

"Is not that worth Persepolis?"

"I admit," I answered, "that you gave Dryden, who had otherwise a pedestrian muse, the finest poetic inspiration he ever possessed. But I am still puzzled

TALK WITH ALEXANDER THE GREAT

over this destruction of Persepolis, for I cannot marry it with other acts of yours. You restored the tomb of Cyrus, and we know that at Thebes you bade them spare the house of Pindar, when temple and tower fell to the ground. Yet why, also, did you destroy Thebes itself, since you knew well its legendary history, and yourself owed much to Greece?"

"I restored the tomb of Cyrus because I was incensed with the thieving Magi, who robbed it when they should have guarded it. Nor had I any war to wage with the dead Cyrus, who was in any case a better man than Darius the Third. As for Pindar, I knew his verses well, and loved

> "the pride and ample pinion
> That the Theban eagle bear,
> Sailing with supreme dominion
> Through the azure fields of air."

"I have, as you see, a liking for poetry. But, if one goes conquering, one has to make examples of those who oppose one; therefore it would have been folly to spare Thebes because of its legendary origin. And the destruction of the city has done the legend no harm. To the end of time men will learn how Amphion built the walls of Thebes, charming the stones to their places by the sweet strains of his lyre, and will read the tale of Amphion and Niobe. These are the things that, though they never happened, are indestructible; and the stones of Thebes are of no import. Apollo and Artemis slaying the children of Niobe are eternal, though the altars of the gods of Greece are gone for ever; and Niobe turned to stone upon Mount Sipylus would so remain, though the mount itself were sunk beneath the sea."

THE ORIENT EXPRESS

"Then, at least, you acknowledge a debt to the Greeks?"

"Debt! Yes, I had a tailor in Athens," said Alexander, smiling. "As for the Greeks, they called both my father and myself barbarians in our lifetime, and would not call us Greeks. Nowadays they are very anxious to claim me as a Greek, and even set forth a claim to Byzantium because it acknowledged my sway. That is the way of the Greeks. But I did not conquer for them, for I was a Macedonian, as they truly said. I had no such great opinion of those Greeks of yours, except in the kingdom of art. They made for themselves a refined and wonderful society, living in leisure and tended by slaves. Old Aristotle used to talk to me about the φύσει δοῦλος. The Greek intellectual regarded his hewer of wood and drawer of water as a slave by nature, whose sole duty was to subserve his higher needs. But that is a game which can be played in a different way. I was a conqueror, not an intellectual, and I made the arts my slave. To me the Greek, with his philosophy and his poetry, was φύσει δοῦλος, one who had much to teach me, but whose business was to serve my pleasure. Athens and Corinth set the fashion for us, both in philosophy and smart clothes. Actors and artists, tailors and cooks, for such I owed the Greeks much, and they never forgot to send me the bill. But what of that? Englishmen are enthusiasts for German music, and Germans have succeeded in explaining Shakespeare to Englishmen, but has that made you love each other more? You are now on affectionate terms with France, but for many years it was not so, in spite of the fact that Englishwomen went to Paris for their frocks and

TALK WITH ALEXANDER THE GREAT

Frenchmen kept their tailors in London. These things do not rule the world. There comes a storm, or there comes a man. It is men who make history."

"What made you a conqueror?"

"Just taste. I wanted to see the world, like you, more especially the East, and that was my way of doing the grand tour, after Aristotle had given me a university education. Issus and Arbela were to me no more than a column article to you; a means of livelihood and a fulfilment of my profession. Had I not caught cold after that bathe——"

He paused, as though pursuing his thought in silence.

"So, after all, there is something you regret?" I asked.

"Nay," said he, quickly. "You mistake me. I have no regrets. But in another hour it will be dawn, and the gun will soon arouse the camp. Therefore I bid you farewell."

He was gone, and so was the flagon of wine. As I turned towards my tent I reflected that he whom I had seen was indeed a super-ghost. None but a superman could turn the world upside down, for good or evil, all for his own sport, and at the end of all have no regrets. And none but a super-ghost could carry this *insouciance* beyond the grave.

CHAPTER XIII

THE PROBLEM OF SHIRAZ

SHIRAZ, a city of forgotten glories, is a name that has all but passed from the lips of men. To a select few it is still one of the most magical names in all the East. It speaks of perfumed rose gardens in a fair green valley, overlooked by the Pass of God is Great. It has been sung by the greatest Persian poets, and there you may still make pilgrimage to the graves of Sadi and Hafiz. Here, too, you may see the Bazar-i-Vakil, the most renowned bazaar in all Asia. But in the time to come the British public is likely to hear much of Shiraz in a more intimate sense, for the collapse of the Persian Government in Fars is bringing it more and more into the circle of Imperial responsibilities. Difficulties thicken, and it seems safe to say that Shiraz will soon be recognized as an Imperial problem of the first class.

In the present confusion of lawless tribes and private feuds in the province of Fars, it is impossible to state the whole of the issues, or to put before the English reader all the mazes of tribal politics and family intrigue. But it may be worth while to attempt an outline of the main difficulties confronting any one, Persian or foreigner, who has to deal with the existing situation in Fars.

I think that even the most casual and unreflecting

THE PROBLEM OF SHIRAZ

traveller in Persia at the present time would speedily come to the conclusion that there can be no security in this country till there is a general disarmament. Deadly brawls were common enough in Europe when every one carried a cutting weapon. What the Middle Ages would have been like had every private person carried a modern rifle can be imagined. Yet in Persia to-day, when the Central Government has lost all authority over the tribal chiefs, and the tribal chiefs in turn have lost a great deal of their authority over their men, modern weapons of precision are nearly as common as blackberries in England. North and south, east and west, every town possesses stores of rifles, and the bazaars are full of Mausers, Winchesters, Martinis, Mauser pistols, and Belgian Brownings, exposed for sale to any purchaser who will pay. The recent activity of the British in the Gulf is supposed to have checked gun-running, and it is to be hoped that the bonded warehouse established by the Sultan of Muscat may produce good results. As regards rifles, the stable door is being shut, if it is shut, after the steed is stolen. There are enough rifles in Persia to keep the country in turmoil for a generation. But the most disquieting feature is that there is nowhere apparent any lack of ammunition, and in fact it is still being introduced in large quantities. Recently there has been a very slight rise in the price of cartridges, but this is the only sign of tightness. It is probably due to the lack of transport on the roads, and it is not likely to affect the tribesmen at all, who make their own arrangements for obtaining ammunition and do not buy in the bazaar.

In a country where no one is punished for his ill

deeds, and where weapons are easy to obtain, honesty is by no means the best policy. Villagers and road-guards have not unnaturally embraced robbery as a profession. Besides the larger tribal bands, Fars is full of masterless men who have cast off, or never had, any tribal allegiance, and live by plunder. The main difficulty, however, lies in dealing with the tribes. The nomads of Fars are better armed than the Bakhtiari and other tribes further north, magazine rifles, chiefly Mauser, being very common. It is said that in the year 1900 the Kashgai tribe did not possess two hundred rifles, whereas they may now have about fifteen thousand magazine rifles and perhaps eight thousand of older models.

No estimate of the strength of the tribes can claim accuracy, for in Persia trustworthy figures are never obtainable, and the local estimates are quite obviously grossly exaggerated. From a comparison of various estimates and from other evidences it is, however, possible to make general calculations which may be somewhere near the mark. In spite of the very much larger figures sometimes given, it is very difficult to believe that the total nomad population of Fars can number more than two hundred and fifty thousand souls. This includes a large number of small but well-armed tribes, of whom the Boir Ahmedis are the largest and the most rapacious. They may possess twelve hundred fighting men, and in the summer they carry their raids almost as far north as Isfahan itself, and eastwards on the road to Yezd, while their headquarters are around Behbehan, in Arabistan. It will thus be seen what a large tract of country they cover and terrorize. But the two great tribal divisions of

THE PROBLEM OF SHIRAZ

Fars are the Khamseh and the Kashgai. The Khamseh consist, as the name implies, of a combination of five tribes: Arab, Baharlu, Basiri, Ainalu, and Nefar. They probably number seventy-five thousand souls, and may have twenty thousand armed men. The combination is, however, of the loosest kind, and it would never be possible to assemble more than one-fifth of that number for one purpose. They acknowledge a common chief, who is generally a member of the Kavam family and is at present Kavam-el-Mulk, who has recently been acting-Governor of Shiraz. Otherwise they have little in common. The Arabs, though knowing Persian, speak a debased Arabic among themselves; the Baharlus, on the other hand, are Turks. Their lines of migration also are different, the Arabs moving northward in the summer to the district of Dehbid and Abbasabad, while the Baharlus, moving from Darab, keep further east and frequently raid the Bunder Abbas-Kerman road. In September 1911, the Khamseh tribes, rallying to the cause of Kavam as against the Kashgais, sent three thousand fighting men to Shiraz, and it is not unlikely that this represents the maximum force which they can put in the field at one time.

On the same occasion Sowlet-ed-Dowleh, *Ilkhani* of the Kashgais, was only able to muster about two thousand men, and this though every circumstance appeared favourable. Just before the migration is the best time to ask a tribesman to fight, as he is then willing to move. Sowlet-ed-Dowleh promised him, in addition, the loot of the Kavam's quarter and the Jewish quarter in Shiraz. By common report the Kashgais are said to possess fifty thousand tents. In reality they may possess twenty thousand, and to these must be added some twelve thousand or fifteen thousand families which have ceased to dwell in tents and have become villagers, but are still to be reckoned as offshoots of the Kashgais. Of these the Boulvardis and the Surkhis are the best known. Including these, the tribe may have twenty-five thousand armed men, but no such number can be put in the field.

The Kashgais are governed by an *Ilkhani*, whose appointment is supposed to rest with the Central Government. It is the duty of the *Ilkhani* to collect the *maliat*, or property tax, from the tribe and hand it to the Government of Fars, which in turn remits it to Tehran. In actual fact no *Ilkhani* has paid over any *maliat* for nearly five years. And, just as the authority of the Government has weakened over the chiefs of tribes, so has their authority over the petty khans weakened in turn. The Kashgai tribe, like most others in Persia, is torn by family feuds. Of late the principal protagonists have been the two brothers Sowlet-ed-Dowleh and Ikhtisham-es-Sultaneh (formerly known as Zeigham-ed-Dowleh). Sowlet-ed-Dowleh, who was formerly *Ilkhani*, is at feud with his brother, with the Kavam family, with a section of the Arabs, and with the Bakhtiari. The last Governor-General of Fars threw in his lot with Sowlet-ed-Dowleh. The treacherous murder of Nasr-ed-Dowleh, head of the Kavam family, the *bast* of Kavam-el-Mulk in the British Consulate, the indignation of the Bakhtiari, who controlled the Central Government, and the final deposition both of the Governor and Sowlet-ed-Dowleh, were the result. After bombarding Shiraz itself, the pair were induced to leave the town in September 1911, by the

THE PROBLEM OF SHIRAZ

threat of the British Minister that Great Britain would be forced to act if they remained.

Kavam-el-Mulk then left the British Consulate, and acted as Governor till the arrival of the new Governor-General, Mukhbir-es-Sultaneh. Sowlet's enemy, Ikhtisham-es-Sultaneh, who stood well both with the Bakhtiari in Tehran and with Kavam-el-Mulk in Shiraz, was likewise appointed *Ilkhani* of the Kashgai tribe. The wheel, in fact, came full circle. But there was little profit in the change. For a spell Shiraz enjoyed comparative peace, but outside the town things grew worse. The Kavam has no authority over the nomad Arabs, and has been able to do nothing whatever to prevent their raids on the Bunder Abbas road. Ikhtisham-es-Sultaneh was nominally *Ilkhani*, but the tribe refused allegiance. Sowlet-ed-Dowleh installed himself where he could command the Bushire road, and his brother was powerless against him. Finally, in September 1912, the tribe openly deserted Ikhtisham-es-Sultaneh, and are at present without a recognized *Ilkhani*. In Shiraz itself, also, the authority of the Kavam failed, and British residents were repeatedly fired at.

One most unfortunate result of the treacherous attack on the Kavams, followed as it was by the prolonged stay of Kavam-el-Mulk in the British Consulate, was that Great Britain has been forced into a position which to the Persian seems a partisan one. It is the deep conviction of the Persians that England supports Kavam-el-Mulk in his private feud with Sowlet-ed-Dowleh. That this should be believed is the fault, not of Great Britain, but of those guilty of one of the foulest acts of treachery which can be imagined, when under the guise of an offer of safe conduct to Bushire they planned a murderous attack on the two Kavam brothers. Nevertheless the impression is a very unfortunate one, and it was regrettable that colour should have been given to it by handing over to Kavam-el-Mulk £5,000 of English money, to be spent on "restoring order." Needless to say this money, for which the Central Government had to pay interest, was wasted. Not a penny was accounted for. It came like water, and it went like wind—apparently to meet the strain on the Kavam's private purse. The Kavam was rightly the object of sympathy when he was treacherously attacked, but that he possesses more virtues than Sowlet-ed-Dowleh is, it is to be feared, an unproved assumption. In any case he represents no one but himself, and is no more capable of restoring order in Fars than in the Balkans. The Swedish gendarmerie officers would have spent the money to more advantage in attracting a better class of recruits, and, had they been entrusted with it, they would likewise have been able to furnish an account of where it went.

CHAPTER XIV

THE TRIBES AND THE ROADS

It will be seen that in actual fighting strength the Kashgais and Khamseh are probably pretty nearly matched. The new Governor-General's task is to reduce these turbulent elements to order, and it is worth while to consider what are his prospects of success. The familiar usage of previous Governors has been to lean either to one side or the other, to give special patronage either to Kashgais or to the Kavam family. But the violence of the previous Governor and of Sowlet-ed-Dowleh, who would content themselves only with the extermination of the Kavams, has put this method out of court as a policy of State. The new Governor cannot call in the one to redress the balance of the other, without giving a fresh fillip to the local Armageddon which bids fair to end Southern Persia. Sowlet-ed-Dowleh appears to be the only Kashgai who retains much personal authority, and his wealth inspires respect. To deal with him, and to turn the poacher into gamekeeper, was probably at one time a possible policy; for he could, were he so disposed, keep order on the Bushire road. But events have unfortunately prevented such an experiment, and now it is too late. Even were there any prospect of its success, as some are still found to urge, it would be exceedingly difficult for the Central Government to enter into such an arrangement, or for

THE ORIENT EXPRESS

the British Government to support it, without great loss of "face." And so much face has already been lost that neither of these two Governments can spare any more without serious risk that no tribesman will any longer recognize their features.

Neither by any negotiation, nor by using one set of enemies to chastise the other, can the Governor-General hope to produce peace in Fars. He must find a force of his own, sufficient to produce and maintain order. The immediate question is the policing of the roads, southwards to Bushire and northwards to Isfahan. Here there is an initial, and most serious, difficulty, before the tribal question is reached at all. The caravan which ventures upon the road may, or may not, fall among thieves. The chances are that Boir Ahmedis or Kashgais will fall upon it, carry off mules and loads, and even strip the muleteers of their clothes. But if it escape these dangers, it cannot by any means escape the *tufangchis*, or riflemen, whose supposed duty is to guard the road. A dozen or so of these scoundrels, strong and fine-looking men most of them, with a physique far superior to that generally seen in Northern Persia, are to be found in every village and at posts all along the road. Formerly they were a sort of local gendarmerie who received pay and took no toll from caravans. In those days they were few, and far from wealthy. Nowadays they get no pay, but are exceedingly numerous and prosperous. They have abandoned all pretence of guarding the road, and, being well armed, are simply blackmailers, taking toll for every man or beast that passes. So pleasant and remunerative is their existence that every villager near the road who can get a rifle, and

THE TRIBES AND THE ROADS

is strong enough to hold his own, seeks admittance into the local confraternity of *tufangchis*. The groups have feuds with one another, and when a traveller who has paid for the " protection " of one group is so exacting as to suggest that they should make some show of earning the money by escorting him to the next stage, he is generally met with the reply that they cannot accompany him more than a few hundred yards, as the next group are their blood enemies, and would fire upon them.

First, then, the Governor-General has to deal with the *tufangchis*, for even if regular robbery were unknown their exactions add so much to the cost of transport as to make the price almost prohibitive. Unless he is possessed of means of overawing them, to turn these riflemen into peaceable road-guards by the mere process of offering them pay is not a course open to the Governor-General. Their numbers, their wealth, and their arrogance have grown far too great. No ordinary pay would content them, and in any case no one has any pay to offer them. How, then, is the Governor-General to overawe them? It should be remembered also that the Bushire and Isfahan roads do not constitute the whole of the problem. Shiraz is much more than a half-way house to Isfahan. In normal times it is a great distributing centre to a vast district, and it is of little use to fill its bazaars with goods from Bushire unless these can in turn reach the surrounding districts. The trade with Lar and Laristan has come to a standstill; and there is also the question of opening the Bundar Abbas and Kerman road.

Besides the Swedish gendarmerie, the Governor-

THE ORIENT EXPRESS

General has a few hundred nondescript Persian soldiers. With these it is quite impossible for him to attempt to deal either with Kashgais or Arabs. The task itself is not inherently difficult. Could he command a sufficiently large and sufficiently well-trained force to smash either Kashgais or Arabs separately, he would have little further difficulty with the remainder. The Kashgais are particularly easy to reach. Possessed of vast flocks and herds, they are not, like the poorer Bakhtiari, a mobile force. Their wealth ties them within the narrow limits of their migrations. Every spring, moving northwards to the district of Ardakan, they strike the main road between Shiraz and Bushire south of Kazerun, and follow it to within a stage of Shiraz, when they turn northwards. No other road is easily open to them, and nothing should be simpler than to block their advance in the narrow passes. Five thousand regular troops with two batteries of artillery would, in military opinion, be sufficient to bring the tribe to terms, and would provide a sufficient margin of strength to cover all possible risks.

But the Governor-General had on his arrival no such force, and could attempt nothing until he got it. Therefore, as he justly said, he could do nothing till the spring. In the spring of 1913 there arrived at Shiraz a considerable additional force of gendarmes under Swedish officers, and it will be seen that on the ultimate success or failure of this gendarmerie much depends.

The task before the Swedes should command the sympathy of all, as the manner in which they are bending to it inspires respect. Young and energetic, they were on their arrival in Persia full of an enthu-

THE TRIBES AND THE ROADS

siasm which is rapidly chilling to despair. In Tehran they find little support except from the British Minister. The Russian Government will not allow them to send their men to certain important towns, and would naturally prefer to see nothing but Russian officers in Northern Persia. The Bakhtiari, who control, and are, the Central Government, are jealous of the creation of an efficient, armed force. Local governors and officialdom dislike them, because they represent reform. The Treasurer-General is not overburdened with cash, and with all these influences at work it is not surprising that the gendarmerie are not his first preoccupation. Nevertheless, the Swedes hammer along. They came totally without experience of the East, and have to buy it at great expense. Indeed, a sympathetic contemplation of their tremendous efforts tends to confirm one in the view that Mr. Shuster was right in thinking that Anglo-Indian officers were above all others the most naturally suitable for gendarmerie work in Persia. There is, perhaps, a little too much "mailed fist" about the Swede. The Anglo-Indian in general knows what are the points on which a Mohammedan is sensitive; he knows, too, that there is no profit in making enemies of villagers; and, even if he is not by nature sympathetic towards natives, he has behind him a long tradition of responsibility towards them, and he has before him the fear of Press and Parliament at home.

But the Swedish officers are able and adaptable men, and they are rapidly acquiring experience. The pity of it is that their pay is poor and irregular, and their contracts are only for three years. At the end of this period, just when they will have thoroughly learnt their work in strange conditions, their contracts will expire, and it is extremely doubtful whether all of them can be induced to remain. The reports which they send home may make their Government unwilling to lend successors, in which case the gendarmerie will collapse, but even if successors are appointed the experience gained may be lost. That they will be able, ultimately, to send to Shiraz a force either sufficiently large or sufficiently trained to cope with the tribes is somewhat doubtful. This, however, is the only hope of success left to the new Governor-General, and the effort deserves, as it will doubtless command, the support of the British Government. Money is a prime necessity, and Great Britain will do well to see that a due proportion of any money she may lend to Persia is allotted to the Swedish gendarmerie.

CHAPTER XV

BRITISH INTERESTS IN SOUTHERN PERSIA

That the British made their title good in the waters of the Gulf by hard work is beyond doubt. There has been, perhaps, some exaggeration as to what has been done in the past in the matter of lights; and when the assertion was made that we have "buoyed and beaconed" the Gulf, its author was guilty of a slight rhetorical flourish. As a matter of fact there are no lights whatever in the Gulf outside the Shat-el-Arab, but that is about to be remedied. A lighthouse is to be built on the island of Tamb, and red and white lights are to be shown from the Residency flagstaff at Bushire. The old buoys were laid down by the British India Steam Navigation Company, but they are tended by the Indian Marine, and a new and extensive scheme of buoyage is now being undertaken.

But the Gulf is one of the hottest, as it is one of the most inhospitable, places in the world, and all honour is due to the successive generations of Englishmen who toil in that inferno, have swept its waters clear of pirates, and still police it for all the world. Admiral Bethell, in the *Highflyer*, with the whole of the Persian Gulf flotilla, was stationed at Muscat during the autumn of 1912, watching what, it is hoped, were the last gasps of the expiring trade of the gun-runners. The Sultan of Muscat's bonded warehouse had just

THE ORIENT EXPRESS

begun operations, but preparatory to its opening there was a final flare of gun-running on a large scale, all the merchants engaged in the trade hastening to send their cargoes up the Gulf before the bonding began. Consequently vast quantities of rifles and ammunition, including several million caps, were run in in the early autumn. One consignment of eight hundred rifles was captured in September, but in general it was impossible to stop the inrush. It would appear, however, that the end has come. The system of bonding can be strictly enforced at Muscat, and it will be difficult for the gun-runners to find an alternative port higher up the Gulf. Doubtless, however, some effort will be made to run through from Jibuti, and there will still be need for the exercise of vigilance. In the matter of rifles irreparable damage is already done, as both Persia and Afghanistan are full of them. But if the supply of ammunition is cut off, that will be a great gain. Doubtless the arms factory in Afghanistan and the trade of the Shiraz gun-maker will revive again, and ammunition also will be made. But the local ammunition is a poor substitute, and the Afghan and the Persian are very dependent on European caps.

That Great Britain has considerable interests to safeguard in Persia is generally admitted. What is the precise extent of these interests, how far they are purely commercial, how far they are political and wrapped up with her prestige in India, how far they are purely strategic—these are questions for which the public at least has no definite answers. Whether the Government knows precisely the answer it would give, if forced to formulate them, is a matter of surmise. Presumably it does. There have been frequent

BRITISH INTERESTS IN S. PERSIA

indications that it has not always done so. The vagueness of its Persian policy, on occasion the apparent lack of policy, might justify the suspicion that it was not quite clear as to what it wanted. Nevertheless it would be both ungenerous and unjust to criticize it ruthlessly on this ground. The times have been admittedly critical and difficult, and if the results so far obtained by living from hand to mouth are very unsatisfactory, it is equally true that hard-and-fast views might be disastrous. The Anglo-Russian Convention, or rather the Anglo-Russian Entente, has dominated the situation, and that needs delicate handling in a country where the material interests of the two Powers cannot always coincide.

But the more critical are the times, the more urgent it is to have a policy. If, therefore, it be true, as some suggest, that there still exists some vagueness in the mind of the British Government as to the precise extent of its vital interests in Persia, the time has come when it should decide where those interests lie, what supposed interests can reasonably be sacrificed, and what must be safeguarded. It is the business of a Government not only to govern, but to formulate its own policy. The Foreign Office and the Government of India command so much information that no one should be able to compete with them in passing judgment on the situation, and it would be presumption to make such a supposition. Certain facts of the situation are here recorded, in order that the public may have an opportunity of judging in what direction British policy is likely to lie.

From previous chapters it will have been seen how little room for hope there is that the Persian Government will be able to restore order in Southern Persia. Even if the British Government lend money freely, and give all possible support to the efforts of the Persian Government and to the Swedish gendarmerie, it is possible that things will become worse instead of better. The tribes may become more and more disorderly; and Fars become a closed country, a no man's land with no relations either with Tehran or elsewhere, a country such as Central and Northern Albania were for so long in Europe. The Bakhtiari khans, also, who sit at Tehran, are losing their authority in their own country.

What interest has the British Government to interfere in such a situation? Three courses seem to be open to it. It is possible to argue that, when it comes to the point of spending men and money, the internal condition of Persia is no affair of ours. It was pleasant to have the trade, no doubt, and it seems very important to certain Manchester firms. But, taken in comparison with the total volume of our trade, the Persian market is nothing, and its loss would not matter. At any rate, why spend more money on an expedition than the whole trade is worth? We are sorry for the traders, but it is not our business to protect them with bayonets in a foreign country where trade has really become impossible. The attack on Consul Smart was not organized or premeditated, and was no one's fault. Let us close the Consulate at Shiraz, and retire to the coast, where our real interests lie. British goods will still be landed to a certain extent, but, instead of our having British firms represented in the interior, the Persian merchants will be their own buyers; and once the goods are landed at a Gulf port, the rest will be their affair. We have spent vast sums and infinite pains to make our frontier defences at Quetta and elsewhere impregnable. It would be folly to "scrap" these defences and move forward to a much wider, and less defensible, position. The existing frontier and the Gulf are our true line of defence; and, with the desert and the Navy to help us, we are ready for all comers, and whoever likes may have Persia.

This policy, or something very closely resembling it, was, I have reason to know, under the very serious consideration of the Government. It appears to have been decided that, though desirable, it was impossible. It has the advantage of solving, or shelving, many difficulties for an indefinite period in the future. Certain objections must, however, be stated. It would appear to involve the discountenancing of all railway schemes, since, if we resolutely abandon the interior, the desert frontier becomes more important than ever; and, also, the railway field is left to others. Other results are almost inevitable. It is, of course, now recognized by all who have any appreciation of the situation that Northern Persia has passed definitely under Russian influence. It will take Russia some years to consolidate that influence down to the southern limits of her sphere—Kermanshah, Isfahan, and Yezd. At the end of that period, finding herself confronted with a lawless district all along her sphere of power, it is impossible to believe that she would not take action there, if we would not. She would not be separated, as we are, from Shiraz and Arabistan by the desert on one hand and the sea on the other. Fars and Arabistan could not be ignored. They would be her turbulent neighbours, disturbers of her trade and of the peace; and they would in turn inevitably fall beneath her supremacy. Those who advocate this policy must, of course, be prepared to see other Powers step in where we refused to tread, and would reply that it does not matter, as we shall still retain the frontier of our choice. But when that time came it would probably be impossible to prohibit the advance of railways; and there is also the difficulty of adhering sternly, over a long period of years, to a policy which the advance of other Powers might make increasingly unpopular. And a political, and more especially a commercial, position once abandoned is not easy to recover. The loss of prestige is also an argument which weighs heavily with Government.

If we turn from the purely British point of view to more general considerations, it is interesting to note that the Nationalist and the humanitarian points of view, with both of which most plain people have in their hearts some sympathy, are here entirely antagonistic to one another. The adoption of the policy outlined would satisfy the former and sacrifice the latter. To leave Persia to herself might indeed be to leave her to stew in her own juice, and it would certainly be to leave her to the mercies of another Power, but it would satisfy the sentiment which forbids meddling with the internal affairs of other nations. It would certainly not satisfy the Persians, who, in spite of all that a devoted group of Nationalists in Tehran may assert to the contrary, desire nothing so much as foreign intervention. Neither at home nor in India do people fully realize how radically the situation has changed since the Russian ultimatums of December 1911 and the expulsion of the American Commission.

BRITISH INTERESTS IN S. PERSIA

Before that time it was possible for an optimist to believe in the renascence of Persia without foreign intervention. Intervention was then a thing to dread; now it is a thing for which the Persian hopes. It is, in fact, the only hope he has. Those who are opposed to it are only those who profit by anarchy—plundering tribesmen and thieving officials. Pan-Islamic leaders in India who oppose any British action in Persia could not do better than make a journey through the country and talk to the people.

The second and third policies can only be very unwillingly considered. The British Government has done a great deal to convince the world of its unwillingness to send troops to Southern Persia, and the longer it finds it possible to exercise patience the better. The Central India Horse, which were in Shiraz at the time of my visit, have since been withdrawn. It would, perhaps, have been better if they had never been sent at all. It was not a fair position in which to put fine troops, to send them in a small body into a disturbed country, and then to condemn them to complete inaction. If there were reasons of State for which it was done, the British officers might have been expected to understand them, but it can hardly be supposed that the Indian *sowar* would do so. As it was, they showed the most admirable restraint in very trying circumstances. Both officers and men were repeatedly fired at and subjected to insults. And for these no one was punished and no redress was ever offered.

There was a squadron at Isfahan at one time, and when I left on the southward road, Captain Eckford rode with me a few miles. Almost immediately afterwards this squadron was ordered to join the regiment at Shiraz, and there I saw something more of this very gallant officer. Only once did any of the regiment betray the discontent, which I knew to be there, at the situation in which they were placed. An officer, who came to see me start on the journey from Shiraz to Bushire, remarked as he said farewell, with the air of one taking leave of a doomed man: "For your sake I devoutly hope that you will get through to Bushire all right, but I am bound to admit that if you get 'scuppered' it will suit our book."

Evidently he thought the cup was full, and that it needed only one more incident to make British indignation brim over. I had a shrewder idea of my own insignificance and of our imperial capacity for patience. No one "scuppered" me on the way, but the day I reached Bushire I learned that Captain Bullock, a British officer, had been robbed and beaten on the Bakhtiari road and his native orderly so severely wounded that he died. Seven weeks later, at Port Said, I read a telegram containing the news that Captain Eckford of the Central Indian Horse had been shot dead by tribesmen on the first stage south of Shiraz, on the very piece of road over which I travelled on the morning when his colleague had wished me the good luck which fell to my share.

And still we exercise, and I think rightly, our imperial patience. One hears the most diverse comments on British policy. There is a section of opinion abroad which believes that England is only seeking a pretext for occupation, as if there were some trouble in finding one. In Shiraz and Bushire there is general Persian astonishment, and no gratitude, that nothing is done, and it is attributed either to fear or indiffer-

BRITISH INTERESTS IN S. PERSIA

ence. The most delightful explanation was that of the Persian who thought it all a Machiavellian scheme. "Inglisha kheili yavash kar mikunand—The English work very slowly. They are sending officers and travellers into the country now, and arranging for them to be robbed and beaten. They are eating dirt and saying nothing. They are encouraging us to insult them and injure them. Then when they think we have gone too far they will turn round and say to Europe, 'You see how the Persians treat us, and that we are forced to take their country'"

There is, in fact, nothing easier than to be cynical about England's unwillingness to intervene in Southern Persia, if in the end she sends an expedition. There have been so many examples of this same unwillingness with the same result. Yet those who have had an opportunity of judging know how genuine and deep-rooted this unwillingness is. Both the British and the Indian Treasuries have a better use for every penny they can find; and there is no profit in adventuring into a poor and sparsely populated country. Above all, let those who may idly suppose that there is some fire-eating military party in India try to imagine for themselves the actual situation. As an inventor lavishes care on his model, or a trainer on his horses, so the Indian military authorities have spent themselves on the defences of the North-West Frontier, in order to make them as perfect as possible. And in proportion to the care they have taken and the success they have achieved is their dislike for any step which may ultimately involve a shifting of the frontier further forward, and to a line of country far less easily defensible. For my part, I trust that nothing that is here said may be taken as advocating a British expedition to Southern Persia. I know of nothing that will ever make it acceptable save necessity. On the other hand, I do not hesitate to record my belief that, however much one British Government or another may seek to avoid it, however long they delay (and the longer the better), however many shifts and devices they may resort to (and it is well that they should resort to them), in the end they will be forced to accept responsibility in Southern Persia. This is the universal penalty of great empires —that there is no finality until a boundary that marches with a settled country is reached. In India, as elsewhere, history is strewn with former frontiers, from the days of Clive onwards, each of which was to be final.

This brings us to the consideration of the second and third policies. If the time ever comes for British action, one plan would be to come to a definite understanding with Russia and to partition Persia. That has the merit of simplicity, but is hardly likely to commend itself in England. A third plan would seek to keep Persia in existence, and to restrict intervention to the narrowest possible limits. A sufficiently strong British column would have little difficulty in dealing with the Kashgai tribe, at the time of their spring or autumn migration, at the point nearest Bushire, where they strike or leave the road between Bushire and Shiraz. If the Kashgai were disarmed the Khamseh would probably immediately be amenable to reason. It would also be necessary to station a force at Kazerun, and a smaller one at Shiraz, to deal with any recrudescence of trouble on the road. If the existing gen-

BRITISH INTERESTS IN S. PERSIA

darmerie were employed in the towns and in the villages off the road, and were used for the sufficiently strenuous task of collecting revenue, and a road gendarmerie under British Indian officers were raised to keep the road open up to Isfahan, it should then be possible to do without the Indian troops. A similar gendarmerie, or at any rate the presence of a British Engineer officer, is likely to be required on the Bakhtiari road also, unless the Bakhtiari improve very much upon their present performance.

The consolidation of Russian influence in the north requires a readjustment of conditions in the south. Now that the Russian Minister at Tehran is practically a Russian Resident, it is no longer desirable that the Governor-General of Fars and other officials in the south should be controlled by the telegraph wire from Tehran. If, therefore, some pacificatory measures such as those described were carried out, and if the southern Governors were placed in a more independent position, if money was lent by Great Britain for necessary purposes, and if British Consuls were given powers of control over expenditure, it is permissible to hope that Persia could be maintained in being, and that any more drastic action might be avoided, at least for a period of time. But as a preliminary a new understanding with Russia appears to be needed. The Convention, with its Russian, British, and neutral spheres, represents a state of things which has passed away. It was supposed to relate to a Persia much more independent than the Persia of to-day. The neutral sphere at that time enjoyed peace and comparative good government, and the Convention declared it neutral with regard to commercial concessions. It was never contemplated that in the event of its falling a prey to disorder it should be a neutral ground for political influence. Nor, indeed, has anything of the kind ever been suggested. Russia has recognized in the fullest manner that she has no interests in the neutral sphere at all commensurate with those of Great Britain. She was fully cognisant of the British Note of 1910, which proposed that British officers should organize a gendarmerie for the road from Bushire right up to Isfahan. And lately British troops were sent to Isfahan, where they remained till September 1912, although Isfahan itself is in the Russian sphere. There should, therefore, be no difficulty in coming to a definite understanding with Russia which, while safeguarding for her the commercial equality of opportunity which was envisaged in the Convention of 1907, shall limit the political and military action which Russia has taken, and may in future take, entirely to the northern sphere: Within that sphere she has enough scope for her activity for a long time to come, for it includes many places where as yet she is comparatively unknown, and some, as for instance Isfahan, where the trade has hitherto been almost entirely British.

CHAPTER XVI

THE DECAY OF PERSIA

IF the downfall of Persia is now so complete that not even her most enthusiastic friends can hope for the establishment of any form of government worthy of the name which shall not mean foreign domination in one guise or another, it is perhaps worth while to pause and examine how this result has come about. It is true that it is idle to cry over spilt milk, and there is no pleasure in the apportionment of blame, but there are profitable lessons for all concerned in even the most recent history, and the candid historian of the future will undoubtedly endeavour to find the balance of responsibility.

If this future historian possess the gift of invective, there can be no doubt that in dealing with the Persian *buzurgan*, or aristocracy, he will feel that an occasion has arisen when he may use his damnatory powers to the full, without risk of obscuring the truth by any excess of language. All that Macaulay said of the Bengalee, or of Sir Elijah Impey, might aptly be said of the nobles of Persia as a class. Nothing is more astonishing than the dearth of new men in Persia, the total failure of the constitutional movement to bring to the front an array of middle-class zeal and talent, and the success with which the princes, nobles, governors, and the whole official world, who had wrought the downfall of the old *régime,* succeeded in imposing themselves upon the new. Nothing, in fact, was changed, except that the authority of the Shah was gone, and that a Parliament was in existence which, though individual members were corrupt, was collectively patriotically inspired, but—provided the old gang of officials did lip service to the Constitution—far too weak to exact a new standard of honesty. The leopard does not change his spots, and a Parliament that had to work with such tools was not likely to make startling progress in reform. No scorn can be too great, and no words too harsh, for the men whose grandiloquent and magnificent titles might in themselves have been a reminder that *noblesse oblige.* The Pillars and the Meteors of the State, the Lions and the Confidences of the Kingdom, the innumerable band of ed Dowlehs and el Mulks, possessed, with a few lonely and honourable exceptions, neither common honesty nor moderate capacity. Not all the high-born grandees in Persia could produce between them a spark of the clear flame that lit the spirit of Takeh Zadeh, the bookseller's son from Tabriz. Him they hounded forth, untitled and unhonoured, to the exile that is still his fate, fearing the honest eloquence which made the common people hear him gladly.

Intrigue was their only art, and lying their most cultivated talent. Their sole inspiring motive was greed, and the embezzlement of public funds from a stricken Treasury was their principal pursuit. While throngs of wailing women clamoured daily at his gates for arrears of salaries due to their husbands, or for some small instalment of pensions long unpaid, a constitutional Minister of Finance bought up claims

THE DECAY OF PERSIA

for a trifling sum in his own name, and helped himself to their face value from a Treasury that could not pay its civil servants. The Governor and the great men of Tehran combined to form a corn ring, and not all the miseries of the population from the famine price of bread could make them forgo a single kran of their ill-gotten gains. During the siege of Tabriz, when the famine reached its height, so that the poor were to be seen dying in the streets and the town was in the last straits for food, the Persian leaders of the defence retained large warehouses full of grain, for which they had not paid a penny, and refused to sell except at the ruinous price which they had fixed for their own profit.

These are but a few instances out of many. They excite no surprise and earn no condemnation. Their authors continue to enjoy power and prestige, and pass from one office to another in successful careers of colossal peculation. And from the European who professes friendship to Persia strict silence on such subjects is expected. Against dishonesty so flagrant it is recognized that there is a Western prejudice, and in view of this it is incomprehensible to a Persian that any friend should feel called upon to state the whole truth. Criticism, however well-intentioned, must, in their opinion, be always the act of an enemy, and it is no part of one's duty to violate the grand conspiracy of silence.

The merchant classes, and townsfolk generally, though no strangers to chicane, are unable to challenge comparison with their shameless superiors. There is a large residuum here which, while corrupt according to Western standards, is intrinsically far from worthless, and is often attractive. Fidelities are frequently possible to the faithless, and high ideals dance before the eyes of those who follow baser practices. The Persian populace is far from being wholly bad, and much may be forgiven to the large section of it which is very poor. Here, as elsewhere in the East, the rural peasantry are the best of all, and strike a readier chord of sympathy in the European breast than does the French-speaking, vicious *flaneur* of the towns, with his glib political conversation. The peasant is not very different from peasants all the world over. He presents frequently the same appearance of crass stupidity, and possesses the same curious observant shrewdness. He has the same inveterate objection to innovation, and the same grasping thrift. Also, and this it is which differentiates him from the Persian of the town, who seeks to come by money quickly, by a little work and a little chicane, he possesses the same laboriousness as the peasant of other lands, the same indefatigable patience in wresting a livelihood from a resisting soil. Wherever the desert yields a little water his grateful patch of cultivation is to be found, and the system of *kanats*, or deep underground watercourses, by which he has devised an irrigation, is a striking testimony to his persistent industry.

Yet it must be said that the canker which comes from above, the shameful product of the wealth and education of Persia, has gone through all ranks, and has reached even the peasants in the villages of the wilderness. In Turkey an honest villager is as common as an honest pasha is rare, but the Persian peasant does not often use the truth. The highest standard is to be found among the peaceful nomads,

THE DECAY OF PERSIA

whose morality is in every way superior to that of the villagers. In the outward graces, too, they commend themselves to the stranger. It is an unpleasant characteristic of the poor Persian who can make a show of rendering any service, though it be only the offering of a withered flower, to ask an immediate reward. Nothing is ever left to the stranger's instinct of generosity, and long before he has time to put his hand in his pocket he is told what is expected of him. But among the *iliat*, or nomads, it is not so, except in the neighbourhood of towns. They will even entertain a passing traveller with bread, milk, and cheese, and persistently refuse a reward on the plea that it is not their custom to accept it.

Among the armed tribes of nomads, of whom the most famous are the Bakhtiari and the Kashgai, there is a traditional combination of robbery and hospitality; and not the least of the excitements of Persian travel lies in the fact that one does not always know which of these two very different alternatives one may expect. Sometimes there is a mixture of the two, but the traveller who has lost all his property hardly feels adequately consoled by the offer of tea and cigarettes. The tribesmen often share the pleasant manners and the singular charm of the Persian townsfolk. But their morals, also, are said to be no better than those of the towns. Disease is rife among them. And there is the same grasping avariciousness which everywhere repels. Every European resident in Persia remarks that the subject of chance conversations overheard in the streets is invariably *pul* (money). The more prosperous are arguing over 'tomans, the poorer over krans and shahis. It is one of the surest signs of degeneration that money is everywhere sought for its own sake. Persia would be an appreciably richer country were all the wealth that is hoarded in her mud walls brought into circulation.

A consideration of the warrior tribes brings us to an important contributory cause of the passing of a famous nation. The utterly unwarlike character of the bulk of the people, and their lack of physical courage, might be appropriate in a secure civilization where the arts of peace were free to flourish. The victories of peace are greater than those of war, but the great ideal of the pacifists is still far remote from the actual conditions of the East, and a nation which claims to be free must be prepared to maintain its freedom by the sword. There is still no other way, for, even in this our modern world, slavery will certainly overtake a feeble empire. In Persia the warlike elements have unfortunately preferred to war with one another. Only one tribe, the Bakhtiari, has at any time in this troubled period shown any conception of a higher patriotism, and has been ready to place its services at the disposal of the Central Government for the task of restoring order.

It must be confessed, however, that the lights that the Bakhtiari have followed have been somewhat broken ones. They too, like the Kashgai, have their internal feuds; and the genuine services that they rendered, under the guidance of Sardar Assad, have often been marred by the rapacity of the various khans. These have not always been able to subordinate the aggrandizement of their tribe to the welfare of their country, and the taste of their followers for loot appears to be incurable. In any case, their fighting strength has been vastly exaggerated. The figures that have been given have never been genuine, and the Persian Government has found money for many men who had no existence except upon a pay-roll. At no time during the last four years, though they professed to put forth all their efforts, have the Bakhtiari been able to put more than three thousand men in the field, and of these not all were either well armed or well mounted. Among them there may be as many as a thousand fine irregulars, who would fight stoutly except against well-directed artillery, of which, like most tribesmen, they have an exaggerated awe. If we include Bakhtiari, Kurds, and Shahsevens, all of whose performances I have at various times had an opportunity of witnessing, I doubt whether there are in Northern Persia much more than two thousand really brave men—that is, men who are prepared to risk their lives freely in war. In the south the tribes are better armed, and it may be a slightly different story, but I incline to think that the tribesman is an overrated warrior whose prowess lies in terrorizing helpless villagers.

This does not mean that there is not everywhere in Persia excellent material for the training of troops. Subjected to the same training, even Persians of the towns would probably produce as good results as have the Egyptian fellaheen. But the few brave men of to-day have not been all on one side, and the Persian Government has had no force with which to maintain order. The devoted little band of Armenians and Caucasians, whose courage was of a finer quality than anything Persia can produce, were the real authors and guardians of the Persian Constitution of 1909.

THE ORIENT EXPRESS

Yeprem, the Armenian bricklayer's son, with one hundred men could strike terror into a thousand Kurds. But Yeprem is dead, and many of his braves have fallen also. The rest are disheartened, and the Armenian Dashnaksuṭian has formally abandoned Persia to its fate, declaring it unworthy of the ceaseless efforts and many lives that that most formidable of secret societies has lavished for it in the last five years. Many of its warriors also have had to flee from Tehran to escape the hand of Russia.

A Government which had no homogeneous force capable even of policing its roads could naturally not enjoy a prestige abroad which it lacked at home. A Balkan State with a small but efficient army can command the respect of diplomatists, and had Persia possessed any army worthy of the name she would not have been utterly negligible. As it is, she is the merest pawn in the hands of her neighbours.

CHAPTER XVII

THE VALUE OF THE MEJLISS

It might be thought that the corruption and disorganization which I have tried to depict must in themselves have inevitably led to the passing of Persian independence, and that nothing could save a country so far diseased. The assumption may be true, but it is by no means one that can be made with absolute certainty. All great revolutions have been the product of misgovernment, and some have marked the end of what had seemed a period of fatal decay. Nations have raised their heads from the dust before now without passing under anything approaching foreign rule. It is true that the Persian revolution was not in any way a great one. Superficially the Constitutional movement had its origin in a gigantic *bast* at the British Legation, the initial object of which was merely to get rid of a temporarily objectionable Grand Vizier, whom the Constitutionalists themselves later made a Cabinet Minister. It was diligently fomented by a contractor, who made a large haul by catering for the twelve thousand people who picnicked in the grounds of the British Legation. As *basts* on this scale can only come from persons who are against the Government, on the establishment of a Constitution this gentleman promptly went over to the other side and endeavoured to organize reactionary *basts* at the Russian Legation.

THE ORIENT EXPRESS

But, when all is said as to the general ignorance of what a Constitution was, as to the large part which a handful of Christians and foreigners played in the actual struggle, and as to the worthless character of many of the Constitutional heroes, it remains true that the Constitutional movement represented a real stirring of the dry bones and the breath of new life in the mass of corruption. There can be no doubt that the majority of the people—north, south, east, and west—were weary of the despotism of the Kajar family and imbued with a thorough hatred of their Shahs. It may be true, as many constantly assert, that the East loves a despot, but, if so, the fact has not come under my observation, and I do not know what is the evidence for this unnatural and inherently improbable taste. It is fair to remind the critics who tell us that Constitutionalism will "never do" in the East, that despotism has not been a shining success, and that nothing but its bankrupt failure to provide a tolerable government at home, and to maintain national prestige in the face of encroaching Western nations, made possible the Turkish, Persian, and Chinese revolutions.

It would appear inevitable that a brand-new Parliament in a hitherto despotically governed country must spend most of its time in making mistakes. It has been flung in the water, and its first efforts to swim are more likely to submerge it than to keep it afloat. In the nature of things it is heir to poverty and disorder, the embarrassing legacy of the despotism it succeeds. English parliamentary government, in the sense of good government, was the slow product of many centuries. Any one who will honestly try to recreate for himself a picture of England in the

THE VALUE OF THE MEJLISS

Middle Ages, of the state of the roads and the inns as a foreigner would find them, and of the plight of the people everywhere during the Wars of the Roses, will realize that centuries of muddle and misgovernment went to the making of modern England. There is no obvious reason for supposing that if an Eastern country could by some miracle be secured from all outward dangers and left entirely to itself it could not, after several generations and many failures, make a tolerable success of parliamentary government. It would buy its own experience, and evolve in course of time its own instrument to suit its own conditions; not necessarily a Chamber on the Western model, but something which, like all permanent successes, would be the fruit of previous failures.

But how, in the modern world, is an Eastern State to obtain this long period of respite from foreign complications, wherein to make its mistakes without losing its independence? The new Constitutional State, the child of revolution and the inheritor of disorder, is bound to be weak. There was a time when disorder was so common in all European States that weakness and disorder in one—as, for instance, in England during the Wars of the Roses—did not necessarily expose it to attack by others. But there are now so many ordered military States in the world that the position of the disordered State is exceedingly insecure. In the first place, it is a real embarrassment to its neighbours, for the course of their settled trade, the lives of their citizens, their strategical and political plans, are grievously affected; and, in the second place, in the modern race for influence, markets, and territory, its weakness is a temptation to a strong neighbour to assert its own authority in what Mr. Balfour once called "the area of depression." In the case of a nation which, though passing through a period of revolution, yet possesses great fighting strength, it may successfully resist the pressure from without, and derive from this pressure a powerful impetus to internal union. The menace from abroad rendered revolutionary France an inestimable service, and enabled the military genius of Napoleon to turn the national revival into a military channel, and to make France, in turn, a menace to the rest of Europe. There were some who believed that Turkey possessed sufficient fighting strength to repel the attack which came upon her in her period of post-revolution floundering in the waters of parliamentary government, but the event has proved the contrary. In the case of Persia, a country totally negligible in war, there was no possibility that she could successfully resist foreign pressure in any form. Unless it was definitely directed to sustain her, it was bound to submerge her.

So bad, in truth, was the internal situation that the Mejliss could not hope to deal with it at all, unless it was prepared to employ foreigners. There was a complete dearth of administrative ability of any kind. The restored Mejliss met in the autumn of 1909, and during the next year the Governments of England and Russia lost no opportunity of declaring that Persia should take foreign advisers. In January 1910, they joined in urging the Persian Government to appoint a French financial adviser to succeed M. Bizot, who had been adviser at the time of the first Mejliss but had since returned to France.

The Persian Mejliss was not a very wise body, nor

THE VALUE OF THE MEJLISS

were its individual members generally of the highest integrity. Wisdom, indeed, was not to be expected in this ready-made Assembly, which could only hope to attain political sense by making a fool of itself for generations, as other Assemblies have done. It was ready enough to be led, but it could never get an Executive which would attempt to lead it. It is a common charge, to which the Regent has given currency, that the Mejliss interfered with the Executive at every turn. Nothing, in my opinion, could be further from the truth. Any Executive worthy the name could have driven the Mejliss, but no Cabinet ever tried to do so. Ministers prepared no time-table for the session, rarely visited the House, and neither initiated nor took charge of its legislation. Sometimes for a whole week not a Minister was to be seen on the front bench. The House was left to itself, and spent its time in passing laws without any advice or assistance from Ministers, and without any attempt at co-ordination. Sometimes a law, when passed, was found to be at variance with some existing concession or some foreign privilege. Then Ministers would go down to the House and explain to it that it had been wasting its labour, and that the law must be amended. And when a decision of any importance had to be taken by the Cabinet, it immediately invoked the Mejliss, for if Ministers showed the House scant courtesy in the matter of attendance, they treated it with exaggerated awe in leaving everything to its decision. To say that this was the fault of the Chamber and not of the Administration seems to me entirely to reverse the truth. There is no country in the world wherein it is easier for those who do not fear responsibility to acquire power than in Persia. When, for instance, the Government brought forward definite proposals, such as the Treasury laws drafted by Mr. Shuster, they were promptly adopted. The Chamber longed to be led, and would readily have followed a leader. But, however often Cabinets were made and remade, it could find only men who feared all responsibility, offered no guidance, and found it more profitable to sit in their offices and sell their signatures at the foot of documents for as high a price as they would fetch.

Yet, whatever errors the Mejliss made in these unpropitious circumstances, it was responsible for one act of striking statesmanship. It realized the hopelessness of the administrative chaos, it called in foreign advisers, and it gave them *carte blanche*. For a revolutionary Parliament, full of the most hot-headed national sentiment, that was probably an unparalleled performance. Those who remember the constant, and generally unavailing, efforts of the Powers to induce Abdul Hamid to accept any kind of foreign adviser in Macedonia, the succession of notes, and finally the concerted naval demonstration of December 1905, that preceded the coming of financial agents, and the stubborn refusal of the Turks at all times to give any foreigner any executive power, will appreciate the magnitude of the Persian venture. But there has, in fact, for any able foreigner in the Persian service, never been any insuperable difficulty in acquiring large powers. The Persian has never shown the same jealousy as the Turk, and the European is everywhere a highly privileged and respected person, in spite of Persia's disappointing experiences with the

THE VALUE OF THE MEJLISS

various European "reformers" whom the Shahs from time to time took into their service.

It must be admitted that when the Mejliss actually proposed to call in foreigners, and to give them large authority, Great Britain and Russia showed none of that pleasure which might have been expected from previous declarations that nothing else could save Persia. In the first instance it was proposed to employ Frenchmen for the Treasury, but as soon as this became known, in the autumn of 1910, the British and Russian Ministers were instructed to inform Persia that this proposal was not acceptable. It appeared that since January the two Powers had changed their minds, and now agreed to oppose the appointment of subjects of any first-class European Power, other than themselves, to any important administrative post. The idea of appointing French financial officials, and likewise of having Italian officers for the gendarmerie, had therefore to be abandoned, and Persia made application to America for financiers and to Sweden for gendarmerie officers. Even these revised proposals were not very welcome, for the Russian Ambassador in Washington represented to Mr. Knox that it might be better that no Americans should be sent to Persia, while, owing to similar representations in Stockholm, the Swedish Government has since decided not to sanction any large increase in the number of Swedish officers now serving in Persia.

In spite, however, of these not too encouraging omens, foreign administrators arrived in Persia, the Mejliss gave them full powers, and showed every disposition to add to their numbers from time to time as many more as they might deem necessary. They soon found, among the many obstacles to their work, some which must inevitably bring them into relations with the Legations. Nothing, for instance, can be more embarrassing to a country which aims at good government than the pernicious custom of *bast*, by which it is open to all who fear the arm of the law to take refuge in sacred shrines, or in foreign Legations or Consulates. The British and Russian Legations and the Turkish Embassy are those to which Persians principally have recourse, and attempt is often also made to use them, not to escape penalties, but merely for purposes of political demonstration. The British Legation has of late years done much to mitigate the evil by setting a strict watch to prevent *bastis* from getting within its precincts, and by refusing its protection to all except those whose lives are actually in danger, and who are not "wanted" as ordinary malefactors. But it is obvious that *bast* and the possession of foreign citizenship by Persians are serious difficulties in the way of government. Nevertheless, those Constitutionalists who now so bitterly denounce *bast* are open to the charge of ingratitude. In the days of despotism it was the greatest asset of the revolutionary. The Constitution had its origin in a *bast*, and but for the protecting gates of the British Legation many a Constitutionalist would not be alive to-day.

But, if due allowance be made for difficulties of every kind, it cannot be said that the task set before Mr. Shuster and his assistants was in any sense impossible. If the skein was very tangled, it should be remembered that it was also small. If we judge it by its population, the Persian Empire is not a very large country. Its foreign debt is very small, and

THE VALUE OF THE MEJLISS

its actual taxation very light. The bulk of the population are singularly peace-loving, and extremely submissive to any proper authority wherever they can find one. Official corruption and intrigue were the giant obstacles. Mr. Shuster is admittedly a remarkable man, and he possessed a remarkable personal ascendancy over the Persians with whom he had to deal. He had already begun to work miracles in the matter of controlling the official world. He was, moreover, rapidly organizing a Treasury gendarmerie, and would in time have had a large and well-drilled force at his back. There seems, therefore, no reason to doubt that, had it been possible for him to remain in Persia without foreign complications, he could, with plenty of assistants, have set Persia upon the path of prosperity, and made it an ordered country. The task will ultimately have to be achieved by some one, and for Russians or English it will be the same problem as it was for Mr. Shuster. It is only a question of having a sufficiently large number of sufficiently able Europeans, backed by a sufficient force.

It will thus be seen that we have arrived at a stage in our argument at which it is possible to conclude that, though the Persian rulers were contemptible and though the country was chaotic, the Mejliss, by its large importation of foreign administrators, had justified its existence, and had taken steps which might have saved the country. Mr. Shuster, however, came to an open breach with Russia; he and his assistants were ejected, the Mejliss was dissolved, and the whole experiment came to an end, leaving behind it nothing but the desolation of despair which I have already described.

CHAPTER XVIII

A LOOK BEFORE AND AFTER

THERE will remain for the historian the question whether the responsibility for this failure lies with Russia and England, or with Mr. Shuster. It is a question to which I do not attempt here to give a final answer. It has still a root of bitterness which must prevent it from being usefully raised in any such direct form. But there are one or two general considerations which may profitably be submitted. Those who undeservedly condemn Mr. Shuster for what are called headlong characteristics should also remember that these were the defects of certain definite qualities. The strong personality and the driving energy which brought him into collision with the Powers were precisely what hypnotized the Persians, and made them do his bidding. Had he been trained in diplomacy and made the susceptibilities of the two Powers his first consideration, he might have secured their support for his proposals, but he would have lost all the confidence of the Persians. He would never have been able to translate his programme into action, for the goodwill of the Powers would have been no use to him without actual force behind him. The Persians would have obstructed him at every turn, and he would never have succeeded in raising or controlling a gendarmerie.

A LOOK BEFORE AND AFTER

Whether he did or did not possess tact, Mr. Shuster would appear to have fallen because his position as Treasurer-General was believed to be in conflict with Russian policy. On the point of tact, it should be remembered that, though he unfortunately did not in any real sense know the British and Russian Ministers till he had been more than three months in Tehran, his personal relations with them after that period and up to the day of his departure were of a most cordial character, and, if Russian policy had been directed from the Legation instead of from the Consulate, it is possible that he might be in Tehran to-day. The actual causes are probably to be sought deeper, and operated in St. Petersburg and London. In regard to the two points on which Russia's ultimatums were formulated, the question of Shua-es-Sultaneh's property and the appointment of Englishmen to posts, certain facts must tend to confirm this view. Of the five Englishmen whom Mr. Shuster appointed to posts, four remain under M. Mornard's *régime* without protest of any kind. One, whom Mr. Shuster appointed to Shiraz, a nomination naturally welcomed by England, is now actually employed by M. Mornard in the Russian sphere, at the Treasury in Tehran. Another, whom Mr. Shuster appointed to Isfahan, but finally dismissed in deference to Russia, was reappointed by M. Mornard to the same post, and has now been transferred to Yezd, another town in the Russian sphere. A third case, that of M. Lecoffre, was not in any sense a fresh appointment, as Mr. Shuster merely transferred him from Tehran to Tabriz. He has since been nominated to Shiraz by M. Mornard. A fourth appointment, that of Mr. New, to the Telegraphs, had been unsuccessfully urged by the British Legation for some time previous to Mr. Shuster's arrival, and has never been the subject of criticism. The remaining case was that of Major Stokes, to whose appointment Sir Edward Grey in the first instance agreed. In regard to Shua-es-Sultaneh's property, the Russian Consul-General based his objections to its confiscation on the ground that the Russian bank had a claim upon it. No such plea, however, was put forward by the bank itself, nor, in fact, had it any lien on the property.

It need not be inferred from these facts that Russia is opposed to the execution of any programme of reform in Persia. In the light of history, however, it does appear to be established that the position taken up by the two Powers at Tehran is such that it is impossible for any large scheme of reforms to be carried out successfully except by the nominees of these two Powers. In British policy during the period under review two objects have been visible—to maintain our friendship with Russia, and to maintain the independence of Persia. The first of these is, however, regarded as the more imperative, and in so far as conflict has at any time arisen between the two objects, the former has always dominated the issue. Whether it would have been possible for a more vigorous diplomacy to combine the pursuit of both objects more successfully is not a question that can ever be definitely decided. Yet history will hardly reckon as among the worthier achievements of a singularly conscientious and high-minded statesman the conversation in which Sir Edward Grey suggested the dismissal of Mr. Shuster to Russia, at a time when

A LOOK BEFORE AND AFTER

the formulation of the first Russian ultimatum alone was under discussion. The idea of dismissal was first raised through the British Embassy in St. Petersburg on November 6, 1911, but was rejected by M. Nératof, the acting Foreign Minister. On November 14, Sir Edward Grey returned to the point, and instructed Mr. O'Beirne to urge Russia to concentrate on the Shuster issue, to formulate her complaints, and to make a demand. These instructions were carried out on November 15, when for the first time M. Nératof entertained the suggestion, but replied that further consideration would be necessary. Writing to Sir George Buchanan on November 16, 1911, Sir Edward Grey thus reports what he had said on the same day to the Councillor of the Russian Embassy in London: "If the Russian Government were satisfied that they had grievances which demanded redress, they must, of course, formulate their own demands for redress. That was no concern of mine. If they thought that no satisfactory settlement could be reached without the dismissal of Mr. Shuster, I could urge no objection. I did not wish to suggest the dismissal of Mr. Shuster, but I mentioned it lest there should be an impression in St. Petersburg that I was prepossessed in his favour. As a matter of fact, he had given me endless trouble by his inconvenient appointments of British subjects, in spite of all I could say to him."

On November 17, Sir Edward Grey telegraphed to Sir George Buchanan, "to make it quite clear that any demand for Shuster's dismissal will be met with no objection by his Majesty's Government." On November 20, M. Nératof expressed great satisfaction at this communication, but was of opinion that if the first ultimatum were accepted the step would not be necessary. "If, on the other hand, the troops had to proceed beyond the frontier, then it might be necessary for Russia to increase her demands, and she would then probably insist on Shuster being dismissed." It was not till November 22 that the Russian Government, on what it considered fresh provocation from Mr. Shuster, finally determined to expel him.

Doubtless Sir Edward Grey, as he says, did not wish to suggest the dismissal of Mr. Shuster. But, if so, it would surely have been simpler not to have made the suggestion, coupled with an assurance that he would not object to its adoption. If one may make a criticism of the general policy of the Foreign Office, it is that in general it has made a bad choice of points on which to emphasize its own views as against its partner's. It has shown extraordinary tenacity in resisting all suggestions that the ex-Shah should return to Persia. In the present plight of the country it is difficult to see that it can make so much difference whether the ex-Shah does or does not return, whereas the efforts spent upon this point might, at some earlier stage and in some other direction, have possibly secured some substantial advantage.

I have endeavoured in this summary to provide materials for some future estimate of the events of the last few years. There can be little doubt that the impartial historian, after having weighed all considerations, will be driven to the sad conclusion that, although Persia was quite capable of destroying her own independence, that melancholy privilege has not been left to her. Lest at any time, by some freak of fortune, she might escape her fate and raise her head

A LOOK BEFORE AND AFTER

again, Great Britain and Russia have stood by with bludgeons, not indeed with conscious intent to injure, but rather as the baleful instruments in her malign destiny, and have smitten her to the ground whenever one of her more convulsive death-struggles bore the appearance of an attempt to rise and walk. With the two Powers, therefore, must rest the final responsibility for her end, which might otherwise have been justly charged to the venality and folly of her rulers, and the cowardice and corruption of her people.

The oft-repeated statement that the British Government desires the independence of Persia is in itself sincere, and is entirely true in the sense that an unambitious artisan desires to be a millionaire. Even as Sir Edward Grey, Lord Morley, and the Viceroy of India make public declarations of the fervour with which they desire the independence of Persia, so might the artisan with equal truth issue a statement that one of the dearest wishes of his heart was to be a millionaire. But his life is ordered, and his projects are framed, without any regard to the realization of this abstract desire, and in such a way as to secure that he shall remain a workman on forty shillings a week. Were he, while in practice limiting his existence to this narrow outlook, to make continual public reference to his hopes for a million, many would accuse him of folly or suspect him of chicanery. And in the last resort, when all facts have been sifted, it has to be admitted that for English statesmen to talk of the independence of Persia is either wilful self-deception or that kind of current political cant which we all pardon, but which we know in our hearts to be arrant humbug. In every true and vital sense Great Britain no more seeks the independence of Persia than the workman seeks a million, and the whole drift of her policy must as inevitably prevent any such independence as the workman's way of life precludes the possibility of his becoming a millionaire. Only in word does she desire Persian independence; in act, both England and Russia have opposed, and will continue to oppose any such consummation.

Had Mr. Shuster not come into collision with the Russian Government on the particular issue on which he fell, he must inevitably have met its opposition later upon others. The Russian Government itself nominated his successor, and chose a man thoroughly familiar with its position, policy, and interests in Northern Persia, who had given proofs in another capacity of his desire to preserve the friendliest relations. But even M. Mornard has discovered that it is impossible to serve two masters, and whenever he has assumed that he is the servant of an independent Persian Government, this carefully chosen and supple official has found himself in direct conflict with Russia. And it must not be forgotten that though in some ways English methods are different, the position taken up by the British Government in the south is in all essentials the same as that of Russia in the north. Had it been possible for Mr. Shuster to come to terms with Russia in the north and to set the Persian house in order, he would sooner or later have come into conflict with the English in the south. The independence of Persia is quite incompatible with our protectorate over the Sheikh of Mohammerah, with whom we have our own treaties, to which the Government at Tehran is not a party. Were a powerful and progressive

A LOOK BEFORE AND AFTER

Government at Tehran possible, it would certainly find this anomaly intolerable. Moreover, had Mr. Shuster proposed to send a Russian or a German official, I do not say to the so-called British sphere, but even to any town in the neutral sphere—to Shiraz or Bushire, for example—such a step would probably have been even more distasteful to the British Government than were his appointments of Englishmen in the north to the Russian Government. The latter has, indeed, allowed M. Mornard to make a few such appointments in the north, but it is difficult to conceive Great Britain making a corresponding concession in the south. Our special position in the Gulf also, which no British Government is likely to allow Tehran to impair, is equally at variance with Persian independence, and it has more than once proved a source of difficulty to M. Mornard in the exercise both of the Customs and the Treasury administration.

The future of the country, therefore, lies with England and Russia. Their policy cuts too deep for change, and actual independence is a vain dream. It is plain that the two Powers are now set in a position and upon a path from which there will be no retreat. Their duty towards the world, and towards the unhappy country which is caught in the wheel of their policies and interests, is so to understand one another that war shall be avoided, that Persia shall not be made a great military frontier camp, that it shall be preserved as a single country, dominated indeed, but undivided and unannexed, and that its two overlords shall develop its resources and give peace to its people.

CHAPTER XIX

THE DARK AGES IN MACEDONIA

"When God made the world," runs the Balkan legend, "and was distributing stones over the earth, the bag that held them burst and let them all fall upon Montenegro." While in this vein, one might go on to argue that when the social and political weather destinies were being given out, the bag of storms and battles burst over all the Balkan peninsula. No spot so small in all the world has seen more blood and intrigue, more glory and shame, more wondrous human achievement and more appalling human misery. From the days of Achilles and his Myrmidons, of Pericles, of Philip and Alexander, of Pyrrhus and his Albanians, of Pompey and Cæsar, and of Trajan, to the coming of the Slavs and the Bulgars, the Russian, Latin, and Byzantine Empires, and last of all the Ottoman Turk, strife has never failed and rarely flagged. As it was in the beginning, so it is to-day, and there are as yet only faint signs of the time when all the Balkan lands shall have the rest they sorely need. The Netherlands have been called the cockpit of Europe; the Balkans are the cockpit of Europe and Asia, the gate betwixt East and West, where migrant hordes from the East and conquering nations from the West have met and must meet.

It was upon an ill-conditioned Balkan peninsula—

THE DARK AGES IN MACEDONIA

when was it otherwise?—that the Ottoman Turks advanced. Latin and Byzantine, Serb, Bulgarian, and Hungarian Empires rose and fell. Everybody's sword was in his hand, for the Byzantine Empire was only a great name and Constantinople a capital without an empire. Where the carcass is, the eagles are gathered together; and the virile people who felt in their bones the world's old passion for empire-carving, whether it be called land-grabbing or legitimate expansion, the Hungarians, the Bulgars, the Serbs, the Roumanians, and the Albanians were carving and quarrelling for all they were worth, succeeding in turn and disappearing, but always with intent to reappear. Then came the Turk, and laid his dead hand upon them all on the fatal field of Kossovo in 1389. The swords fell, the clock stopped, time rolled on in Europe but not in the Balkans; whence it comes that if any one wants to project himself back into the Middle Ages, he need not strain at Sir Walter Scott or swallow Mr. Harrison Ainsworth. The Orient Express will whirl him there in three days.

The clock has begun again in these latter days, and it has begun where it left off. Time has brought its revenge with a grudging hand. Once again Constantinople is the last stronghold in Europe of a falling empire. The terrible Turk, the scourge of Europe, is at last dying slowly, very slowly, but surely; and once more the eagles, the same old eagles, are gathered around the carcass. In the nineteenth century, Greece, Servia, Roumania, and Bulgaria have all fought free of the yoke, and the Serbs of Bosnia and Herzegovina passed from Turkish to Austrian rule. And in the debatable land that still remained to the Turk till the

THE ORIENT EXPRESS

year 1913, every race, Albanian, Roumanian, Greek, Serb, and Bulgar carried on a propaganda and laid claim to a territory against the day when their overlord should disappear. All remained as of old. The Greek Church carried on the old intolerant Phanariote policy, with the result that there was exactly the same ecclesiastical quarrel between the Greeks and the other races as divided them when the Turks entered Europe. Now, as then, the Church is the outward symbol of nationality and a willing political instrument. Religion, literature, dress, customs, passions, all are mediæval. Cut off for centuries from any communication with, or knowledge of, Western Europe, without education, and living in poverty and in nameless terror, the peasants turned to the past for that something which makes life other than "nasty, brutish, and short." While the Turks were a conquering nation, the future had no hope for them, and they lived in the past. Every Serb has heard from his father the history of the old Servian kings, and the exploits and the territories of Tsar Dushan, celebrated in many a song. No Bulgarian with a goodly family omits to call a son after Boris, the great Bulgarian king, and he knows that Simeon ruled from the Danube to the Adriatic. The Montenegrins wear mourning once a year on the anniversary of Kossovo. Songs that to us are but a record

> "Of old, forgotten, far-off things
> And battles long ago,"

speak to the Balkan peoples of national sorrows or triumphs, as of yesterday. In this way and with the help of a Church, which may therefore be forgiven

THE DARK AGES IN MACEDONIA

many sins, they have each with sure instinct preserved through centuries of political death and precarious existence the spirit of nationality, a national language, and a national costume. When it has passed through such an ordeal, one may smile at those who suppose nationalism to be a deplorable accident, a political epidemic, which the world will shake off; in some form it will last while the world stands.

The threads of national life, hidden underground for centuries, have come once more into the sunlight, and there is surely great profit and much fascination in watching them. Here we have not old and spent, but young and virile nations resuming with all the appliances of civilization their development where it was arrested centuries ago. Their nationality is somewhat crude perhaps for weak stomachs. With long concentration it has grown bitter in bottle, and Balkan people do not understand that the intensity of your patriotism is not necessarily in exact ratio to your hatred of your neighbours. Race hatreds are deeply engrained, but for all that the Balkan peoples are a portent; they are young and eager, and their future may be their own.

The free lands of the Balkans, as they were before the great struggle with Turkey which began in the autumn of 1912, have been described by many travellers. I hope that their writings may induce you to go there, for you are likely to carry away memories, like mine, of days so good in themselves that one can never think them wasted. You can travel in Greece, where the very names of the railway stations have been stolen from your classical atlas and bring you back to the days of the Persian and Peloponnesian wars. Or

THE ORIENT EXPRESS

you may climb to Rilo Monastery, in Bulgaria, and order your dinner in Latin from a cheerful monk, who will have no other language in common with you. Or you may wander among the merry peasants and gipsies of Roumania, and for a change look in at the smart civilization of Bukarest, the little Paris of the Near East, where rank and fashion inhabit. Servia, too, you must not miss, nor the rugged citadel of Montenegro; nor yet Bosnia and Herzegovina, which, though they are not free lands, repay a visit, for there you will see how Imperial Austria can govern a province. But my purpose here is only to give some sketches of the Turkey which has ceased to be, the Balkan country which formed part of Turkey in Europe till it passed, presumably for ever, from the possession of the Sultans in 1913. Let us look at three pictures. The first will be a sad one, and we can pass from it quickly. It is a picture of Macedonia as I first saw it, in the year 1905, when Abdul Hamid sat upon the throne, a still unchallenged despot. Later we shall see the coming of the Constitution, and the gayer scenes that shaped themselves in the enchantment of the false dawn, the most beautiful hour of an eastern day. And finally we shall have a glimpse of the last phase.

A ride across the Turkish frontier in the days of Abdul Hamid was a passage from freedom to bondage. The free lands are young, and they have some of the faults of youth, but in them at least the traveller felt that both foreigner and native could do what they would, provided they did no wrong. In Turkey it was different. At the frontier one was taken in charge by dignified officials with charming manners and

THE DARK AGES IN MACEDONIA

doubtful uniforms, who explained, over ever-recurring coffee and cigarettes, the elaborate precautions which they had taken for the safety of the English effendi; for there were "troubles" in the country, and the effendi might be molested by wicked men. And from that moment the free citizens of a free country found that their inheritance had for a season disappeared; they marched with an escort, they slept with a guard, and if they were to have speech with the people of the country, or to see more than broken roads and the rifles and bristling cartridge-belts of the soldiers, they had to defy the constant vigilance of cavalry by day and sentries by night.

From the frontier post between Kustendil and Egri Palanka, where in 1905 I first set foot in Turkey, a road in the making wound through a narrow, sun-dried valley; here and there were fields of indifferent maize, or stacks of corn, but for the most part the parched soil climbed down from the barren hills to the empty river bed and the broken road without crop or stock. Scarcely a cottage could be seen to right or left, but on the road gangs of grimy peasants worked to make a military way, while soldiers with loaded rifles kept guard over them. Palanka is a poor place and a small, but it was garrisoned for a siege. At midnight on Saturday, August 19, a force of two hundred soldiers of the garrison raided a collection of some half-dozen hovels, which passes as a village in Macedonia. Konopnitsa is a Bulgar village near the road to Kumanova—an hour's ride from Egri Palanka—and the Turkish authorities had received information that there was a Bulgar revolutionary band in it. The Turk is slow to start, and though it was true that a band had rested in the village, it had left three hours before midnight. The story of what happened is confused, as is natural in such a midnight scene, but from a comparison of the Turkish and the villagers' versions it would seem that the soldiers surrounded the khan, and on looking in discovered two peasants drinking, probably the khanjee and a client. Seeing the soldiers, the peasants put out the light and endeavoured to save themselves, whereupon the troops opened fire in the dark, acting, according to the local version, on the order of the bimbashi in command. It is the custom in the stifling summer nights for the villagers to sleep in the yards or at the doors of their houses. At the sound of firing they started up in terror, with their infants in their arms, and, according to the Turkish version, they got in the line of fire. But I saw a babe of three of whose skull but a hollow fragment remained, and I cannot believe that the child was not clubbed.

It was on Monday, August 21, that we reached Palanka, and though the Kaimakam showed me every courtesy, and mounted a guard in front of the khan all night as a preservation against all possible dangers, no news of the story of Konopnitsa reached our ears. No peasant could pass the military rampart to tell "the English" of his wrongs, but on Tuesday an opportunity was found, and, "in consequence of information received," we insisted, to the evident perturbation of our escort, on visiting the church of Konopnitsa, which is hidden up the hill-side a mile from the road. We climbed on foot, but the horse-soldiers did not fail in their duty, and followed at our heels. The villagers had dispatched some messengers

THE DARK AGES IN MACEDONIA

across country to Uskub to inform the foreign consuls, and kept the dead unburied in the church in the hope of an inquiry. A group of weeping women stood by the gate, and, apart, a larger knot of silent men, as they had waited and watched by the dead all day long. The priest came forward to greet us, and I followed him into the church. The bodies were laid on low biers side by side, their feet towards the altar, and the priest removed the covering that I might see the faces. It is not a sight to describe, for they had lain for three August days. I saw the bodies of one man, of two young wives, of one young girl, and of three infants, aged one, two, and three years. A bullet between nose and mouth had killed one child; part of the brain of another lay in the remaining fragment of its skull. All accounts agree that there were eight killed, but I did not see the face of a boy, and I concluded that he shared a bier with another body; on one bier the priest raised the coverlet at either end to show me the faces of two of the children. In Palanka town there were seven wounded, six of whom were women and children, and one a man. The dead man left a family of five. In one family the mother and two children were killed; the grandmother, aged seventy, lay wounded at Palanka.[1]

From Palanka to Kumanova is a long day's ride through dreary, desolate country, which looked to my inexperienced eye as if its barren hills might be as rich in metal as their sides were certainly poor in crops. There are no hamlets by the roadside, but after a time one learns to pick them out where they hide amongst

[1] For the official account of the affair of Konopnitsa, see Blue book, Turkey No. 1, 1906 [Cd. 2816], p. 34.

the slopes, their brown thatch and brown sides blending in the sombre landscape as animals efface themselves in the snow. The day we reached Kumanova a Turk killed a child of three days old, and for the previous eight days there were eight murders proved in the kaza of Kumanova. Ten days before a soldier thrust a child roughly out of his path, and when its father, who stood by, uttered a word of remonstrance, the soldier shot him dead. In the same week a policeman shot a Christian shopkeeper for the crime of having his shop open after sunset. In the neighbourhood of Uskub horror was equally rife, and we heard authentic cases, not a fortnight old, of murder, rape, and torture. The Uskub district was allotted to the Austrians for reformation under the Mürzsteg scheme, but in Macedonia there was no longer even the thinnest veil of pretence that tinkering at the gendarmerie could ever heal the sores of the country. This did not mean that the officers did not work hard, but only that the task was impossible. There was an Austrian at Palanka, for they had an officer in every kaza in the Uskub district, but he was powerless to prevent the Konopnitsa affair, for he was given no authority over the soldiers. There was an Austrian at Kumanova, young, energetic, and sympathetic, but alone: a solitary European in the midst of a hundred and nineteen villages. A few months previously the troops encountered a small Servian band, which, finding itself hopelessly outnumbered, surrendered at once. The seven prisoners were disarmed and brought to Kumanova town with their hands bound to their sides, and there, in front of the Austrian officer's windows, every man was butchered.

THE DARK AGES IN MACEDONIA

So perished Europe's reforms of 1903. "We thought that the Powers would do something for us," said one to me; "but now we are worse off than ever. We are desperate. Will not England help us?" Southward in Salonika the tale was the same, and everywhere all men asked, in the words used by a foreign officer to me, "Of what use to remodel the gendarmerie unless you are going to reform the course of justice? There is no justice in this country."

From Salonika a railway line, that came by German enterprise, runs up through lovely country, between blue lake and brown mountain, to the hills of Monastir. But in Vodena and Florina there was strife, for the Turkish Government was taking a census, and each of the races was anxious to claim as many of the inhabitants as possible. It was not the Ottoman policy to discourage the feuds of the subject races; it was always better to encourage the "under dog," and since the Bulgarian rising of 1903 the Greeks had been selected for encouragement. In the Salonika district, Greek bands containing Turkish officers and Greeks in Turkish uniform attacked villages to force their adhesion to the Patriarchate. In Monastir, the Turkish soldiers killed a member of a Greek band, and were about to bring his head in triumph to the town when they discovered, to their chagrin, that the trophy belonged to a Turk!

On Sunday, August 27, Turkish troops raided the village of Mogila, near the town of Monastir. Their pretext was a search for komitajis, but their object was to avenge the death of a notorious Turkish bandit named Sheffsky. The truth of this was beyond question, for all knew that Mogila was doomed, and a month earlier a warning appeared in a London newspaper that evil would befall it. There were no komitajis in Mogila when the troops arrived on Sunday, but they went away on Monday leaving nine peasants dead in the maize. The consuls and the Italian officers visited the spot the same day, and made a report on the things that were done, so if any chance European chose to read a tiny, very tiny, fragment of modern history in Monastir he had the power to do so; but he would have been wrong in supposing that the soldiers were punished.

It was August 29 when we reached Monastir, and all visible trace of the previous day's work had been removed. On the night of August 31 a fire broke out in the Christian quarter of the town. A shop blazed up furiously, for Turkish houses are fine fuel, and in the twinkling of an eye there arose an indescribable tumult. The narrow ways were filled with a swarming throng of Greeks and Bulgars, Jews and Turks, Vlachs, Albanians, and Serbs, all roaring directions to one another but listening to none. The flames played on a red sea of faces which ebbed and flowed in the crossways, where staggering salvage porters forced their way through, shrieking warnings to all the world. Fire brigade there was none, but hand-pumps arrived and were lustily worked by scores of hands, and would have served well enough had there been water; but after one bold jet the stream ever died away, and a long interval of jostling, swaying, and yelling in five tongues ensued. The water only made the flames more spiteful, and they roared more fiercely, gripping new walls and roofs, where weird figures toiled with axes, breaking away tiles and timber in the vain hope

THE DARK AGES IN MACEDONIA

of checking the fire. Gendarmes prowled about and made sudden rushes, without apparent reason, on single persons, thrusting them back into the dark alleys; but for the rest the crowd did as it liked, and one had the novel sensation of being allowed to view a fire from whatever point one might select. It burned all night, and in the morning there were fifteen houses in ruins. On all sides one heard that it was the work of incendiaries, but no one knew the truth of this report.

The most tranquil portion of the vilayet of Monastir was in the west. At Resna and Ochrida the Christian population is predominantly Bulgar, consequently there was not internal strife as in more evenly balanced districts. At Resna, by the shore of Lake Presba, there was an Italian officer, and at Ochrida another. In both districts assassinations were too frequent to suit a European palate, and at Resna the troops had bastinadoed the peasants in making perquisitions, but so well did these parts compare with less fortunate regions that all held them "tranquil," and the peasants considered themselves in better case than many another.

Ochrida was desolated in 1903, and the gloom of that summer rested over it like a pall. We walked on a Saturday evening to the village of Velgoshti, for Ochrida, the Macedonian Switzerland, is cool beside its mountain lake, and summer walking is possible. We found a mass of black and ruined cottages, and some hovels hastily built for shelter. All the women wore on their heads a black handkerchief, the mark of widowhood, and uphill to the cemetery we saw aged women toil, singly and in groups, bearing large bunches of sweet wild flowers to lay on their husbands' graves, as is their weekly custom. They bring also a dish of food to the church for the priest's blessing, and afterwards eat it with their families by the graveside as a sacred meal. Men were scarce in this village, but graves were plentiful, and to strangers the women could not speak for tears; for there were seventy males and ten women killed in 1903. The men told us they had paid no tithe the previous year, for it was clear they could not. That year they had sent a telegram to the Sultan on his birthday, begging exemption; but they had had no answer, and the tithe had been paid. The Government had given nothing for sustenance or for rebuilding; they did not know what they should have done but for some kind English people, to whom they were very grateful.

The English Relief Committee did its work well in 1904, and it earned for England a gratitude which could not find words. In truth the simple English folk, parsons' wives and poor men's widows, knowing nothing of politics and caring less, who sent of their store to Macedonia when they heard of burned villages and dead breadwinners, did more for England's prestige in the country than diplomacy can easily do. Here one might well feel proud to be an Englishman, if anywhere, for all looked to her as a Power, great, generous, and disinterested. On Sunday afternoon a caique containing a party of Bulgars pursued us across the lake. In Macedonia it was difficult for Bulgars to have free speech with strangers, and they had watched their opportunity. In mid-lake their caique came alongside, and we had to accept a complimentary *raki*. When we landed on the further shore, they found us, and enacted a scene as embarrassing as

THE DARK AGES IN MACEDONIA

possible for modest men. While we ate the watermelons and drank the coffee which they forced upon us, the two males of the party raved—there is no other word—of England. England in her greatness and goodness was like the Madonna, the Holy Virgin; nay, England was as God Himself. They raved of Gladstone, of Queen Victoria, of King Edward, and of Macedonia's love. Then the women of the party were solemnly ranged in order, and sang in unison a long, sad song of Macedonia and its struggles for freedom; when we had thanked them we endeavoured to escape, but our hands were seized and covered with kisses, and when at last we shoved our caique off shore, a chorus of affectionate farewells followed us.

That night we were awakened by an earthquake which shook the house to its foundations. But unless the house falls an earthquake causes little comment in those parts. Turkey tottered, but no man cared.

CHAPTER XX

THE MILLENNIUM

I HAVE seen the British people drunk with the news of victory in South Africa; I have seen vast, popular political demonstrations in England and in Ireland; I have seen victorious armies in the field; I have been in Athens, Sofia, and Belgrade in the hour of victory. On all these occasions there was excitement in the air. But I have no hope that, though my days be as many as the sands of the seashore, I shall ever see again the like of the Turkish revolution, or feel the communicable thrill that ran through Macedonia like Greek fire in the summer of 1908. Liberty was in the very air, an intoxication which every human being breathed. There was no escape from it, so that even the most hardened sinners reeled, and sober consuls of Great Powers, grown old in watching one another, confessed themselves rejuvenated.

The Turkish Constitution, with the exception of that first fine rapture, has as yet had a sorry history. It is therefore the more important to record the reality of the rapture, and to confess that though I found it good to be in Salonika with the Greek army in 1913, and to see that historic town embarking on a fresh era to the great content of the population, yet I neither felt myself, nor saw any evidence that others felt, anything like that never-to-be-forgotten delirium of

THE MILLENNIUM

1908. Looking back through old files, I find that I had a presentiment that things were far too good to last, for this is what I wrote—

"When I reached Salonika and had taken breath I telegraphed home that the millennium had arrived. I said also that it was impossible to describe it; nevertheless, I suppose that one must try. For the memory will pass, since the millennium is not made of years, but of crowded hours, and our old human hungers and angers will quickly overlay it. But even if the shadows of the ancient prison-house should again begin to close around the Turkish Constitution and the Macedonian peasant, the recollection of the dazzling light of liberty will remain. For—let there be no mistake about it—at the present moment there is only one country in the world where the liberty of all without the licence of any is an understood and accomplished fact, and that country is, of all others, Turkey. Destiny has played a trick upon Dr. Watts, and it is not enough to have been born 'a happy English child.'"

Even while the train shot southward across the great heat-wilted plain of Hungary one felt the coming change. These were not the old familiar gates of the East. The dining-car was filled with happy exiles— Young Turks from Paris, London, and Geneva, who wore their fezes with a jaunty rake and laughed with sparkling eyes as they talked to one. And all their talk was of equality, of freedom, and of the coming greatness and glory of the Turkish Empire. "Stambul! Stambul!" they cried, and boasted how they would find Constantinople a repentant mother, ready to gather them back to her arms. All night we pounded on through Servia, the train singing a song

THE ORIENT EXPRESS

in our ears, as though impatient of its own slowness and anxious to beguile the hours; and in the morning, after a momentary halt at Ristovatz, on the Servian side, we crossed the Turkish frontier and drew up amidst a cheering crowd in Zibeftche station. In the old days, to cross the frontier from any other country was, by contrast, to step into the shadow from the sun; one had the feeling of entering a prison. But now the cowed or scowling faces were gone. The outward and physical change was one which to be believed had to be seen. It was as though all fear—and fear, whether bodily or mental, is the worst thing in life—had fled for ever.

A show was made of examining my passport, but it was merely an exchange of smiles and compliments. The custom-house officer patted my kit affectionately with his fingers, but displayed no curiosity as to its contents. There was a wait of an hour, and I strolled back across the frontier to Ristovatz. A fortnight before such a thing would have been impossible, but the soldiers at the frontier only smiled at me as I went and returned. Then the festive journey began again, and every wayside station broke out in joyful shouts as the train steamed in. An excursion train, a *train-de-plaisir*, in Macedonia! Who that knew that hitherto sullen and blood-stained country had ever in his strangest dreams imagined such a thing? Yet that was what I saw, and not one train, but several. At Uskub and Kuprilu, vast, seething, good-tempered, happy crowds, composed of all the nationalities of the vilayets, thronged the station. Smart Turkish officers, swaggering Albanians, Bulgar peasant men and women, Serb "popes" in the flowing robe of the Orthodox priest, Greek merchants, Jewish pedlars,

THE MILLENNIUM

and a medley of boys and girls, all wore the red-and-white rosette that celebrated the Constitution. Every one seemed to wish to shake his neighbour by the hand incessantly, and Turkish officers might be seen embracing Bulgar priests, and kissing them affectionately on both cheeks. Bands paraded, surrounded by a forest of banners bearing the white crescent on a crimson ground or a Constitutional motto on a green one, and an army of little children carrying the flags of liberty followed them.

The great event of the day was at Kuprilu, when a train arrived bringing home twelve hundred Uskub excursionists who had been junketing at Salonika. The engine was dressed with red-and-white streamers, and every inch of the train was decorated with palm-branches and flowers. On the roof, close to the engine, was a band, and the rest of the roof was packed from end to end with men standing poised beside heavy banners,—which tugged against them in the breeze,—or squatted Turkish fashion on the carriage-tops. The crowd in the station roared a welcome, and vehement answer came from the train. Gay Albanians fired their revolvers in the air by way of a *feu de joie*, and general ecstasy ensued.

"Why are you all so happy?" I asked one.

"We have been in a dark cavern," he said quite naturally, "and now that is all over for ever. We are free."

"But are you not afraid that some of the old evils may return?"

"No," he answered quite decidedly; "after this it is impossible. No one could bring them back."

Another who was no less radiant was more anxious about the future and the intentions of the Sultan,

THE ORIENT EXPRESS

"Qui sait?" was his cautious reply. "Qui vivra verra."

Evening papers in Macedonia! Yes, so it was. There were the boys running in and out amongst the crowd, crying the latest word of liberty and selling not merely Turkish papers, but yesterday's journals from Sofia and Belgrade.

All day long, as the train crawled southward, the tale was the same. At a lonely post a strange figure of a bagpiper played a wild dance upon his pipes to the incessant tapping of a drum, and in the evening from the fields came the sound of drumming, for all the world as though it were a June night in the Ulster country-side when all the Orange lodges are out practising for "the twelfth."

All this was marvellous in Macedonia, but there were greater marvels. The truth, the astonishing, bewildering truth, was that for the moment Macedonia —the cockpit not of Europe, but of the world, where murder is more common than measles—governed itself of its own goodwill. Every one did what he liked, and no one liked to do ill. In Salonika there was only the veriest handful of police, for the Turkish Government never made any pretence of policing the town, and street murder ordinarily went unpunished. And now in this unpoliced city there was not a single prisoner. The vast prison, besides its great contingent of political prisoners, of whom many were political assassins, contained also many common criminals of the lowest kind. But all had been released, and the murderers came out first. The two thousand political prisoners, after waiting six hours for their expected release, finally determined to break out, and found, to their surprise, that there were only six gendarmes in

THE MILLENNIUM

charge of them, the regiments of the guard having gone away! But there was not a crime of any kind to record. The bishop had offered his candlesticks to the burglar, and the burglar was overcome. Salonika swarmed with thieves and cut-throats transformed for the time, by the grace of generosity and by a tide of public good-feeling the like of which has rarely been seen since the days of the early Church, into citizens of goodwill.

The whole gigantic revolution had been wrought by goodwill and with singularly little violence. A few spies had been shot and a few had been hanged. The shooting of Osman Hydet Pasha was a most unfortunate mistake. He had to read a telegram from the Sultan to the Monastir garrison in reply to its demand for the Constitution, and the telegram, according to the Sultan's wont, began with threats of condign punishment and ended with fair words and many promises. Osman would have done well to read it backwards or to suppress the threats, for it was a long telegram, and he was shot before he got to the promises.

When the English papers arrived in Salonika we read how the komitaji bands in Macedonia had given up their arms. This was a natural mistake, for the telegrams had spoken of their surrender. But a "surrender" in Macedonia was a much more pleasant process than might be imagined, and I may be permitted to recall a warning written at the time—

"Though at present peace reigns, let it not be supposed that the bands have been disarmed or that all danger is past."

A "surrender" was, in fact, a glorious junket. Men who had held the hills for years, sleeping by day and waking by night, came down to the town that lies in the valley and rejoiced. Wild, fierce figures, with whom no brigand that has ever trod the stage of a theatre could compare in dressing for the part, shaggy men with Mannlichers, knives, revolvers and a double-burdened belt of cartridges marched in proudly and were greeted by the whole populace as heroes. For years they had seen life only from the mountain-tops, fighting in the dark or by the blaze of burning houses. Only in occasional expeditions across the frontier into free Bulgaria had some of them held up their heads in the sunlight in the streets of towns and moved freely in the pleasant ways of ordinary men. Now they ate, drank, and made merry; they tasted such civilization as a Macedonian town affords; they were embraced by the Turks; they were embraced by the Greeks; they were embraced by everybody. The chiefs came to Salonika; the rank and file dispersed to their homes to resume the long-interrupted life of the fields, to plough and sow and reap and mow, and sleep in the bosom of their families. But no one asked them to give up their arms, nor would they ever have consented to do so. The Young Turks knew well that any attempt of the kind would immediately upset the momentary millennium. Some even assured the Bulgar "Voivodes" that if any attempt were made to tamper with the liberties of the Constitution, they would open the army's magazines to the Bulgars and invite them to march, side by side with themselves, upon Constantinople.

This declaration was literally fulfilled some six months later during the counter-revolution in March 1909, when Mahmud Shefket Pasha distributed arms from the arsenal at Salonika to the Bulgars who

THE MILLENNIUM

accompanied him when he made his triumphal march to Constantinople and deposed Abdul Hamid from his throne.

The most dramatic of all the surrenders was that of the great chief Apostol. Apostol was a lake-dweller rather than a mountain man. For years past his had been the only writ that ran in all the district of Yenidje-i-Vardar, some twenty miles from Salonika. Hidden in the reeds, he ruled, and none might fish in the lake unless they were his tributaries. His name was feared far and wide, and yet he earned much gratitude and love, for though he forced the villagers to sustain his men with supplies he was a strong protector from the Turks, and was counted just and simple in his dealings. Much violence lies to his account, but no treachery towards his friends. In the marshes and the island swamps he saved himself from pursuit, and the Turkish troops hunted him in vain. They encountered him in many a fight, and often he lost many men, but his own life was never forfeit, for all the large price upon his head. He had grown to be a legend, and wonderful tales of him ran through all the country-side. His escapes had been miraculous, and I remember to have seen an account of his death four separate times in English newspapers. On the last occasion all men thought him drowned, and the troops rode home triumphant, for Apostol had been driven to the lake, and swam out from the shore while a hurricane of bullets smote the water. But in a few weeks' time he proved very much alive again, and the Turks learnt, to their amazement, that he had dived and saved himself amongst the reeds.

Imagine the feelings of this outlaw with a price upon his head, when the Turks sent him an emissary who greeted him as a brother and a friend, invited him to come and meet them in Yenidje-i-Vardar, and informed him that Turkey was free and the Constitution proclaimed. If men read the telegrams in London with a certain scepticism, can it be wondered at that incredulity wrinkled the brow of Apostol in his lair? There was in Yenidje a priest of the French Catholic Mission, and Apostol bethought him that this was a man who would tell him if there was treachery afoot. So he sent a messenger to the priest, and the answer came back: "There is nothing to fear; the Turks are in good faith." But Apostol doubted. "Are you sure?" he asked, in a second message, and the answer was the same. Thereupon Apostol came, but, thinking that if there were a trap it were well to come in force, he marched into Yenidje at the head of all his men. And then was seen a marvellous sight, for at the end of all the decimation of the country-side, the band-hunting, the perquisitions, the searches for arms, the raids, the beatings, the tortures, three hundred shaggy warriors, well armed with Mannlichers and with every belt stuffed with cartridges, came swinging proudly into Yenidje-i-Vardar, and at a word from Apostol fired three volleys into the air. The inhabitants fled into their houses in terror at their approach, and shops and booths were hastily shut. Only the Young Turks, the military officers and the local members of the Ottoman Committee of Union and Progress, remained to greet Apostol. They poured into his astonished ears the story of liberty, and he soon yielded himself to their persuasions. Turks and Bulgars embraced, and many of the popular kisses which marked the new era were exchanged in the street of Yenidje-i-Vardar. Afterwards Apostol, with his

THE MILLENNIUM

principal lieutenants, came to Salonika, and was the hero of the hour.

Sandansky, notorious for many exploits, but most famous for having carried off Miss Stone, an American missionary, in 1903, and held her in the hills a prisoner for ransom, was also in Salonika. There, too, was Panitsa, who treacherously shot Boris Sarafoff and Garvanoff with his own hand, and wounded Colonel Elliot, the British chief of gendarmerie at Drama, in an attempt to kidnap him. Garvanoff I knew for a sincere lover of his country; Sarafoff also I had known, a man with murder on his own hands and many ugly flaws in his brilliant personality, but one who deserved a better fate than to be shot by a pretended friend in the very act of farewell salutation. It gave me no pleasure to see Panitsa enjoying the benefits of this marvellous amnesty, and posing as a hero in the struggle for freedom. I had little doubt that he was a doomed man, for Sarafoff's friends had vowed vengeance. But threatened men live long, and I saw Panitsa again, walking the streets of Drama, in January 1913. I was assisting in the organization of relief work there during the Balkan War, and a Bulgarian officer came to me with a request that he might introduce to me Panitsa, who was anxious to assist me. Panitsa and I had met once years before, but though we saw each other daily in the streets of Drama, it was not our habit to bow to one another. By various accidents I have at one time and another made the acquaintance not only of many people who have subsequently met violent deaths, but also of a great number of men who might technically be described as murderers. I cannot honestly say that I have had even the smallest feeling of superiority in their company, or felt the slightest objection to shaking their hands. I do not at all know whether this is a serious discredit, but for the sake of honesty wish to state that this is so, and also that the case of Panitsa is an exception. There are few kinds of criminals of whom one might not say: " There, but for the grace of God, go I." But Panitsa's treacheries were such that if ever deeds deserved to be branded as unnatural, his are entitled to that stigma. I therefore replied to the officer that I did not wish to renew my acquaintance with Panitsa, more especially as I had known Boris Sarafoff.

" But all that is forgotten and forgiven long ago," argued my friend. " Panitsa has done excellent service during the war; moreover, his information will be of the greatest value to you, as he knows the villages in the neighbourhood better than any one."

" I have no doubt that he does," I answered, " and that the villagers also have only too good reason to know him. But if you assure me that he can be of any service to the relief work, I am quite willing to meet him."

Seeing that the affair was not to my liking, the officer, who had begun the conversation by stating that he could himself bring Panitsa to call upon me that afternoon, now said that he was not sure that he would himself be free, but that he would tell Panitsa to come. Apparently he did not give a very enthusiastic message. In the somewhat primitive hotel at Drama there is one public room, which is really a long and rather wide corridor running the full length of the building. At three o'clock that afternoon I was writing at a table at one end of this corridor, when I heard the door, which was at the other end, slowly opening, and

THE MILLENNIUM

Panitsa appeared. He stepped inside the room, and stopped and looked absent-mindedly at me. I sat behind my table and looked at him. And so we remained for about two minutes, with the length of the room between us, neither of us making any sign of recognition. Then Panitsa turned and quietly went out.

Some words, which were written in August 1908, in the first flush of the millennium, and unfortunately foreshadowed the troubled sequel, will serve to conclude this chapter—

"Sandansky and Panitsa have no connection with the Bulgarian Internal Organization, which has always condemned their actions. This organization, apart from the Turks, is the strongest force in Macedonia. It has for years formed a kind of secret Government, an underground republic, with its own court of justice, its own police, its own militia, its own postal system. It represents and is trusted by the bulk of the Bulgar population in Macedonia, and if the Young Turks and the Internal Organization can come to a definite understanding the future outlook will be good. At present there is mutual respect and much friendly intercourse. But there are some rocks ahead. For the Bulgars desire a Federal Parliament for the empire, with local autonomy in Macedonia, and to this the Young Turks are opposed. They are prepared to develop local institutions, but they do not desire autonomy. There is a constitutional struggle ahead, but in the meantime the Bulgarian militia system remains in existence.

"The Internal Organization asks for a Chamber for Macedonia, with representation in the Imperial Parliament at Constantinople. There may be Arab,

Albanian or other parties in the Imperial Parliament also desirous of local autonomy and federation, and with these the Bulgar deputies will co-operate as far as possible; but they intend to remain a Macedonian party. Meantime the Bulgars declare themselves willing to accept any instalment of their programme, and they ask for the development of the local administrative councils, the retention of such a local institution as the Financial Commission—as to which Europe will also have a word to say—and official recognition of the Greek and Bulgar languages in local government, so that Christian Macedonians may be introduced into the Civil Service as soon as possible. How far Greeks and Bulgars will unite in these demands and make common cause remains to be seen. The programme of the Greeks has not yet crystallized.

"But the Turks have far other ideas. When they speak of equality they mean equality with the empire as a unit, one and indivisible; which means that they will always be in the majority. They want an Imperial, but not a Federal, Parliament.

"They propose that Christians and Turks alike shall serve in the army, but they do not propose to enrol the Christians in separate regiments. Turk and Christian are to serve as brothers side by side, wherever the necessities of imperial defence may call them. The Macedonian Bulgars will ask to be enrolled in separate regiments and to serve in Macedonia. Here is matter enough for a young Parliament to settle. Is Turkey to start with her Irish question, or to be like Austria, an empire in unstable equilibrium? The Young Turks have done well. If this problem is solved without bloodshed, now or hereafter, they will do better."

CHAPTER XXI

THE YOUNG TURKS

THE story of how the Young Turkish organization was created is wonderful. In all the history of secret societies living in the shadow of a terror there can be no parallel to it, either for secrecy or for success. In the end the organization included an army of which the private soldiers had taken the oath. Yet no one knew. Spies flooded the country, but could not break the charm. There was a national conspiracy of silence. The East is not always silent; for it is, in fact, a very mother of lies, and the rumours that run rife in the bazaars often leave truth at the bottom of the well. But, when there is great work afoot, the East can be silent as well as patient. Macedonia was studded with observant pairs of European eyes belonging to gendarmerie officers, consuls, and vice-consuls, whose vigilance was rarely relaxed; yet I found no one who did not confess himself surprised beyond measure by what had taken place.

A Young Turkish organization had long existed, but its members were chiefly exiles, and its centre was Paris, where Ahmed Riza Bey and his friends laboured to promote a liberal propaganda in Turkey. But the ramifications of the system of espionage made the difficulties of the task insurmountable for an outside organization. Moreover, the ideas of the Paris Committee were not in harmony with those of the reforming Turks at home. The exile becomes exacting, and the Eastern exile who does not put off the virtues of the East and put on the vices of the West, tends to an unpractical idealism and the cherishing of dreams. The Young Turks of Paris did not merely demand the deposition of Sultan Abdul Hamid, they asserted that the only way of safety lay in a republic. Republican ideas are not in fashion in Turkey. If the revolution were to grow, the Salonika leaders saw that, whatever might happen to Abdul Hamid, they must not propose to abolish the royal house or to interfere with the semi-religious character of the Sultanate. The empire was Mohammedan, and Mohammedan it would remain, though they hoped to make it a possible place for Christians. The Young Turks of Macedonia were right. They would not have got their revolution on any other terms. But a question which I asked in the earliest hours of their success may perhaps here be fitly reproduced.

"It is just here," I wrote, "that the root of the trouble and the whole danger for the future lie. Will not the exigencies of a Mohammedan empire ruin the liberalism of the Young Turks, sincere though that liberalism is?"

There was high debate between Turkey and Paris. Then, in 1905, relations were broken off and the last phase of the Young Turk movement, which culminated in a successful rising in European Turkey, began with the formation of a secret Committee of Liberty in Macedonia, with its most active centre at Salonika. The wiser heads in Paris recognized that this was something real and valuable, and sent an emissary

THE YOUNG TURKS

with a proposal that in order to promote common action, the new Society should adopt the title of the Paris organization, the Ottoman Committee of Union and Progress, and should appoint the members of the Paris Committee as its delegates. This proposal was adopted, and Ahmed Riza Bey and his colleagues became the trusted agents abroad of the Committee in Turkey.

The new organization consisted chiefly of servants of the Government, civil and military, with a goodly proportion of young officers. The nature of the force which produced it is now evident. The old discontent with the misgovernment of the country had never resulted in any effective movement for reform. It was the European reform schemes, dating from 1904, which laid the train and kindled the spark, and the Powers, with quite another intent, were the indirect cause of this amazing revolution. To the Turks the coming of European officers and the imposition of reform from without were unspeakable mortifications, and engendered the bitterest hatred of the corrupt *régime* at Yildiz Kiosk, which, by its impotence, its tyranny, and its provocative attitude towards the *rayah*, exposed the empire to continual humiliations. The ineptitude of the Government was demonstrated in a striking object lesson by the fact that the foreign officers, although their authority was cut down to the lowest point and their activities hampered at every turn, succeeded in turning the gendarmerie into a smart, well dressed, and well drilled force, for which the insistence of the Powers secured regular pay. The contrast between the condition of the gendarmerie under foreign supervision and the condition of the army under their own corrupt and shiftless rulers was a bitter one for officers and men, and the reforming energies of the International Financial Commission impressed the civil servants also with a disgust and hatred of the old *régime*, which exposed them to the mortification of foreign tutelage. The plunder of the country by European concession-hunters, and a long series of ignominious incidents, of which the Italian naval demonstration in order to secure the establishment of Italian post-offices throughout the empire was the most recent example, increased the hatred of the Palace. There seems to have been also a conviction among the Turks in Macedonia that the attitude of the Sultan towards the Macedonian question, his encouragement of the bands, and stubborn opposition to reform, would inevitably end in the loss of the whole of European Turkey. The meeting between King Edward and the Tsar at Reval, in June 1908, when the Macedonian question was the principal subject of discussion, and England and Russia agreed upon the necessity of imposing a far more drastic scheme of reform, brought to a climax the anxieties of the Young Turks for the future of the empire.

The Salonika Committee had set vigorously to work in 1905. It saw clearly that the only way to wring a Constitution from the Sultan was by force, and conceived the plan of a general strike of the troops upon some critical occasion. The Third Army Corps stationed in Macedonia was made the special object of its attentions, and the new propaganda infected the officers with extraordinary speed. Local committees were formed everywhere, no unit of the army being neglected. Great pains were taken with the secret organization. Books were smuggled in and officers

THE YOUNG TURKS

sat up at night studying the history of the French and most other revolutions, collating the methods of the Jesuits and the Jacobins, striving to penetrate even the Eleusinian mysteries and the records of the Essenes—ransacking, in short, the literature of secret societies. The famous Greek Hetairia, over which Prince Ypsilanti presided a hundred years ago in the Greek struggle for independence, was a mine of suggestions. And the existing Bulgarian organization was another useful model. A ritual of signs, countersigns, and formulas was elaborated, and interwoven with this strand of organization was another—Freemasonry. The masonic order, secret and forbidden, grew prodigiously in Macedonia between 1905 and 1908. On Constitution Day in 1908 it came proudly into the open, and the Salonika Freemasons were photographed in all the glory of aprons and decorations. A strange feature of the secret organization was that the Committee had no officials of any kind either in Salonika or elsewhere. A chairman was elected to preside over each sitting, but he had no further authority, and meetings were summoned by the members, almost always by word of mouth. It was not till the revolution was accomplished that the Committee had a recognized rendezvous, where business was transacted and members could ordinarily be found.

The work throughout was done with singularly little expense, as the emissaries in general worked for "love," whilst officers and officials all contributed their mites whenever money came their way. The feudal beys of Macedonia were also for the most part ardent supporters of the Young Turks, and a good harvest brought some gold to the Committee's treasury. But naturally the other parts of the empire were not ignored. The Second Army Corps at Adrianople was inoculated with the leaven, and special attention was also paid to Asia Minor. Doctor Nazim Bey, who was supposed to be in exile for his liberal opinions, escaped to Asia Minor, disguised as a *khoja*, or preacher, and for eighteen months was busily engaged in sowing the good seed amongst the Anatolian battalions, disguised at one time as a pedlar, at another as a cultivator of leeches, but carrying ever in his basket the leaflets and instructions of the Committee. It was chiefly owing to his efforts that the Anatolian battalions, brought from Smyrna to crush the movement at Monastir, declared themselves friends and were sworn to the Constitution as soon as they arrived.

It was not to be expected that the activities of the Salonika Committee should entirely escape the notice of the ubiquitous spies of the Palace. A system of small bands was organized on the Bulgar model in order to protect the Young Turks in case they should have to fly to the hills for safety. Spies mysteriously disappeared, and were, in fact, put to death by the Committees. In March 1908 official suspicion became acute. A series of raids and perquisitions was made, and a commission was sent from Constantinople to collect evidence against suspected persons; but so widespread had the propaganda become among the officials and officers that it continued unchecked, and the Committee, in fear of discovery, prepared to strike its blow at an early date. In default of a more favourable opportunity, plans were evolved for rising on the anniversary of the Sultan's accession, September 1, or in the spring of 1909. But events forced the hand of the Committee, and the Revolution broke out in July. There were two political reasons in favour

THE YOUNG TURKS

of this earlier date. One of these was the visit of Munir Pasha, the Turkish Ambassador at Paris, and a favourite agent of the Sultan, to Athens and Belgrade, where, rumour ran, he was engaged in making humiliating agreements in return for an anti-Bulgarian combination. The other more urgent reason was the desire of the Young Turks to forestall the application of the new reform scheme which was expected to result from the Reval meeting. But the actual precipitation of events was due to a purely local train of circumstance.

It is noteworthy that in this great conspiracy, every member of which knew that any suspicion which fastened on him would cost him his life, women played a heroic part, which some might have expected would have been denied to them in a Mohammedan country. The wife of Assim Bey, an active spirit of the Salonika Committee, wrought great service, and often kept the door to guard against surprise when the conspirators met in the dead of night. And in the event which brought about the final rising another woman played a singular and dramatic part, which may be here recorded.

The *commandant de place* at Salonika, one Nazim Bey—who must be distinguished from Doctor Nazim Bey already mentioned—was principal police spy, being himself *aide-de-camp* of the Sultan. After the familiar manner of the privileged *mouchard* he conducted himself as above authority, and was *de facto* superior to the actual commander-in-chief. In 1908, however, Essad Pasha was appointed to the chief command at Salonika, and quickly showed himself disposed to assert his position. The new commander, by setting his face against corruption and removing some of the most scandalous offenders, soon found himself at war with Nazim Bey and the whole party of reaction. Feeling against Nazim ran high in the army. The Committee of Union and Progress considered the situation and decided that Nazim must die. Now his wife was the sister of Major Enver Bey, a young officer who had been *aide-de-camp* to Hilmi Pasha and a leading member of the Committee. This lady, though married to a police spy, was herself an ardent revolutionary, devoted to the cause of the Committee of Union and Progress, and often an instrument in its designs. She knew of its decision to procure the assassination of her husband, and did not shrink from playing a part which many may think revolting in a wife, though doubtless praiseworthy in a conspirator. She offered to assist the murderer in his task, and on June 11, the day of the Vali's fête at Salonika, an assassin stole to the window of the room in which Nazim Bey sat dining with his wife. The latter had carefully left the curtains undrawn, so that a clear view could be obtained, and had placed a strong light behind her husband. In this wise husband and wife sat and dined, he talking in high good-humour, all unconscious that she who sat opposite him was waiting for his death with an expectation which grew tenser as the moments rushed on. Suddenly a shot rang out, which may well be called the first in the Young Turk Revolution. The would-be assassin missed his aim, and Nazim was but slightly wounded. There was a stir of sentries and the alarm was immediately given, but the conspirator escaped.

Six weeks later, when the miracle of the Revolution had been successfully wrought, one of the first acts of the Committee of Union and Progress, then in a mood of mercy and proud of the bloodless character of its triumph, was to condemn Nazim Bey not to death, but to exile. They banished him to Benghazi, one of the furthest and most forlorn outposts of the empire, far away on the north of Africa and since become a portion of Italy's Tripolitan conquest. The Committee would have made a heroine of his wife, but Enver Bey was greatly astonished to learn from her that she proposed to go with her husband and share his lonely exile.

"But, my sister," said Enver, "it is unthinkable that you should suffer such a terrible fate. Moreover, the man is an infamous spy who deserves death. Why should you share his public disgrace?"

"He is my husband," she answered, "and I love him."

"You love him! But were you not already a consenting, and even abetting, party to the death which was intended for him?"

"That is true. I was willing that he should die for the sake of our cause; but as he is to live, I shall live with him. Where he goes I shall go."

So together the husband and wife went to Benghazi. For he had no suspicion that she had shared the councils of the Committee and aided in the attempt made upon him on June 11. Whether he still lives and has survived the tides of war and vengeance in Tripoli and the many changes that have since shaken the empire from Constantinople, I do not know. If he is still in ignorance of the part which his wife played in the drama of 1908, I trust that the revelation here made will not be the means of undeceiving him. So long ago as 1910 Enver Bey, from whose lips I originally heard the tale, gave me full liberty to publish it, and said that even if some rumour of it should reach remote Benghazi, his sister's devotion to her husband had been so great that she need no longer fear the truth being known. The story seems to me worth telling, for I know of no other which, in an understandable fashion of unexpectedness, affords a better illustration of the fact that the way of a woman is past finding out.

The immediate result of the abortive attempt upon Nazim's life was to produce a crisis in the affairs of the Committee. Nazim fled to Constantinople and gave information that the Young Turk party in Salonika was so strong that his life was no longer safe. A new commission was appointed by the Sultan, nominally to concern itself with the arsenals of Salonika, but really to unearth the Young Turk leaders, and the commission and the *commandant de place* repaired to Salonika. One of the first to be denounced by Nazim was his own brother-in-law, Enver Bey. The denunciation resulted in the invitation which has led to the bottom of the Bosphorus before now. Enver was invited to Constantinople, with a promise of great promotion and reward upon his arrival. He understood at once the meaning of the treacherous offer, and realized that he could only save himself by flight. It was clear that the Committee was in danger of being broken up, and of losing its members, as Salonika and the provinces were being flooded with spies. It was resolved to act, and to act quickly.

When the Salonika Committee found itself in imminent peril, Resna was chosen as the scene of revolt. There was a twofold reason for this choice. There was the obvious advantage of having a stronghold far removed from the sea coast, so that time might be obtained to make sure of the Asiatic battalions which would be summoned to quell the rising. The second and determining consideration was that the garrisons in the Monastir vilayet were known to be even more loyal to the movement than those of Salonika. There was scarcely a soldier in the districts of Monastir and Ochrida who had not sworn the oath of the Constitution months before Niazi Bey and his followers took to the hills.

Niazi Bey, who raised the flag of revolution on July 3 in the Resna hills, and was promptly joined by Enver Bey, had been, as a Turkish officer, a determined enemy of the Bulgar bands. Adjutant-Major of the Fourth Battalion of the 88th Regiment and *commandant de place* at Resna, he was a terror in the neighbourhood. I do not malign him, for I had the story from his own lips. He was the most ruthless *chasseur* of all; in searches for arms, in beatings, in raids, he spared none. Always he complained that he could stamp out the bands, if he were allowed to do so; but the Turkish Government would not let him do so, and often sought to make him punish the innocent instead of the guilty. His sympathies were with the people, for he himself was born and bred at Resna, and one has only to look at this sturdy Turkish officer to realize that some Bulgar blood flows in his veins. The Young Turks chose him of set purpose to raise the flag. "I was counted cruel," said Niazi, "because I served a bad Government. I wanted to show all men that under the Young Turk flag I stood for justice, equality, and the principles of the Constitution." The Committee certainly began with a very interesting object lesson.

So at dead of night on July 3 Ahmed Niazi put

himself at the head of a group of Turks, seized the money in the battalion treasury, seventy-five Mauser rifles, and one ammunition chest. This done, he distributed the arms to his followers and made for the hills. The same night Lieutenant Osman at Presba collected the rifles and cartridges of his own detachment and reached the Albanian village of Asumati, where he assembled and armed the villagers and, followed also by another subaltern, a handful of soldiers and a young sergeant-major of gendarmerie, hastened to join Niazi. Next day two hundred Musulmans, nearly all of whom were Albanians of the kazas of Ochrida and Monastir, joined the little army, and Niazi found himself at the head of seven hundred men. On the night of the 5th the Committee placarded the town of Monastir with its Constitutional Manifesto. Next night the officers of the garrison of Monastir deserted to Niazi with their regimental ammunition. At Resna and Ochrida the civil and military authorities quickly declared for the rebel, and took their orders from him.

Pourparlers were at once begun with the Bulgarian Internal Organization, which replied in effect, " We shall not merge ourselves with you. We shall watch your movement sympathetically, and if the Sultan crushes it, our bands will provide you with shelter in the hills and give you safe conduct across the frontier." This offer was gladly accepted, and the Bulgar bands, therefore, showed no sign of life from the moment of rebellion. The Turkish army did not move from Monastir. Niazi met with no opponents, and consequently there were no casualties, except the Monastir assassinations and the shooting of spies. Bands with officers at their head visited both the

THE YOUNG TURKS

Christian and Musulman villages and rapidly won over the population. The fire flew, and soon the officials who remained faithful to the Government had no force at their disposition. Desertions of both officers and men in the army and in the gendarmerie increased in numbers from day to day, and the Albanian bands also came pouring in. The Committee decided to make a demonstration in force at Ochrida, and thence to march on Monastir. On July 19 the Monastir garrison, previously reinforced by two battalions from Salonika, was increased by two thousand five hundred men from the Smyrna army corps, but these soon proved to be infected with the revolutionary virus. Shortly after midnight on the 22nd Niazi entered Monastir with two thousand men, captured Marshal Osman Pasha, the *commandant*, and returned with him to Ochrida. Next day at noon a vast crowd of Musulmans and Christians, headed by their clergy, the local authorities, the army, and one thousand insurgents, assembled on the parade ground at Monastir, and the Constitution was duly proclaimed with a salvo of guns. The same thing happened in Florina and other towns. This was on Thursday, the 23rd. At one o'clock on the morning of the 24th, after many telegraphic messages, and in face of the Young Turk ultimatum "Surrender or we march upon Stambul!" the Sultan's gracious gift of the Constitution was received. At noon on Friday Hilmi Pasha, pale and nervous, proclaimed it from the steps of the Konak in Salonika.

CHAPTER XXII

HILMI PASHA

It would be hard to decide who are the cleverest and most interesting men in Europe, but all things considered I think that somewhere, not very far down the list, a place ought to be found for Hilmi Pasha. If, as is generally reckoned, European Turkey is not really Europe, then there is this interest added to Hilmi: that until 1910, when he first travelled in the West, he had never set foot in Europe at all. To-day he is Turkish ambassador in Vienna, and a pretty good judge of European politicians. But in the old days of Abdul Hamid, who always refused his repeated requests for leave to visit Europe, his knowledge of the West was entirely derived from his own dealings with the agents of Western Governments in Turkey, and from reading French books. But his is a marvellous intelligence and an incurable thirst for information. And it was curious to witness this overdriven man of affairs, who longed for opportunities of general knowledge, and whose intellect was often working almost in a vacuum. What mental picture, indeed, could this brilliant man make of the Europe he had never seen, but against which, as Inspector-General of Macedonia, he daily pitted his brains in the struggle with the "reform agents," financial commissioners and gendarmerie officers sent by the Great

HILMI PASHA

Powers? One concession the Sultan made him: he allowed him to connect his own house in Salonika with the International Financial Commission by telephone. That, as far as I know, was the only telephone in the Turkish Empire in those days, for to Abdul Hamid the instrument was anathema. It was the first telephone that Hilmi had ever seen, and I shall never forget the delight with which, soon after its installation, forgetful for the moment that I might possibly be already familiar with them, he explained its workings and its advantages to me. I remember another occasion when, after a dinner-party at which some British and other European officers were present, the talk turned upon the campaigns of the Franco-Prussian War. It was good talk, and Hilmi Pasha sat silent, drinking in every word, with the rapt face of a man who finds himself in a new and wonderful world. Then suddenly, when the subject seemed in danger of being dropped, he broke in with eager questions, and when he left us that night the company had few ideas and little information left to give him about the events of 1870.

It was a favourite theme of Hilmi that all the trouble in Macedonia was due to the theological dispute between the Greeks and the Bulgars, and that for this religious quarrel there was no help, inasmuch as nothing would stop the Christians from fighting one another. In 1910, in the period of rest that fell to him after his resignation of the office of Prime Minister, he fulfilled his long-cherished design and visited Europe. In London his thirst for information was insatiable. There was no institution which he was not prepared to visit. And amongst many other

THE ORIENT EXPRESS

places, his wandering footsteps strayed—I know not at whose instigation—into (if my recollection is correct) the Kensington Workhouse. There, as everywhere, his examination was carefully minute. The inmates were having tea, and Hilmi Pasha noticed a number of old ladies at a separate table apart from the main body. "Why is this?" he asked, and was told that these were the Roman Catholics, and that it was found better that Roman Catholics and Protestants should have their meals apart, as sometimes they quarrelled. Hilmi was delighted, and told me the story the next day. "You see," he concluded, "it is just the same here as in Macedonia."

For five weary years Hilmi Pasha, as Inspector-General of Macedonia, was the man with whom Europe had to deal while the tragic farce of reform was being enacted in a blood-stained country. In Macedonia there was no god save Hilmi, and around him the foreign gendarmerie officers and commissioners were compelled to buzz, like mosquitoes attacking a waxwork. A wonderful man is Hilmi, a man of tact and charm and great ability, and a capital workman, the faithful servant of a bad Government, the loyal follower, in those days, of Abdul Hamid, who trusted him with a completeness of confidence not elsewhere bestowed. For five years Hilmi played a difficult part, for it was his duty to maintain the *status quo* in Macedonia and to neutralize the efforts of the foreign reformers without exasperating unduly the European Powers. But when the revolution of 1908 came, he had to play a new and unexpected part, beset with greater personal perils and difficulties. He had to stand between his sovereign and the

HILMI PASHA

Turkish people, for the Macedonian army and the Macedonian people had thrown off the old yoke. In the space of a day he ceased to be only the Sultan's servant, and became also the tool of the Salonika Committee of Union and Progress. Could he fail to forfeit the confidence of both masters whom his fate compelled him to serve?

He was naturally an object of intense suspicion to the Young Turks, and although he kept his nominal position as Inspector-General of Macedonia, the declaration of the Constitution deprived him for the time of all power and importance. He became a puppet in the hands of the Salonika Committee, which issued its orders through him and kept a vigilant watch upon all his actions. The Committee, though all-powerful, was composed of new and inexperienced men, and Hilmi Pasha added to his long experience a great deal more brains than most of its members possessed. Rarely has been seen such a swift triumph of intelligence and skill. In a few weeks he gained the confidence of the Committee and recovered his old position. For me the change was illustrated in the following very striking manner—

On August 13, 1908, I went to the play at Salonika. There is a pleasure in saying that I went to the play at Salonika. If you knew the old Turkey, which had come to an end three weeks before, you will understand the reason. It was a very great occasion, for —except for an ill-fated attempt at Constantinople years ago—it was the first performance that had ever taken place in Turkey of *Vatan* ("Fatherland"), the patriotic drama of the great Turkish poet and patriot, Kemal Bey. Kemal had not lived to see these latter days, yet, being dead, he spoke to his countrymen in a way that Western poets of our era may sigh for in vain. Kemal had come into his own in those last three weeks, and his poems sold like hot cakes and cold drinks in the streets of Salonika. You bought them separately, printed on little fly-sheets in red ink in the Turkish tongue. The urchins who sold them to you—younger Turks, or little Greeks, or the bright-eyed Spanish Israelites of the Levant—had always something new to shout; for there are many poems, and they had never been offered to the public before, so there was a great demand for them at ten paras a poem. But there must have been a great subterranean circulation even in the bad old days, for the man in the street knew all about Kemal Bey. He is the poet of the revolution, the singer of Young Turkey. He was a literary revolutionist also, for he endeavoured to purify the Turkish language, and to drive out the Persian, Greek, and foreign coinage which were debasing it. But in *Vatan* the only revolutionary idea is that it is a glorification of the love of country, instead of an expression of devotion to the country's ruler. "Long live the Sultan!" and "Long live our country!" are cries which should be uttered strictly in that order, but in *Vatan* the order is reversed. That had always been enough to secure its suppression. At the conclusion of the performance in Constantinople the audience so far forgot itself as to shout "Long live Kemal Bey!" Even to mention *Vatan* was a punishable offence after that, and if a spy wished to ruin an enemy, one way of doing it was to deposit a copy of *Vatan* in secret amongst his merchandise or household chattels, in order that, after due notification to the authorities of the probability of finding incriminating documents, it might forthwith be discovered by the police.

But for me, it was not the play that was the thing that night. It was the *mise-en-scène* and, above all, the audience. The theatre was the garden of the White Tower, open to the stars of the magic night. The scent of oleanders was in the air, and in the silence we could hear the Ægean lapping very softly against the sea-wall behind us. In front of us was the simple stage, and in the small garden we sat packed close on small, hard chairs of Austrian bentwood. In the front rows this privilege cost us a pound apiece, and the prices paid for "boxes" in the open galleries which ran down the sides of the garden were *illimités*. A performance at Drury Lane does not produce such a golden harvest, for this was a £1,500 "house." Needless to say, it was a benefit for the cause of Young Turkey, "sous le haut patronage du Comité Ottoman d'Union et de Progrès et au profit de ses œuvres."

The Committee was present in force. Enver Bey and Niazi Bey, the heroes of the revolution, were there, but, with characteristic modesty, they sat unostentatiously in the middle of the audience. In the boxes were the pashas and the great officials, most of them the representatives of the old system, but now the servants of the new. The real rulers sat with the audience below, but they sat quietly conscious of their strength, unwilling to obtrude it. Perhaps there were many in the boxes who did not relish the performance, but they carefully concealed their feelings. So they paid large prices, beamed with smiles, applauded with ostentatious vigour the liberal and patriotic sentiments which they had so long sternly suppressed, and waxed especially enthusiastic over any line which was caught up by the cheering Turkish crowd below because it was applicable to the new situation.

Truly it was a strange sight, the epitome of the revolution. In the front box to the right of the stage sat Hilmi Pasha, the famous Inspector-General of Macedonia. The change in his position was not disguised from the man in the street. Had he made this public appearance a month before, he would have come with much state, with *aides-de-camp* and a glittering escort. All men would have feared him, and bowed themselves in the presence of the great man with the lowly homage of the East. But the Committee had curtailed pomp and circumstance. To-night he came almost unattended, and except for the greetings of his personal acquaintance his presence went unnoticed. Yet in all that audience of enthusiastic souls, drinking in their new-won liberty like wine, applauding every generous sentiment uttered by the amateur actors, Hilmi Pasha was the most interesting figure. They cheered the jet-haired Armenian girl in the soft red-rose frock who played the Turkish heroine, and after the first act fought for her country, disguised as a man in Albanian costume. They cheered her Albanian lover, Islam Bey, whom his country summoned from her side at Monastir to defend the fortress of Silistria against the Russians during the Crimean War. They cheered to the echo the picturesque chorus of Albanians, girdled with weapons, who sang a rousing patriotic hymn in honour of the Osmanli nation. There was also a specially written March of

HILMI PASHA

Liberty, "dedicated to his Excellency Enver Bey," a silent young officer who sat unobtrusively in the middle of the audience, and this the orchestra had to repeat. And all this time the figure in the plain frock-coat and fez, the patient, brilliant man who had played a strange part in a strange and blood-stained history, looked on with the calm eyes of a not uninterested spectator. His hands fingered mechanically the beads of a Turkish rosary, after the custom of the country, or joined in the loudest round of applause of the evening, which greeted the hero's remark that he did not know the enemy's plans, "because it was dishonourable for a Government to employ spies." Who shall say what Hilmi Pasha thought of it all? Perhaps he, too, was sincerely glad the spies were hanged or had fled, for he himself had suffered from them, though he was one of the Sultan's most trusted servants. Perhaps he, too, recognized that liberty is best of all, and found pleasure in the extraordinary change in the faces all around—the change from sullenness and fear to brightness and confidence. Or was there in his thoughts some root of bitterness that liberty should seem to mean that there was none so poor to do him reverence? It is not possible to answer for him; but let it be said that he played his part well.

Some six weeks later, after having made a journey through Albania, I returned to Salonika to say farewell to the Committee and give them such report as I could as to what was happening in Central Albania, of which they were still without news. On the evening of my departure there was again a great performance of *Vatan*, and before it the Committee invited me to dinner

THE ORIENT EXPRESS

in the White Tower garden. No one present held any official position, though most of them have been heard of since, and amongst them were Enver Bey, Taalat Bey, afterwards Minister of the Interior, Djavid Bey, afterwards Minister of Finance, and Jemal Bey, afterwards Military Governor of Constantinople. They told me that Hilmi Pasha was once more in authority, and presently, when we visited the theatre, we saw the outward and visible sign of it. My fellow-diners handed me over to Hilmi Pasha and Mahmud Shefket Pasha, who sat in high state in the places of honour, and they themselves modestly sat in attendance upon the great Inspector-General.

Six months later Hilmi was Grand Vizier of the empire.

CHAPTER XXIII

THE HEART OF ALBANIA

THE world is mostly pegged out in claims now, and the explorer's trade is a decaying industry. Who would suppose that our old, sophisticated Europe—of all continents—holds secrets still, and that her super-civilized sons have not yet overrun her? Who would suppose that there are in this country only one woman, and not half a dozen men, who have ever been in Jakova and Ipek, and that, barring these and an Austrian or two, no "European" has ever made the journey through North Albania from Scutari through Pooka to Ipek? Yet this I believe to be the fact. And Central Albania, through which I stole in a memorable month, holds many secrets still.

It was after the miraculous proclamation of the Turkish Constitution in 1908 that I fulfilled a long-cherished desire. In 1905 I had drawn blank both in the north and in the south. Mahmud Shefket Pasha, since immortal and lately assassinated, was then a provincial governor, Vali of Uskub to wit, and he did his best for me by sketching a tour through Novi Bazaar to Podgoritza, but when I begged for Ipek, he shook his head in sorrow. Ipek and Jakova were forbidden fruit. So, not contenting myself with Novi Bazaar, I determined to attempt the journey from the south.

THE ORIENT EXPRESS

At Ochrida permission to travel further westwards was refused, in violation, as I held, of a previous understanding with the authorities. Whereupon, with two companions, I took French leave in a fine dawn and broke my first ground in Albania. Soldiers pursued us with emphatic orders to arrest us, by force if necessary, but on our refusing to return and invoking the majesty of Britain by producing passports which no one could read, but whereon the innumerable styles and titles of Lord Lansdowne loomed large and terrifying, our pursuers transformed themselves into an unwilling, but not ungracious, escort. In this wise we made two days' journey to Elbassan, but there we were held up, and no one was allowed, under dire penalties, to let us have horses. We fought the battle for a week by telegraph, living meantime in a hovel and gleaning a great deal of unnecessary information about Elbassan, which chanced at that time to be indulging in a furious outbreak of smallpox. A fortnight later, when we were well set on the return journey, the Ambassador secured us leave from the Porte!

That was in the bad old days. But there are always odd surprises and revenges in Time's lap. It came to pass that I was at Salonika during the revolution in the glorious summer of 1908, and after having spent some weeks there it was clear to me that Macedonia had in general accepted the Constitution, and that the writ of the Young Turks ran throughout that country. But from unknown Albania came all sorts of rumours. Some said that the Young Turks were powerless there; others that the Albanians were brewing revolution and reaction; others also that Albania

THE HEART OF ALBANIA

was more "off" foreigners than ever. The Committee of Union and Progress assured me that the country was quiet; whereat I urged that the best thing possible would be to let me travel through it, so that I might bear testimony to its peace. "For Europe only laughs," said I, "when you tell us that Albania is quiet and has accepted the Constitution." The Committee threw themselves upon frankness. "Go and welcome," said they, "and, to tell you the truth, we shall be glad of your news. We have heard that all is well, but we have no sure knowledge of what is happening in Albania. We can give you no guarantee of safety, but we believe you will be safe." So they gave me an open letter, signed with the wonder-working seal of that most wonderful secret revolutionary society, and setting forth the polite fiction that I was one of the most illustrious people in the British Empire, and that all princes, governors, and others were to render me obeisance and service. Armed with this, I bought a tent and saddle, sent a wire to an Albanian at Koritsa whom the new *régime* had happily released from prison, asking him to meet me at Monastir, and set forth. At five in the morning, on the steps of the British Consulate at Monastir, I bought a horse at sight. He served me well, and I sold him with sorrow a month later for the best offer the public crier could win for his hard-used, weary body, after he had shown his paces through the length and breadth of the bazaars of Mitrovitsa.

At Monastir I left the railway and struck into the interior. I told myself that I was going to see how Turkey was taking to its Constitution, but the interest and fascination of the journey soon proved its own

THE ORIENT EXPRESS

reward. Napoleon professed himself weary of old Europe a hundred years ago, but clearly Napoleon did not know everything. The Tosk country, south of the Elbassan road to Durazzo, has few mysteries left; and the neighbourhood of Scutari is also adequately explored. But there is a heart of Albania which Europe does not know; which the Turks have never really conquered; which remains now, unmapped, unstudied, and unwritten, as it was in the beginning. So, too, by force of its mountains and its rivers, it is likely to remain for long, even under the new autonomous *régime*.

The first two days were spent in a part of Macedonia already familiar to me, and the journey seemed in danger of becoming a kind of festal march. An hour's ride from Resna—the town on the northern shore of the beautiful lake of Presba long famous as *komitaji* country, and now immortal as the place where Niazi Bey raised the flag of freedom—we saw a cavalcade halted by the roadside. It proved to be the Mudir of Resna, with the civil and military authorities and the leading Bulgar "notable," Mr. Tatartchieff, an old friend, who had been in a Turkish prison since I had last seen him. Niazi Bey had forewarned them, and they had come out to meet us. Speeches followed, and we drove in state to Resna, where a ceremonial lunch awaited me. After lunch the cavalcade reformed, and left me later far on the road to Ochrida, marvelling at the change that had come to pass. Strangest of all was the fact that that year, up till the month of July, the Turks in the Resna and Ochrida country had been pursuing a campaign of repression which was unexampled in severity. Musulman bands were formed,

THE HEART OF ALBANIA

with the cognizance of the authorities, for the purpose of assassination and plunder. The authorities themselves were ruthless. Raids, searches for arms, beatings, fines, imprisonments were incessant. The whole of the Bulgar population was in a state of desperation, and there was renewed talk of a last hopeless rising. Turkey has never lacked paradoxes, and lately there have been more than ever. But perhaps the most curious paradox of the constitutional *régime* is to be found in the fact that the leaders of this persecution were the very men who were then working for, and afterwards declared, the Young Turkish revolution. The point of the paradox lies in the fact that they freely avow their past deeds. I have already said that Niazi Bey was the terror of Resna, and so described himself to me. To the Western mind this seems the most curious ingenuity of all; and it is perhaps not surprising that the Bulgars in the early days of July felt strange suspicions of an offer of equality and liberty from their known persecutors.

Another example of the strange situation may be given. The Kaimakam of Ochrida, who was the most unrelenting foe of the Bulgars, was a leading member of the local *jemaat*, or Young Turk Committee. He entertained me to lunch, and at his table I met—incredible fact!—the Bulgar schoolmaster and a "Greekoman" doctor from Monastir. Every one talked frankly and openly as friends. There was no sign of present fear or past history. We discussed the Sultan, Mohammedanism, Catholicism, Protestantism, Agnosticism—anything and everything. A discussion arose as to whether Constitution Day would in future be celebrated on July 23, when the Committee

THE ORIENT EXPRESS

proclaimed it in the Monastir district, or on the 24th, when the Sultan became an accessory after the act.

"At any rate," said the schoolmaster, "I shall keep the 23rd, because it was on that day that I was released from Monastir prison."

"You were in prison?" I asked.

"Yes," he answered; "I had served two sentences before as a political prisoner, but this time I was condemned for life."

"Thanks to me," said the Kaimakam, smiling at him.

Both laughed at this good joke, and the schoolmaster went on to describe how the Kaimakam had sent soldiers to seize him in his school, who had refused him time even to get his fez and had flung him into prison. But there were all sorts at liberty in Turkey now, and the freedom accorded to such men as Panitsa, Sarafoff's assassin, was a very serious danger. The murderer of Stambuloff also came, in the first flush of the Constitution, to visit Resna, his native town; and is said to have wept tears of joy at the marvellous change he found. This sentimentalist is generally credited with having made the bomb with which the Belgian, Joris, attempted the assassination of Abdul Hamid in 1905. He is even said to export bombs as far as Persia, being, in fact, a kind of *entrepreneur* for delicate affairs which are thought to demand a violent solution.

All the officials at Ochrida, from the Kaimakam downwards, were Young Turks, and the town declared for the revolution at once. For two Fridays before the proclamation they forbade the *khoja* to pray for the Sultan in the mosque attended by the

THE HEART OF ALBANIA

officials. "The Koran forbids us to pray for a Sultan who is a tyrant," was the explanation given to me, "and he was a tyrant." The poor *khoja* who had to carry out this order was no Young Turk, but an old man of the old order. He obeyed with fear and trembling, and after the second Friday took to his bed and died of sheer terror, fearing the Sultan's wrath. Little did he know the liberty that was coming.

Ochrida is cool and fresh, set in the mountains under an old mediæval fortress by a lovely lake of dreams. Some day it will be a paradise for fishermen and a playground for Europe. A sleeping-car company's "splendid palace" hotel will crown the steep, and penny steamers replace the amazing caiques, hollowed out from tree-trunks, that are now the sole craft upon the lake. But those days are not yet, and the Ochrida that has known no rest from bloodshed for hundreds of years holds a fiercer, if less flaunting, charm in its narrow, stumbling streets, dark, dirty and dangerous though they be, and in the quaint balconied houses that almost topple down upon one. Struga, by the western shore of the Lake of Ochrida, is the beginning of Albania. Being pressed for time, I wished to escape the kindness of the authorities in Struga; but I was caught, and the usual ceremony took place. It was dusk when we turned sharp to the right and began to ride the valley of the Black Drin northwards, making for Dibra, which has long been a no-man's-land, forbidden country for foreigners, the home of brigands and the refuge of Albanians who were "wanted" by the Government. After three hours' riding on a road running through a wide marsh, wherein seemed to croak all the frogs of Christendom and most of those of Islam, we came in the dark to the Albanian village of Veleshti, and proceeded to knock up Regib Aga, the chief man of the place, to whom my Ochrida friends had kindly given me an introduction. Here I made my first acquaintance with the patriarchal family system of Albania, and also with the blood feud, which I was soon to learn was the secret of Albania's acceptance of the Constitution. Regib Aga ruled a family of thirty, consisting of his brothers and his sons, and their descendants. Some of these, he explained, had been good brigands for many years, as they nearly all had a blood feud which made it dangerous for them to frequent their house or pursue ordinary occupations. With the help of my Albanian dragoman and the single gendarme who escorted me, I pitched my tent in Regib's garden and afterwards ate the excellent supper which he provided.

"A month ago I should not have allowed a guest of mine to sleep in the garden," he said, "but now you are safe. Only do not sleep in your tent up-country."

Here was another miracle of the Constitution. But, in spite of these assurances, I found that my good host had put three of his sons, well girt with weapons, to sleep outside my tent.

At half-past five next morning I photographed him in a gaudy dressing-gown, seated smoking on a mat before my tent, and by six we were in the saddle. The road quickly degenerated into a rocky trail, winding by the Drin through magnificent gorges. For miles the slopes were covered with trees, but further northward they became bare and brown. We forded the Drin twice, the torrent in the centre of the channel rising high, so that the horses struggled through with difficulty. Patches of cultivation began to appear, and in the afternoon we reached Dibra, a pretty town upon a hill-side, with the white minarets of eight mosques tapering in the air. At the foot of the slope there are vineyards and cornfields, gay oases in barren tracts covered with loose stones. I was told that this was the first time a European traveller of the non-official order had ever been in Dibra. Mr. Sackville West, of the Ottoman Public Debt, visited it a year previously with a large escort. Two foreign consuls from Monastir, each with an escort of fifty troopers, also succeeded in sleeping a night in the town, but could not walk abroad in the streets. One of these was M. Rosskoffsky, the Russian Consul at Monastir, who was murdered by an Albanian soldier in 1902. His visit to Dibra took place in the early part of that year, and had a curious motive. The Albanians of Shpata, between Dibra and Elbassan, had hitherto run with the hare and hunted with the hounds in the matter of religion. In fact, no one knew what their religion was. Their churches were built with the outward semblance of mosques; within they were Christian. Their priests were dressed as *khojas*, but they celebrated the Christian rite. The Koran was read on Friday, and Christ was worshipped on Sunday. But Shpata means, in the Albanian tongue, "the men who have drawn the sword," and in 1902 the inhabitants suddenly decided to live up to their name, and, taking all risks in this world and the next, to plump courageously for Christianity. So they sent a message to the Bulgarian Archbishop of Dibra that they were

THE ORIENT EXPRESS

Christians, and he transmitted it to Monastir. The Russian Consul undertook to verify the truth of this rumour, in order that the community might be enrolled as Christians in the official lists. It was this quest that brought him to Dibra shortly before his tragic end.

But times were changed, and I found the men of Dibra charming. Only a month before they had decided—as they put it to me—that "it is better to live as brothers"; an entirely new doctrine, the practice of which, so far, had greatly delighted them. My escort was a single mounted gendarme. They told me in quite friendly confession that a month earlier I need not have come with less than fifty; they would have suspected me as a foreigner, they said, and also it might have occurred to them to rob me. Now they were converts to the Constitution. Outside my window they showed me the spot where they murdered the Mutessarif a few weeks before, because he opposed the revolution. Needless to say, his successor was a zealous Young Turk! Since July 23 no one had been killed in Dibra, and the town did not know itself. On that day fifteen thousand men were assembled there; all of them had bullets in their rifles, and nearly all of them had "blood enemies," whom they recognized in the multitude—yet not a shot was fired. "Europe thinks us savages," said Riza Bey, my host, to me. "After this, how can they say it any longer? You must tell them in Europe what we are like." Would that I could!

Dibra, which the fortune of war has since given to Servia, is the last outpost of the Bulgars, of whom there is a small community. There is also a handful of Serbs, with a Servian church. In the Balkans

THE HEART OF ALBANIA

bishops and archbishops are as plentiful as blackberries, and Dibra possesses a Bulgarian archbishop. Years ago, in the days of the Eastern Roumelian Commission, he met Lord Fitzmaurice, and now, in the evening of his days, amidst the "tigers" of Dibra, I found this fragment of memory, that linked him with civilization, his dearest subject of conversation. The Albanians assert proudly that the Turkish Government has always been a shadow in Dibra, but sometimes it came down with a heavy hand on the Christian communities, which were now breathing freely. Part of the crime of the late Mutessarif was that he called even upon Albanians for forced labour on the road, which he was attempting to improve. The men of Dibra pay only one tax, the tithe, and that irregularly.

From Dibra we plunged northward into the utterly unknown Mat country. Government comes to an end at Dibra. North of that there is nothing; and for the first time in Turkey I found myself free of the telegraph wire which I had never hoped anywhere to escape. The first day's ride brought us out of the kaza of Dibra to Katchenik, in the country of the Malesi tribe. There is little faring in this direction, and guides were found with difficulty. I carried the Austrian staff maps, but they have been made by hearsay, and are full of inaccuracies. Distances are vaguely guessed at by the number of hours marched, and the reality generally proved a very different thing from optimistic rumour. If Dibra people ever go north to Mat they go by way of Tirana, but their generous hospitality was not to be defeated, and eventually they found three guides for the two days' ride. One was a Mat man who had killed in his own

THE ORIENT EXPRESS

country five years before, and had fled from vengeance. He grasped the opportunity to return with me to his old home, feeling that now he was safe. We were all under his protection, for outside the Dibra country the others were strangers. The blood feud rages amongst neighbours, but when a clan gathers for raiding it harries outside its own borders.

At the end of two hours' ride my friend showed me the spot where six weeks before they had overtaken the flying men of Malesi, who had stolen horses in Dibra. That was before the Constitution! Now we plunged into the Malesi country without a qualm. In any case the penalties for killing are not light; but in the case of a stranger like myself, enjoying protection, they are extra special. For a stranger it is only possible to pass under the protection of the men of the district, who conduct him to "blood friends"; but if he meet the enemies of his friends, he is himself counted an enemy, and to kill him is to avenge an old murder. On the other hand, the murderer of a stranger puts the latter's protectors under the unusual obligation of killing not one, but seven of the murderer's family. "If you are killed, I must kill seven for you," said my sworn friend from Mat. Clearly I was supposed to derive a certain comfort and complimentary consolation from this interesting fact.

Here, in truth, one rode the livelong day as in a dream. This was Europe, and these the Albanians, possibly Europe's most ancient stock. Perhaps they were the Pelasgians who have puzzled Greek historians, and probably they were the Myrmidons whom Achilles brought to Troy; they have kept their blood

THE HEART OF ALBANIA

and their own strange tongue, and Europe's civilization has rolled on and left them in their mountains.

I was in a land without law, and I knew at last why Albania was glad that the Young Turks had brought the Constitution. Life without law had become intolerable. The land is so completely throttled by the blood feud that all ordinary human intercourse has become impossible. The houses are great fortresses, the only windows of which are loopholes for Martinis. In these prisons families, sometimes of a hundred people, lead self-centred lives. There are no villages, only houses, dotted at intervals of at least a kilometre, high up round wide valleys. Every one has killed, and all have enemies who seek their blood. Many men have not left their houses for years, and food has to be brought in to them by their friends. Others, again, have taken to flight after killing their enemy, and, unable to sleep in their homes or till their fields, exist by brigandage. There is no dishonour whatever attached to brigandage, and to this day there continues in Albania that primitive society in which the life of the fighter, the freebooter, and the shepherd is held in honour, while agriculture is despised. Sometimes a truce is granted, and a man who has been in hiding for years will ask his enemy for fifteen days' respite in which to visit his friends or undertake a journey; but delay in vengeance is held dishonourable, and the man who lets years pass without killing his enemy becomes himself an outcast. Till he has taken vengeance he cannot marry, or if he is married, he may give neither his sons nor his daughters in marriage. It would appear that during the last five years, and more especially in the six months previous to the

THE ORIENT EXPRESS

coming of the Constitution, the ravages of the blood feud had become so terrible that a kind of climax had been reached. It was part of the initial good fortune of the Young Turks that everything in Turkey reached a climax in 1908. The Albanians were utterly weary of the blood feud, but this "Law of the Mountains" was the only law or justice there was, and it was also an affair of honour, from which there was no escape. Then came the Young Turkish emissary with his simple and hitherto unheard-of proposal of a grand reconciliation under an honourable oath of loyalty to the Constitution. The ground was prepared for it, and the thing came almost of itself. The Albanians leapt at the way of escape. They know nothing of parliaments, and care less. "Constitution" meant to them one thing only—a cessation of the "blood feud."

By the sun's last rays we came to Katchenik, that is to say, to the single fortress of Ali Chaoush. Ali is called Chaoush because aforetime he was a corporal of gendarmerie, but now he lives the life of an Albanian patriarch, head of a family of thirty. Brothers, brothers' sons, and grandchildren live together. Ali received me in state, and his sons knelt to kiss my hand. The rifles of eight men gleamed on the rack in the raftered upper room where we squatted on the floor and ate our supper. The customary sheep was slaughtered for me, and the soothsayer told my fortune by some weird witchcraft from its shoulder-blades. The fortune was good, so, heedless of the warnings of Regib Aga at Veleshti, I went comfortably to sleep in my tent outside the fortress. Neither dreams nor brigands disturbed my rest. After all, the tent was the best test of the Constitution.

THE HEART OF ALBANIA

It is an ill road that leads from Katchenik to Bourgayet, the centre of Mat, and craves wary riding. In truth, it is no road at all, but a succession of precipices which one's horse negotiates with a kind of luck which one soon learns to trust. In the morning hours we saw far above us on a mountain-top the ruined citadel of Scander Bey, the great Albanian hero. Kruga was his home and Alessio is his tomb, but here he fled for refuge and warred manfully against the Turks. Soon we dropped into lanes for all the world like England: the hedges thick with blackberries and sloes, hips and haws, cape gooseberries and wild strawberries. Stunted willows fringed the river beds; above, there is oak, walnut and beech, and sometimes stately avenues of poplar. Higher still we rode through great forests of pine. Maize and melons, vines, peppers, and marrows grow in the fields; but the cultivation is poor, for the mountaineers carry the gun, and the work is for the most part left to the women. Also the men cannot work safely in the fields, whereas the women can; for the Albanians do not kill women and the blood feud passes them by. There is plenty of surface coal, but no one burns it. There is iron too, but no one mines it. Herdsmen bristling with weapons were almost the only human beings we met. Save for their arms, they made a perfect Homeric picture, tending their flocks of sheep and goats with fierce barking dogs. But the "surge and thunder of the Odyssey" were more insistent still in my ears when I came to Bourgayet. Riding under a gateway, where the retainers made obeisance, I passed into the great courtyard of a Homeric house. I crossed the courtyard to the door of the castle, and, mounting the stair, found myself in a large hall. There was no furniture, save a long rack on which were slung many Martinis. Ten men in the white costume of the country—a shirt that comes below the girdle almost to the knee and trousers with a bag that falls to the back of the knee—were squatted on their haunches in a semicircle by the wall. All rose and bowed, and, when I passed behind a curtain into a smaller room, resumed their crouching attitude. In the small room was the chief with the leading men of his clan. The leading men were splendid, fierce fellows in the dress of the mountains. I looked with interest at the Homeric chief, who came forward to give me an eager greeting. Let the devil be ashamed, for I will tell the truth. The Homeric chief wore a fez, an old frock-coat, and elastic-side boots.

Jelal Bey was young, and he rules Mat from his castle by hereditary title as a feudal chieftain. To secure his loyalty, Abdul Hamid paid him a salary and styled him the Kaimakam of Mat. In return for this Jelal wore a frock-coat. There government began and ended. The whole wide district of Mat paid not a single *metallick* in taxes, nor was there any local rate. There is no telegraph and there is no school of any kind. Jelal Bey could talk Turkish, but his people speak only Albanian. His wife was seriously ill, but there was no doctor nearer than Scutari. There is much sickness, and I doctored several cases of malaria, but for these there is ordinarily no relief. The law Jelal administers is the "Law of the Mountains." The people care nothing for his Kaimakamship, but much for the fact that he is Jelal Bey, their chief. For four hours one may ride continuously through his estate. He told me that he thought it might be worth £60,000, and if it were in "Europe" he supposed it would be worth "millions." But there is little money, and Jelal spends all his substance, for he maintains a large retinue and keeps open house. The style of living is simple in the extreme, and the economy of the household was much strained in order that I might have separate dishes whereon to eat my food, a privilege which I deprecated with a false heart. The male members of the family and the dependants mess in common in the hall, and a wonderful sight it is to see them eating from a great common dish, without knives or forks. There is magnificence, too, in their hospitality, and the kindly manner of the mountaineers weaves a charm to bind the stranger.

Jelal Bey, thirsting for my Salonika news, was all for the Constitution, and in this scattered countryside he was trying to form a committee on the model of the Young Turk *jemaat*, of which I told him what I knew. He was full of ideas for the welfare of his people and the improvement of his estates. He longs for schools and roads, and would like an engineer to tell him about minerals and to help him water his estate; for Jelal is an agriculturist, and his heart is in the land. No one had been killed for a whole month in Mat! One man was a prisoner in the castle because a shot was fired in the night, and he had denounced his blood enemy as having fired it. Not unnaturally he was suspected of attempting to compass his enemy's end by constitutional means, and was promptly imprisoned, but he was to be brought before twenty-four elders of the people, and if he would swear that he told his tale in unleavened sincerity, and not from a revengeful motive, he would be released. What befell I know not.

In the cool of the evening I held a reception in my tent. The men of Mat came to call upon me. No European had ever visited their country before, and their eagerness to hear some news of the world was wonderful to witness. So likewise was their simple and perfect courtesy. My friend from Dibra unfortunately found his brother at Mat, whom he had not seen for years, stricken with fever. His brother was the Cadi, or Judge. Long ago he had been to Asia Minor and met an English "Mister," who was his friend. I do not know who this Englishman was, but the Cadi paid his memory a very perfect compliment when he heard of my coming. "I must not let the Bey Effendi go without seeing him," he said, "and if I see him I shall be better." So he rose and came to my tent from the far hill that was his home, though I would gladly have visited him. Then a strange thing happened, for, as soon as the Cadi came, my laughing and talkative friend rose up, silent and humble, and seated himself outside the tent with eyes cast down. Not till the Cadi had encouraged him did he venture again to take his share in our society. So strict is the family system in Albania and so great the reverence for age. "My brother the Cadi is an older man than I," Sadik explained to me afterwards. "Also," he added, with regretful admiration in his voice and a merry twinkle in his eye for his own shortcomings, "he is a juster man than I. I do not know a juster man." In truth, the Cadi's face went well with the long robe and white turban of his office, for honesty shone from his eyes, and a gentler or a juster-seeming man one need not wish to meet.

So we talked till the sun went down. But my proposal to sleep in the tent aroused immense and embarrassing enthusiasm. Hitherto no one had dared to sleep outside a house. Here was a great opportunity to celebrate the happy truce in the blood feud. Behold, they would all sleep in my tent—Jelal Bey, and the Cadi, and Jelal's men. Now this was to defeat the object for which I carried a tent in my baggage, but the matter was difficult of explanation. In the end, however, the diplomacy of my dragoman succeeded, and a compromise was reached. I slept in the tent, and all my friends, including even the sick Cadi, slept outside beneath the stars. I feared that I might kill the Cadi; but I believe that I cured him. In the morning he bade me farewell with a kindly greeting that I shall long remember.

"The fever has left me," he said; "I am better since I have seen your face. I shall ever pray that you may come again."

"I, too, hope that I may come again."

"Inshallah, Bey Effendi," he answered. "It is in the hands of God."

CHAPTER XXIV

THE MIRDITE CLAN

From Bourgayet I struck straight north, making for the heart of the Mirdite country. Mat is entirely Mohammedan; Mirdita is entirely Catholic. Between the two lies Kthela, which is mixed.

To the outward eye there is very little difference between Mohammedans and Christians. The Moslem women go unveiled and do not hide themselves from men. The Christian women wear veils for ceremony, like their Mohammedan sisters, and are in general no less in the background of the picture; they have also their own quarters in the house. The mosques have no minarets and, save for the absence of the Cross, are indistinguishable from the rustic churches. The blood feud rages everywhere, but between Albanians in the mountains there is no religious quarrel whatever. I found a family living under one roof in Kthela in which some were Christians and some Mohammedans. The Catholics of Mirdita take Mohammedan wives from Mat, who dutifully accept the religion of their husbands. Polygamy is possible for the Mohammedans, but is rarely practised, and the moral standard is high.

The feudal chiefs of Mirdita are called bairaktars, that is, bannermen, or captains. There are five cap-

THE MIRDITE CLAN

tains in Mirdita, which has therefore five banners, to which the Mirdites gather for councils of war or peace. Jelal Bey has drunk of the blood of the son of the captain at Orosh, which is the centre of Mirdita, and the son has drunk Jelal's blood. Consequently they are blood brothers, and the Mohammedan chief was in a position to pass me safely into the Christian country of Mirdita. He gave me two of his young retainers, who were to be my cards of introduction, and I set off at sunrise. For four hours we rode by cool and pleasant forest paths through Jelal's estate, resting once at his *chiflik*, or farm-house. The two boys, John and Ali, were great friends and in high spirits. At intervals they fired their Martinis in sheer glee, dexterously swinging these behind their backs and up under their left shoulder so that the bullets went whizzing upwards, past the ears of the Bey Effendi whom they delighted to honour with this inconvenient exhibition of their skill. John is a Christian and lives in Kthela, so he took us all to lunch at his home. There are forty members in his family, which is not considered large.

In Kthela there are three captains with three banners. This was a new world, for Kthela had not yet accepted the Constitution. Consequently the blood feud was not yet checked, and men who had enemies hid themselves and walked with greater care than usual, fearing lest their foes would hasten to wreak their vengeance before the truce was made. This was the very day of deliberation on the Constitution, and as we passed the open place of assembly the clans were already gathering. They pressed me to stay, but the meeting would not be till evening, so regretfully we pushed on to John's house. There, while we ate, a party of warriors dropped in from the wayside to share the open hospitality of the house, according to the custom of the country. "Are you brave?" was the greeting of the grizzled leader to me. Fortunately it is not necessary to answer this customary question except by direct *tu quoque*. Coffee was freshly roasted and served for all. We smoked in a semicircle, and fell to talking. The grizzled leader and his party were fresh from an exploit, and told us their story. The day before, with the view of forestalling the Constitution, a man had killed not his enemy, who was hiding himself, but his enemy's friend whom he took unawares. The murderer had fled; so my new acquaintance and his friends had that morning burnt his house and all his goods, to their great satisfaction.

"Had he a wife and little children?" I asked.

"Yes."

"What will become of them?"

"We shall do something for them; we shall take care of them," he answered.

Weary with this hot morning's work, the party was resting at John's house before going on its way to the meeting for the acceptance of the Constitution. It looked as if the Albanians were prepared to fight like devils for conciliation!

Of what the Constitution meant, and of the manner of its coming, they knew nothing. The head of John's family, an old Christian in the corner by the charcoal, crooned of the new liberty the Sultan had given. He called him "the king," for the Albanians have their own word—*Mbret*—for king, or sultan. The younger men said the *jemaat* had done it themselves. "But how can it come without the king? There must be a king. It is he who has done it," persisted the old man. The young men, Mohammedans for the most part, laughed at him. They understood that the *jemaat* could surround the king and tell him what he must do. But the old man could not understand how such a thing could be.

"Are you a consul?" the leader asked me. "The consuls at Scutari disturb everything in this country. I think this Constitution is something you have made the king do." More questions were fired at me. "Is it because they want us to go and fight some enemy that the Turks have made the Constitution?"

"Would you go?" I asked in return. He made no answer, and silence fell on the whole group.

"What will you do with all the rifles now?" I asked. "If you live at peace amongst yourselves you will not need them any more."

"Ah, we shall keep them to fight the Giaours," he said quickly. By Giaours he meant non-Albanian Christians, for the Albanian Catholics are not reckoned Giaours.

"But why should you want to fight the Giaours? Are you not all to live as brothers now? I am a Giaour; are we not friends?"

"Ah, that is different. You are with us. You will speak for the Skipetari. Let the Skipetari, the sons of the eagle, be free in their mountains."

And with that the party rose, and bidding me a hearty *toongatyeta*—Godspeed—went on its way to inaugurate the Constitution.

Gladly would I speak for the sons of the eagle had I the power. I realized that the Young Turks would have to walk warily if they were to tame these wildfowl of the mountains to the sober limits of the Constitution. What would happen when Mat and Kthela and Mirdita were asked to pay taxes I did not know. But on the whole I was glad that I was not the tax-gatherer. The ancient Illyria meant the "land of the free"; and *lirija* to this day means "liberty" in the tongue of the Skipetari.

John and Ali took the road again, and, after shots had been fired to celebrate the start, they burst into song. It was a song of Jelal Bey, and told how, six weeks before, a young man had carried off a girl from her parents and fled with her to the mountains. Thereupon Jelal Bey had sent pursuers, who had burnt his house and all that he had, thus avenging the parents and fulfilling the law of the mountains. We fell in with more company than usual, and should have fared ill without John and Ali, but they were a sufficient passport. When friends meet they butt each other on each side of the forehead like calves, at the same time clasping hands. John and Ali rubbed many foreheads that day, and after dark they brought me to the castle of Captain Marko at Orosh. Again I was received in patriarchal style, and this time my Homeric chieftain did not fail me. Captain Marko was away on a great errand, so Captain Noah, his brother and the next in seniority in the famous Mirdite family, was my host; and Captain Noah, like his retainers, was clad in the fashion of the sons of the eagle.

The trouble about travelling in Albania is the lavishness of the hospitality. I arrived nightly, late and tired and always an unexpected guest, but no mere hasty meal was considered sufficient to set before me.

THE MIRDITE CLAN

I had to wait three hours while a lamb was brought from distant fields, killed, and roasted whole; wheaten bread had to be cooked, for the maize bread in store was never thought good enough. There was also a soup, a pilaff, several made vegetable dishes, all excellent and better late than never. Grapes are eaten all through dinner, as though they were salted almonds. Captain Noah gave me a royal supper in his almost royal castle, while his own son and Marko's son, who has drunk blood from Jelal Bey's arm, acted as noble waiters. The centre of the castle is in ruins, for the Turks destroyed it with artillery thirty years ago in the days of the famous Albanian League. Captain Noah showed me the ruins, and explained the plans Mirdita was now forming to rebuild it for the exiled chief, Prenk Pasha, to whom the Young Turks had given permission to return. Time and again the Turks tried to destroy the rule of the captains and to establish their own governors; but always the new-comers were driven out. Once they sent a Bimbashi as Kaimakam, and Captain Noah slew him with his own hand. For this a price was set upon his head, and for twenty-two years the captain had not been out of his own country nor taken the road to Scutari. Was it strange that men were weary of these wars and wanted to move once more in the face of their fellows, free from the shadow of death?

Mirdita is such a strange world to find in Europe that it deserves more than a passing notice. It covers a district which on the map is some thirty miles by twenty, but in reality its superficial area is greater. The northern portion is occupied by the mountains of Gajani and the Mundela range, which attain heights of 5,000 and 5,500 feet. In the East is the elevated plateau of Monte Santo, some 4,200 to 4,700 feet high. South and West are an infinity of wooded heights, averaging 1,200 to 1,800 feet, and intersected by the valleys of the Greater and Lesser Fandis and innumerable smaller streams. The only level ground to be found anywhere is near the bottom of the river valleys, and the greater part of the whole area is forest-clad. Sandstone and granite are common, and there is limestone at Monte Santo.

Mirdita owes the independence which it has so long preserved very largely to the fact that there are in general only two ways of entering it, for the way by which I came from Dibra is no way at all. It can be approached from Scutari, or from the sea, but both these ways lie for several hours through narrow gorges with steep sides. Except for punitive expeditions, Mirdita has been left alone ever since the first Turkish occupation in the second half of the fourteenth century. After the death of Scander Bey in 1467 and the fall of the confederate chieftains in the following years, it seems that the family of Count Paolo Ducadjini, who had ruled over the territory lying to the north of what is now Mirdita, took refuge in these mountains, possibly at the Benedictine Abbey of St. Alessandros at no great distance from Orosh, which subsequently became the seat of government and chief village of Mirdita. The name Orosh is not improbably derived from the Slav word *varosh*, signifying "town," inasmuch as it was the only collection of houses. At its most flourishing period, Orosh is said to have consisted of no less than one hundred houses, encircling the *serai*, and situated so close to one

THE MIRDITE CLAN

another that "a rat could pass from one end of the town to the other without quitting the tops of the houses." The legislation of the Ducadjini was the traditional canon of Lek Ducadjini, which to this day remains the only law recognized in North Albania, and had already been adopted by Scander Bey and applied to the whole territory under his sway. In the absence, therefore, of any direct representative of their natural chief, Scander Bey, the Mirdites readily accepted the dominion of the Ducadjini, whose descendants, according to tradition, have continued to govern to this day. Since the beginning of the eighteenth century the ruling family has been known as the Dera Gion Markut, that is, the dynasty of John Marco.

The early Sultans seem to have left the Mirdites full liberty, the sole condition of this autonomy being that they should supply a fixed contingent of mercenaries in time of war. There is a tradition that Murad II, delighted by the prowess which the Mirdites had exhibited at the battle of Kossovo (1389), ordered a charter of privileges to be inscribed on a tablet of brass and presented to their chief, Captain Tenekia. *Teneke* is the Turkish for "sheet of metal," and either this was the origin of the captain's name, or the captain's name was the origin of the tale. In 1690 Suleiman II granted the chiefs a present of a hundred horse-loads of maize, and the record of this is also said to have been inscribed on a tablet. This custom has persisted to the present day, and every year seventy horse-loads are given by the Sultan to the governor and thirty to the elders of the five clans. If the Sultan be recognized as the suzerain of the new Principality of Albania, which the Powers are creating, the custom may even survive that *annus mirabilis* 1913.

The accompanying genealogical table was compiled many years ago, when he was Vice-Consul at Scutari, by Mr. H. H. Lamb, now Consul-General at Salonika, and I am very greatly indebted to him for permission to use it and a great deal of other information on the subject of the Mirdites. From this it will be seen that a direct line was maintained in the ruling family from the seventeenth century to the death of Bib Doda Pasha in 1868. Prenk, his son, was then aged twelve, and the Porte appointed Bib's cousin, Captain Gion, as chief, styling him Kaimakam. Prenk was sent to Stambul, ostensibly to be educated, but really as a hostage. During the war with Montenegro in 1875 and 1876 the Porte called upon the Mirdites to furnish their customary contingent, whereupon they demanded as a condition of compliance that Prenk should be sent back to them. In the autumn of 1876 he was sent back to Scutari with the titles of Pasha and Mutessarif of Mirdita, but his ambiguous conduct and his intrigues with the Prince of Montenegro resulted in two Turkish expeditions being sent against the Mirdites in the following years, in the course of which the old *serai* was devastated, as I have already described. There followed a period of disorder, and great impoverishment of the family. In 1878 Prenk made his peace with the Sultan, but in 1880 he was again taken to Stambul and subsequently banished to Anatolia. The English Government, mindful of the fact that his father, Bib Doda, had fought gallantly in the Crimean war, is said to have interceded for him, and he was allowed to return to Stambul some fifteen years ago. His

THE MIRDITE CLAN

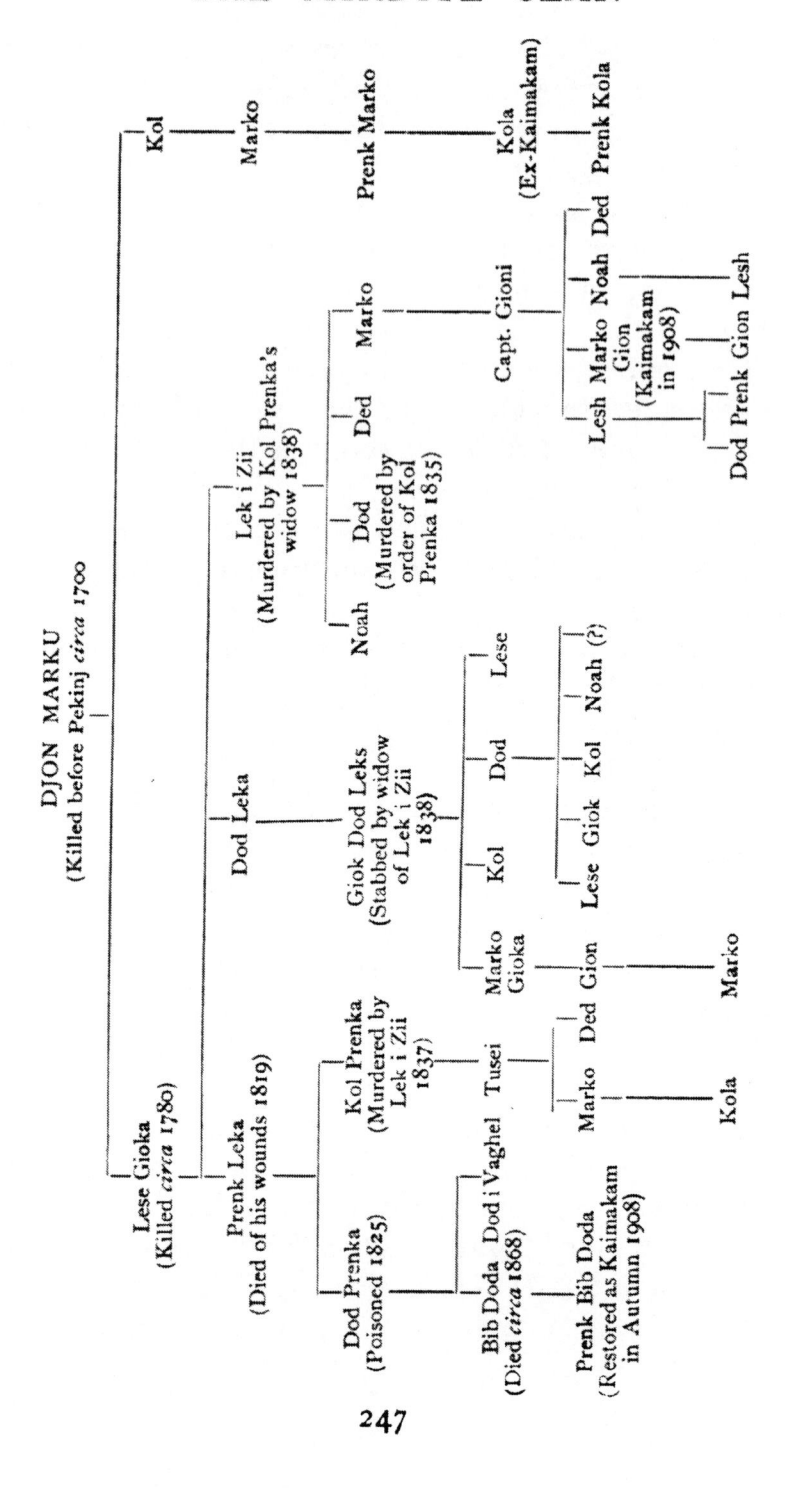

DJON MARKU
(Killed before Pekinj *circa* 1700)

- Lese Gioka (Killed *circa* 1780)
- Kol
  - Marko
    - Prenk Marko
      - Kola (Ex-Kaimakam)
      - Prenk Kola
- Prenk Leka (Died of his wounds 1819)
  - Dod Leka
    - Lek i Zii (Murdered by Kol Prenka's widow 1838)
      - Noah
      - Dod (Murdered by order of Kol Prenka 1835)
      - Ded
      - Marko
        - Capt. Gioni
          - Lesh
          - Marko
          - Noah Gion (Kaimakam in 1908)
          - Ded
          - Prenk Kola
            - Dod Prenk Gion Lesh
    - Giok Dod Leks (Stabbed by widow of Lek i Zii 1838)
      - Marko Gioka
        - Kol
          - Lese Giok Kol Noah (?)
        - Dod
        - Lese
  - Kol Prenka (Murdered by Lek i Zii 1837)
    - Marko Ded Gion
      - Marko
  - Dod Prenka (Poisoned 1825)
  - Bib Doda Dod i Vaghel Tusei (Died *circa* 1868)
    - Prenk Bib Doda (Restored as Kaimakam in Autumn 1908)
      - Kola

247

cousin, Captain Kola, was appointed Kaimakam by the Sultan. He in turn was succeeded by another cousin, Marko Gion, the actual Governor at the period of my visit. But during the whole of the latter's rule and up to the present day there have been constant disorders.

Administration is in the hands of the Bairaktari of the five clans, Oroshi, Kushneni, Spatchi, Fandi, and Dibri. Justice is administered in each clan by its own Elders—called in Albanian Kreen or Plece—who, like the Bairaktari or captains, hold their position by hereditary right; the nearest male relative acts for a minor. Capital sentence can only be pronounced by the captains, but is executed by the elders or by the representatives of the aggrieved party. When fines, which are generally in cattle, are imposed, the amount levied is divided between the captain and the elders, the former taking half.

The whole tribe is said to contain over two thousand families, which, if we take an average, not a very high one for the country, of twelve in a family, gives a total of about twenty-five thousand persons. Their pursuits are chiefly pastoral as, although the soil is not unfertile and there is good water, which they convey for purposes of irrigation in a system of open wooden aqueducts, the hollowed halves of tree-trunks, there is insufficient cultivation. There is not enough grain for the whole year, though rye, barley, wheat, and, on the low ground, maize are grown. Charcoal is burnt, and in the undergrowth there is a shrub called "scodano" (sumach), the leaves of which are dried and pounded for export *via* Scutari to the tanneries of Trieste. Skins, sometimes the skin of a bear, wool, sheep, goats, pitch, resin, pinewood, and honey are brought by the

THE MIRDITE CLAN

Mirdites for barter to the bazaars of Scutari, Alessio, and Prisrend. It is a good fruit country, and the vine, white mulberry, the wild pear, and the cherry are all plentiful. There are oak forests at Dibra, but at a height of fifteen hundred feet pine replaces the oak. Fir, beech, plane, poplar, elm, and yew are all to be seen. Iron is plentiful; silver, lead, antimony, and copper are said to exist, and in more than one place I saw surface coal.

To Mirdita there are three allied bairaks, or banners, Selita, Kthela and Kansi. And Kthela again is divided into Upper and Lower Kthela and Perlab. These belong to Mat rather than to Mirdita, but the majority of the inhabitants are Catholic. And in 1858, when Said Bey Sogol of Mat was in open insurrection, they availed themselves of the opportunity to place themselves under the protection of Bib Doda Pasha. Administratively they are in the Kaza of Kruga, but actually they have, of course, been absolutely independent of the Turkish Government. Kthela is very near the border line between Mohammedanism and Christianity. Polygamy exists, and the priests have much less influence than in Mirdita, where they are a superior and highly respected class.

I paid a visit to the famous monastery of the Mirdites, which lies beyond the castle of Orosh and is the first halt on the road to Scutari. The abbot is a great power in the land and all men speak well of him. He has travelled both in England and America. The Catholics of Albania are allowed many privileges, and priests and abbots all wear moustaches, for in Albania no one is counted a man without a moustache. In the mountains there is also a kind of polygamy amongst the Catholics, for when a brother dies the survivor takes his wife, according to the Mosaic law. The priests set their face against this custom, but they have not yet succeeded in stopping it.

From Orosh, with one of Captain Noah's retainers for my guide, I made a day's journey to Kasanjeti. My host at Kasanjeti was an old man, the father of a priest, and at his door was a school where some instruction is attempted in the Albanian tongue. The old man's sister is a nun, who mingled freely with us without a veil, and for the first time in Albania I was greeted by the lady of the house. Mirdita had not yet accepted the Constitution, and the proclamation was fixed for Sunday. Meantime the blood feud raged. The youngest grandchild of the house, much petted by the nun, was a little boy, whose father had just been killed in the vendetta. We talked of the Constitution and of the forgiveness of trespasses. The nun was intelligent, but implacable. She saw the beauty of the general principle, but she utterly rejected its application to a particular case. "Why," she asked, "should the murderer of this child's father go free? We must kill him or one of his friends. It is our right to kill him." So spake the Christian nun, representing the conservative force of women. The only possible pitch for my tent was some three hundred yards from the house. "*Lark!* (it is far)" they said, "and we have enemies." But on reflection it was remembered that the turn to kill rested with my host, and I was voted safe.

My Kasanjeti host gave me a grandson as a guide, and with him I made the journey to Scutari. Two hours from the town we fell in with an Austrian monk

THE MIRDITE CLAN

on an ambling pad, with a native of the country for escort, and in this company we made the rest of our way. The monk spends his holidays in the mountains around Scutari, holds evening classes for the priests, speaks Albanian, and takes hundreds of photographs of the places he visits. He carried a powerful telescope, and while I was with him he made many stops, sometimes to gaze through his telescope, sometimes to take a photograph. The people of the country declare that he is a monk *pour rire*, and that the cowl conceals an Austrian political agent. What the truth may be I cannot tell. To me he seemed a gentle soul, strange and taciturn, a man not unfriendly, but one who weighed his words and had little store of talk. It may be that men wrong him, and that he seeks the service of his Master in the wild land of the Mirdites, where there is much room for that love which is the fulfilling of the law. We left him at the custom-house at Scutari, a weird figure of mystery to which I have no clue.

CHAPTER XXV

THE SONS OF THE EAGLE

SCUTARI, or "Skodra" as all the Skipetari call it, was the great capital of North Albania. Had any one suggested in 1908 to the pleasant swaggerers who inhabit it that in five years' time their city would fall to a Serb army, and for some weeks belong to Montenegro, he would certainly have been laughed to scorn, and quite possibly have been put to confusion in some physical sense. But this unimaginable thing came to pass, and as a result of the second Balkan war of 1913, Montenegro, in return for her services to Servia in the campaign against Bulgaria, is to have a great deal more Albanian territory than she had obtained by the first war. She is to experience the doubtful joys of attempting to control Jakova and Ipek.

Surprisingly few travellers go to Scutari, but on one point all those who have been will at any rate bear the same testimony. The inhabitants of Scutari are Albanians, they are not Serbs, they are not Orthodox, and they hate a Montenegrin or a Serb of any kind a great deal worse than they hate a Turk. The majority of them are Musulmans, but an important minority is Catholic.

The politics of the town of Scutari are different from those of the mountains. In the mountains there is little difference between Musulmans and Catholic Christians, and no quarrel. In the town there is a subterranean feud and definite distinction. It is true that the Christian women wear veils and baggy trousers, which divide above the ankle, but the veils do not conceal their faces, and their dress is rich and distinctive. Musulman women wear *yashmak* which entirely conceal their faces, and the men wear great white *fustanella*, or kilted petticoats. The town is divided into two quarters by the principal street, and this street is a real frontier. I found the Musulmans of Scutari town as different from the Musulmans of the mountains as chalk from cheese. Amongst the merchants there is some liberty and desire for progress, but the Beys of Scutari have the reputation of being ignorant, fanatical, and reactionary. Under Turkish rule they allowed neither schools nor Albanian autonomy. They were jealous of the great Catholic Mirdite clan and of its feudal princes, and their loyalty was given to the Sultan himself and the Musulman Empire. They were, in fact, Abdul Hamid's spoilt children. If a Vali or a Governor-General displeased them in word or deed they had only to telegraph to Constantinople to procure his instant recall. In the five years between 1903 and 1908 there were six Valis, and some of these had fallen for no greater offence than to be seen publicly in the society of European consuls. The tithe was the only tax which Scutari knew, and there had been an exemption from compulsory military service. Consequently the proclamation of the Young Turk Constitution in 1908 did not fill the breasts of the Beys of Scutari with any joy. "What liberty can it bring us?" they asked. "We are going to lose our liberty. Are we to pay taxes and to serve by force in the army?" The Christians, on the other hand, led by their priests, gave the Constitution an enthusiastic welcome. They had the same privileges to lose as the Musulmans, but they desired a truce to the blood feuds, and more particularly they hoped for Albanian schools and for developments of the industries of the country.

The Young Turk Committee at Scutari had therefore a difficult part to play; it had some Albanian associates, but it was composed entirely of Turkish officers, and for a short time it maintained itself, but chiefly by making no actual changes at all. Hard realities lay in front of it. If the vendetta were not to rage again, law had to be carried to the mountains; and if law were to be administered, taxes had to be imposed. At the time of my visit the Committee had already begun to take a census of the town for the purpose of preparing the electoral lists. But a census prepared for elections can be used afterwards for conscription and taxation, and consequently it was viewed with a suspicious eye. The Catholics were annoyed with the Committee because it had imprisoned a well-known Albanian, who, at a banquet in honour of the Constitution, demanded independence for Albania, and subsequently circulated a pamphlet calling upon the Albanians to bestir themselves with this idea. The Musulmans, on the other hand, were annoyed because the Committee had not hanged this enthusiast, and they might have hanged him themselves had not the Committee kept him in safe custody.

It did not take much political sagacity to see that the Constitution was going to have a rough time in North Albania. To celebrate its declaration in Scutari

THE SONS OF THE EAGLE

everybody naturally fired off his rifle in the customary Albanian way, and by mere accident and exuberance one man was killed and three wounded. Although this did not in any way cloud the gaiety of the occasion, it was in itself an omen, for one remarked that in Macedonia everybody had succeeded in discharging his rifle without hitting anybody else. In point of fact the Young Turks failed hopelessly in North Albania almost from the start, and they soon had a rebellion upon their hands. And this perhaps inevitable failure crippled them severely in their efforts to cope with the disasters, which later accumulated upon their heads, when the Italians struck a blow at their territory in Africa and the Balkan Allies at their territory in Europe.

From Scutari I set out for Jakova by a road which had hitherto been closed to foreigners. The Young Turk Committee which governed Scutari insisted on giving me an officer and four men as an escort. I had come through the Mat and Mirdita region without any official protection whatever, and had, moreover, been impressed by the friendliness and goodwill of the people. I therefore did my best to escape the kindness of the Committee, but my protests were of no avail. And so with a sadly swollen retinue we clattered out of Scutari one early dawn, and took the rocky road to Pooka, in the mountains. An hour's ride brought us to the village of Miet, where there is an ancient Catholic Church, to which the folk were gathering from many miles round for the celebration of St. Mary's Day. Rifle-fire rattled incessantly, for every one carried a Martini, and to fire it is the method of celebration that appeals to the Albanian heart.

THE ORIENT EXPRESS

Outside the churchyard an expectant crowd was massed for the arrival of the bishop of the diocese. Every Martini was pointed in the air, and every one blazed away at intervals. Presently the bishop, with all his robes on, a glorious figure in purple and black, galloped up on a smart horse. Bang went all the rifles, and the bishop rode up to the crowd, which surged round him, and, smiling like a child, he whisked out his great silver-wrought revolver and let off every cartridge in the air. Thereupon he got down, and after giving me a kindly greeting and showing me the church, he said Mass outside to the congregation which was gathered in the churchyard. The women were massed together as in a Quaker meeting and, wonderful in bright garments often shot with silver and gold, formed a solid body before the great silver cross. Around them on all sides were rings of mountaineers, gun in hand and pistol in girdle. It was in this wise that the black-moustached bishop, in his brilliant robes, said Mass in the sunlight.

Night had fallen when we came to Pooka, which was governed by a lonely Kaimakam. Here there were none but Musulmans. There was trouble in Pooka, for law had not yet reached the mountains. A man from Jakova had been betrothed to a maid in Pooka and, according to the custom of the country, had paid her father a solid sum in cash for this privilege; for wives are bought in Albania, but bring their husbands a dowry in the shape of household goods. Subsequently he had been put in prison, for reasons obscure. But when the Constitution came, he was liberated with the rest. A few days before my visit, he had come to Pooka to claim his bride, but her

THE SONS OF THE EAGLE

father refused to give her to an ex-prisoner. The lady, however, was loyal, and the couple eloped. The angry father pursued them, and killed his son-in-law the day before my arrival. He was hidden in the mountains, fearing the vendetta, and the Kaimakam said that there was no way of capturing him. So in the interests of the Constitution, it was decided to fire his house and property instead of letting the blood feud run its course! This seemed a punishment on the murderer's wife and family rather than on himself, but the Young Turk officer of my escort and the Kaimakam, after having taken counsel together, declared that it was the only law that was possible at present. It represented the intervention of authority, rough justice though it was. The mother of the murdered man was willing to compound the blood feud if paid a certain sum by the murderer's family, but this course was not approved. It is, however, not unknown in Albania, where the price paid for killing a man is about £30.

At Pooka, I slept untented beneath the stars, and with the first shaft of daylight we rode to the northeast. Evening brought us to Spas, upon the White Drin. Here the Turkish officer occupied himself in trying to implant the principles of the Constitution in the somewhat unreceptive soul of the local *khoja*, while I was employed in infusing brandy and quinine into the fortunately more responsive system of Tsilka, my Albanian companion, who was in high fever and had, from weakness, twice fallen from his pony in the last hours of the march. He played up gallantly next morning, and forded the White Drin with us in a chilly dawn when we set forth for Jakova. The wonder-

THE ORIENT EXPRESS

working letter from the Young Turk Committee at Salonika, which I carried, had stirred the telegraph from Scutari, and we found Jakova expecting us. It was garrisoned by two battalions of infantry, which marched out to meet us, and escorted through the streets to the Kaimakam's quarters in the barracks a somewhat embarrassed traveller, rather at a loss to know why the inhabitants should be turned out to cheer and why his travel-stained person should be made the centre of a triumphal procession. Apparently it all had something to do with the Constitution. When the official reception was over the Kaimakam and his retinue took us in the cool of the evening to the hill-top above the town, where we found a picnic meal awaiting us, and watched a magic sunset in the intervals of drinking Austrian beer. In the evening there was a great feast and much conversation with fine, swaggering Beys, who professed enthusiasm for liberty, but laughed considerably while they did so in a way which made a curious contrast with the eagerness of the Turkish officers of the garrison, who had been bitten by the Salonika microbe and thought the Golden Age had come. But one of the officers was an Albanian. He discoursed to me on Albania, notwithstanding the presence of the Turks, and as his excitement grew he produced an Albanian newspaper. The interest which this immediately aroused in the Kaimakam was remarkable. He seized the paper and sat down at a table to cope with it. But it was written in Latin characters and the Turk could not read it at any angle, so, after trying it both sideways and upside down, he abandoned, amidst a roar of laughter, his attempt to penetrate this possibly seditious mystery.

THE SONS OF THE EAGLE

It is a rich, fine country between Jakova and Ipek, and an easy journey, so that after a call by the way upon the abbot of the Servian Monastery of Dachan—who is a Russian monk from Mount Athos—we reached Ipek in the early afternoon. Here, again, the wire had been at work, and a deputation of officers awaited us outside the town. They brought me to the house of Nasif Bey, who gave me kindly welcome and informed me that I was his guest. He is the great landlord of the district, and, I was informed, had hitherto been a most unruly subject, ever in rebellion against the Turkish Government. By some means the Young Turks had secured his temporary allegiance to the new order of things, and this was the basis of their success in Ipek, as his word was more powerful than theirs. The visit of courtesy which I paid to the Mutessarif Pasha, the official Governor of Ipek, seemed to be regarded as almost superfluous alike by the Young Turks and the Albanians, for it was evident that Turkish officialdom had no authority whatever. A year later the Albanians shot him. In the evening Nasif gave a wonderful feudal feast, to which he had invited his Albanian colleagues and the Young Turk Committee of Ipek. It was a gay gathering, and as wine, raki, and beer were consumed in large quantities, the gaiety grew to uproar towards midnight, and one felt that the era of liberty was indeed in full swing. The tables were tended and the drinks served by remarkably ruddy-faced and bright-eyed young men, who, when they judged that the Beys and officers had become thoroughly saturated with the spirit of freedom, expressed a desire to have speech with me. To my great surprise I found that they had a political communication to make. They were, they said, pastry-cooks in the town, who had been brought in for the evening to superintend the feast, but they wished me to understand that they were Kutsovlachs and not Albanians. Although Ipek was mainly Albanian, there were a few Kutsovlach houses and also, they declared, some twenty-five Serb families.

The next day found me at Mitrovitsa, and in touch with the world again, for a railway runs thence to Uskub. At Mitrovitsa I was the guest of the Municipality, and stayed in the local equivalent of the town-hall for three days. On the day of my arrival the town was decorated in honour of Abdul Hamid's birthday, but it was a remarkable fact that when we sat down in the town-hall that night to dinner—which the citizens doubtless supposed also to be a loyal celebration—although we drank repeatedly to the Constitution, toasted our noble selves, and made many speeches on many subjects, the one possible toast which no one thought of proposing and which was never drunk was that of the Sultan. He was, indeed, frequently mentioned, but in terms far from complimentary. But politics were discussed here more seriously and with a greater sense of reality than I had observed for some weeks. Haidar Hilmi, the Kaimakam, himself an Albanian who had seen service in many parts of the empire, was a very intelligent official, and there was also Colonel Ahmed Faik Bey, whom I had last seen at Salonika, an important member of the Central Committee and one of the most sensible and sober of all Young Turks. He had come to Mitrovitsa on a political mission, and I gathered that his observations

THE SONS OF THE EAGLE

left him in grave doubt as to whether the leading Albanians were at all serious in their declarations of enthusiasm for the Constitution. He did not see the future through the rose-coloured spectacles which at Salonika were the only wear.

The object of the Young Turks' propaganda was to absorb the movement for Albanian independence, and for a time they appeared to have succeeded. At the moment of the Declaration of the Constitution fifteen thousand Albanians, assembled at Ferisovitch, solemnly swore the *bessa*, or oath, of the Constitution, and trains from Uskub to Mitrovitsa were held up and not allowed to pass until a telegram granting the Constitution had been received from the Sultan. The forest at Ferisovitch was destroyed, but there was no general disorder, and there, as at Uskub and elsewhere, the populace inflicted exemplary punishment upon those who thought liberty meant permission to commit acts of private vengeance. Even Jakova, which is normally probably the most lawless town in the world and is rarely entered by any European, was tranquil at the time of my visit. An Albanian at Jakova who, unmindful of the changed condition of life, insulted his Serb shoemaker and shot another Albanian who, in the name of Equality and Fraternity, reproved him for this conduct, was himself shot by order of the people in the first flush of liberty, "before they rightly understood the methods of justice," and after that the fraternization between the Albanians and Serbs became general. To those who know the country and understand the Albanian contempt for the Serb and the murderous feud which has always existed and rages to-day, this fraternization was almost incredible, but it was none the less true.

Under Turkish rule the principal grievance of the Albanians has always been that they have been denied the educational privileges accorded to other races in the empire. It was the deliberate policy of the Palace to keep in a state of ignorance and, if possible, of fanaticism this magnificent warlike people, on which it relied for soldiers, and which it sought to make a decimating scourge for the Serb and Bulgar elements in Novi Bazar and Macedonia. No Albanian schools were allowed, and although there was a printing-press for Albanians at Bukarest, a second at Sofia, and a third at Rome, none was permitted within the Ottoman Empire. Yet the Albanians combine with their picturesque savagery and defiance of all authority a deep-rooted desire for progress, a longing to be " European," and a sense of shame at their ignorance of letters. They know that their blood and heritage are European, and not Asiatic like those of the Osmanli. The Young Turk party promised that under the Constitution they should have their own schools, and for the moment they were content. It is only in our own day that Albanian has become a written language at all. The question of the composition of the alphabet may still be said to be an open one, and there has even been a question as to whether it should be written in the Arabic or the Latin script. When it became clear that the Young Turk party, although prepared to allow the language, desired to encourage only the Arabic script, Albanian discontent broke out afresh.

Five years have passed and all is changed. The

THE SONS OF THE EAGLE

ecstatic honeymoon between Turk and Albanian ended as honeymoons sometimes do. The Balkan War found the Albanians already scourged by revolution and the artillery of the Government, and in no mood to fight the battle of the Turks, as they had so often fought it before. The Serbs found Albania an easy prey, and even proud, unruly Scutari, after siege, surrendered to the Montenegrin arms. The Powers deprived Montenegro of her conquest, but all the country through which I rode is lost to Turkey. The regions of Mat, Mirdita, and Scutari must now be reckoned as belonging to a Principality of Albania which has just come into existence. Ochrida, Dibra, and Mitrovitsa have passed to Servia; Jakova and Ipek to Montenegro.

It is true that in all these towns, and in Jakova and Ipek almost within living memory, there was once a considerable Serb population. But, with the exception of Mitrovitsa, there is no Serb population to-day. The reason is a simple one, and enthusiasts on either side may be left to throw moral blame on the other. The Albanians have for some hundreds of years been steadily exterminating the Serbs. The day of the Serb has now come. He is proceeding to attempt the extermination of the Albanian. And unless I am greatly mistaken we shall hear of trouble near Scutari and in Jakova and Ipek for many years to come.

For Montenegro has bitten off more than she can comfortably chew.

CHAPTER XXVI

ATHENS REVISITED

THE glories of Delhi and Agra, the pageantry of an Indian native State, and that wistful peace, as of an old Oxford garden, which in these latter days has fallen upon the old Residency of Lucknow, where Lawrence died and every Irishman must feel a pride in life, had force to hold me far into the autumn of 1912. Cairo, likewise, had a lure, and the first round of the war of the Allies against Turkey had been fought to a finish in Thrace before I reached the Balkans.

A few days before Christmas 1912 I landed at Piræus from Alexandria. It was four years since I had last been in Athens, and the comparison between the Athens of 1908 and of to-day is, in spite of the proverb, so little odious, and is otherwise so remarkable, that it may be safely drawn. Souls, I suppose, are stubborn things, and it would be absurd to suggest that the Greeks have changed their soul in four years. They say these things better in France, and *plus ça change, plus c'est la même chose* might be nearer the mark in the end. But let me put it that the present manifestation of the modern Greek spirit is infinitely preferable to the old. One always knew the Greeks for patriots, but the old patriotism was, for the stranger, a little embarrassing. It made political

ATHENS REVISITED

conversation difficult. It leapt, it soared, it swore, it dreamt; it did anything but walk in this workaday world. Some strangers called it chauvinism; others, less kindly, lunacy. Its principal arguments dealt with Alexander the Great and the Byzantine Empire, and nobody felt quite equal to answering them. But what mattered very much was that four years ago this kind of patriotism had brought Greece to a lamentable plight. Politics had become disreputable, and the better sort of Greek was weary of them. Foreign policy consisted chiefly in the financing of bands to enter Macedonia and "convert" Bulgarian villages, and in the issuing of unconvincing manifestoes to prove that only the Bulgarians were at fault. Home policy was an unedifying faction fight. Naval policy had produced a doubtful fleet, and military policy a still more doubtful army, of possibly fifty thousand men. Rich Greeks abroad, whose patriotic generosity had appeared inexhaustible, were weary of sending contributions to a mismanaged cause. Then came the Young Turk revolution, which seemed to promise Turkey a new lease of life, and to put Greece's chance of conquering any portion of Macedonia in the same category as her vain dreams of empire at Constantinople. She sulked, and sank lower still. Revolution muttered in army and navy and among the Athenian mob. The Military League ran its futile and mutinous course, and British warships stood in to the Piræus to be ready in case of need to take the royal family on board.

Then came M. Venizelos and changed all that. Not that he did it all himself, but he must be allowed to stand for a movement in which all the best elements rallied to his aid. He brought Frenchmen to improve the army and Englishmen to improve the navy, and both worked wonders. Also he had the courage to tell his countrymen that they need not think about Constantinople just at present.

And so it came to pass that one sees the Athens of to-day a bigger, a more beautiful, and altogether a more vigorous city than the Athens of four years ago, manifesting patriotism in a much more attractive sense. And how the people played up! Even a year before it was thought folly to hope for a hundred thousand men in time of war. But in the war with Turkey Greece put two hundred thousand in the field. Ill-trained men many of them, no doubt, but full of enthusiasm, like the young ladies who thronged round the Red Cross staff for permission to nurse, and said in modest self-recommendation, "Je ne suis pas précisément diplômée, mais j'ai beaucoup de disposition." "Beaucoup de disposition" will not carry you the whole way, especially when it comes to helping a surgeon in an operation. But it is a good start for a soldier, and the new arrivals, many of whom had no previous training, were being worked "like niggers," and drafted out when they had done musketry training and hardened their legs. And still they came. The great discovery of the war was the number of Greeks there are in the world. The Greek population abroad, like the Irish population abroad, is far larger than at home, but few suspected how large it was. From the ends of the earth they came in their thousands, and those who could not come sent money for the cause. A month earlier I was told in India that one great Greek firm had already had over fifty of its representatives and clerks drafted off. I found another of them on board the P. & O. boat that brought me from Bombay to Port Said. From Cairo and Alexandria the Greeks were answering the call in crowds, and when I got to Athens I found them coming in from America by every boat. The hotel was full of returned bankers and wealthy merchants in the new khaki uniforms of private soldiers. Soft-living gentlemen most of these, who had not for years had their livers so seriously shaken as they were every day now in hard exercise on the hills of Attica after a chilly morning parade. Some of them were frankly horrified at the prospect before them, for, though little news from Yanina was given out, the wounded came in daily, and the tales they told were enough to freeze the blood. There were many losses, and there were many who came back with frost-bitten feet that had to be amputated.

"All very well," said one of the *jeunesse dorée* to me, "for shepherds and such like, but how am I, who have already the gout, to resist exposure of that kind? Now, if we could make an arrangement with Italy about Rhodes, I should like to be sent to Rhodes. I am told that it is a lovely island, with fine scenery. But no, I do not want to go to Yanina. Snow a metre deep on the ground, and sometimes days without food, and hours in water up to the waist. And then they are using the bayonet. *Mon Dieu!* six centimetres of cold steel in one's vitals in cold weather—that is adding insult to injury. Vraiment c'est trop, ça. C'est tout ce qu'il y a du plus désagréable."

That was one point of view, sounding eminently reasonable when stated with this engaging frankness.

THE ORIENT EXPRESS

But it was not the general point of view, be it said, for the Greeks were in the mood for sacrifice. They were also displaying remarkable efficiency. Although far more reservists had arrived, and continued to arrive, than were ever expected, there were warm uniforms and good kits, with—best of all—good boots, for everybody; and the supply of Mannlichers and cartridges—a change, this, from the old Gras rifle of four years ago!—never failed. Everybody was disposed of at once, and found his place. A trained American-Greek complained bitterly that on landing from New York at Athens he found himself posted to proceed next day to Yanina, "without having time to say 'Helloa' to my old mother in Sparta." One wonders what the old lady would have thought of this unaccustomed form of greeting.

CHAPTER XXVII

WHO CAUSED THE TURKISH DISASTERS?

When the war broke out in the Balkans in the autumn of 1912 and fortune swiftly declared herself against the Turks, there was an immediate outcry in many quarters that the Young Turks had ruined the empire, and there was much illuminating nonsense talked about the superior political wisdom of Abdul Hamid. The public memory is a short and fickle thing, and in this instance it had forgotten much. It would, I think, be more true to say that the Young Turks did not ruin Turkey: they only failed to save her—a crime in the second degree. In actual fact they probably postponed the war for four years. Had there been no Young Turk Revolution in July 1908, there would have been a Balkan War almost certainly in the autumn of that year, and certainly long before 1912. Those who followed the history of Macedonian reform after the ineffective Bulgar rising of 1903 will ask for no argument upon this point. But it is worth recording that early in July 1908, a week before the Young Turk Revolution, Mr. Stancioff, discussing the possibilities of Sir Edward Grey's success with his latest proposals for Macedonian reform, and the results likely to accrue from the meeting of King Edward and the Tsar at Reval, told me that he had little hope. He thought that Sir Edward Grey's *démarche* was the biggest effort yet made in the matter of reform, but he felt sure that the inevitable opposition of certain Powers would prevent its success.

"And then," I asked, "what will happen?"

"Then England and Russia must let Bulgaria march," he replied. "We can march early in October."

The Young Turk Revolution prevented that, but when October came the Principality of Bulgaria showed her readiness to fight, if necessary, by throwing off Turkish suzerainty and declaring herself an independent kingdom. Had she "marched" that autumn, or before the Young Turk Revolution, all serious evidence goes to show that Turkey would have been far less capable of offering resistance, and that had the other Balkan States fallen upon her at the same moment, the collapse of the empire in Europe would have been even more dramatic and complete than in those memorable weeks in October and November 1912. The ruin of Turkey, begun long before his day, was completed by Abdul Hamid. The Russo-Turkish War of 1878 proved that she was no longer a great military Power. She had no generalship and no organization; nothing was left save the fighting quality of the soldier, which only found its account in stubborn defence, as at Plevna. Even in the farcical Greek War of 1897, although for the most part the Turks had no enemy in front of them, they advanced with the most extraordinary slowness. The fighting quality of the soldier survives to this day, as Adrianople, Chatalja, Scutari and Janina can tell. But when many declared that the results of the war were a surprise and that the experts were "as usual all wrong," they were less than fair to the experts. The military experts in the Balkans knew well that the Young Turks had improved the army, and it is

WHO CAUSED TURKISH DISASTERS?

true that some of them were so far misled in judging the effects of these improvements as to expect Turkish victories. But the point which I am seeking to establish, which is that in Abdul Hamid's day the Turkish army was in a far worse condition, is supported by the fact that every English military attaché in the Balkans, from the early years of the present century until the Young Turks had taken the army in hand, had warned his Government that the Bulgarian chances in war were likely to prove strong, and that the Bulgarian army was a first-class fighting instrument. The British officers employed in the Macedonian gendarmerie were in 1907 very definitely of this opinion. It was my good fortune to be the guest of the Bulgarian General Staff for some weeks during the latter part of the war, and I found that both General Savoff and his staff held the same view in the most emphatic manner. They believed that their relative superiority to Turkey was greater in 1907 and in 1908 than in 1913, and that had they fought at the moment of the declaration of independence, they would have found Turkey far less prepared and less capable of resistance.

The issue seems to me important. The public loves a scapegoat, and it is the fashion to vilify the Young Turks and to call high-minded and patriotic men, such as Enver Bey and the late Shefket Pasha, adventurers. I hold no brief for the political wisdom of the Young Turks, and all must admit that they have made many mistakes. Few, however, consider whether in reality success was ever possible to them. The Balkan States had staked out their claims in Macedonia, and had written them in blood; they were young and vigorous, and they felt their strength growing every year. Macedonia itself was inhabited by their nationals, who hated the Turkish Empire and were determined to work its ruin. The Young Turks were but a handful of gallant men struggling against tremendous odds, and surrounded by an old gang which had put on the cloak of liberalism. Had they had the tongues of men and angels, the wisdom of the serpent, and the gentleness of the dove, the Young Turks must still have failed to hold Macedonia. It may be admitted that they were not possessed of these unusual qualities. But when a corrupt, cruel, and feeble despotism has worked the ruin of a country and finally of itself, so that it is swept away, and when its bankrupt and luckless inheritor is overwhelmed in the final crash, we are ever told that it is the incompetence of the latter which is at fault and that despotism understood the business better!

It is easy to be wise after the event, and those who —complaining much that no one had ever told them of it before—suddenly discovered the Bulgarian army in the autumn of 1912, and declared likewise that the Young Turks had ruined a very flourishing institution —the Turkish Empire as governed by that sagacious statesman, Abdul Hamid!—are entitled to ask whether the argument that is here set forth is not based upon that ripe, but not difficult, form of wisdom? There is only one convincing answer to this natural question. It may perhaps, therefore, be permissible to make a series of verbal quotations, bearing upon the two points under discussion, from writings of a far earlier date.

The first concerns Bulgaria's military strength and the possible issue of a Turco-Bulgarian War. It is from *The Albany Review* for April 1908, and therefore it must have been written four months before the Young Turks flung their challenge in the teeth of Abdul Hamid.

WHO CAUSED TURKISH DISASTERS?

"The strong and well-organized revolutionary organization of Macedonia has held its hand since 1903. It determined to give Europe time to show its power and its earnestness in the matter of reform. It is now convinced of the futility of the reforms, since the state of the vilayets is worse than before the insurrection of 1903. The peasant organization had wellnigh despaired of Europe's help, and resolved on its own desperate measures, when Great Britain stepped forward at the beginning of this year and proposed to the Concert a more active programme. If Austria's magnificent capacity for inertia succeed in defeating the serious diplomatic effort which Sir Edward Grey and Mons. Isvolsky are at present making, the despair and the resolution of the peasant organization will be redoubled. It may find one ally. Of the frontier states, the action of Bulgaria is most vital, owing to its military strength and to the preponderance of the Bulgar element in Macedonia and Adrianople. It was with the utmost difficulty that the Bulgarian Government resisted the pressure of the army and the people, and avoided a declaration of war with Turkey during the Macedonian insurrection of 1903. The representations of Austria and Russia, who had just made themselves jointly responsible for a new scheme of reform, and were otherwise also in a better position than they are now to make their influence felt, contributed to this result; but a reason no less weighty with the ever-cautious Bulgarian was the fact that his military preparations were not complete. Since then these preparations have been hurried on apace, and last year the whole of a large order of Creuzot quick-firing guns was completed. If a general insurrection were to take place in Macedonia, with the inevitable accompanying

THE ORIENT EXPRESS

incidents on the Bulgarian frontier, it seems difficult to believe that either Europe or Prince Ferdinand or the most pacific government would be able to restrain Bulgaria. The massacres of 1903 threw upon a poor country the maintenance of thousands of refugees, and the people realize that inaction a second time would mean the virtual extinction of the Macedonian Bulgar.

"What would be the issue of such a contest? Mindful of the heroic qualities of the Turkish soldier, of the stubborn resistance at Plevna and the Shipka Pass, of the recent too-little-known feats of unadvertised endurance in the Yemen, and of the brief campaign against Greece in 1897, one might be tempted to prophesy a speedy humiliation for Bulgaria. But such a judgment would be hasty, and the prophet might be doomed to rank with the great army of those who foretold the humbling of Japan. In 1878 the invading Russian army numbered 200,000. Its base was far away, and it had to fight its way across two tremendous obstacles, the Danube River and the Balkan Mountains. The Bulgarian army is admitted by all experts to be a most efficient fighting instrument. It is trained and disciplined with ceaseless diligence in the shadow of war, and every Bulgarian soldier believes in his heart that one day he will fight the Turk. He has already given proof of his qualities, both as a marcher and a fighter, and he would oppose the Turk with a greater *élan* than he opposed the Serb. On a war footing the army numbers over 300,000, and there would be an eager response to the call to arms. The offensive would certainly rest with Bulgaria—for the slowness of the Turk in starting may safely be reckoned with—and Bulgaria has to face neither the Danube nor Shipka. No country has

WHO CAUSED TURKISH DISASTERS?

ever been in a strategic position at all comparable to that of Bulgaria for striking a sudden vital blow at Turkey, and it must be remembered that in a war with Turkey time is the essence of the matter. The Turks are capable of maintaining a magnificent resistance, but they have never been ready with a plan of campaign; and of late years all government has become so highly centralized that when communications with Constantinople are cut complete paralysis ensues. By this expedient the small insurgent force of 1903 made themselves masters of a large part of Macedonia for several weeks. Moreover, though the Turkish soldier is magnificent material, he cannot shoot, inasmuch as he gets no practice—except occasionally at a human target. Lastly, the Arab revolt has cost many men and much money, and has been a far more serious strain than is supposed; so that there are many factors that those who prophesy renewed success in Europe for the Sultan's arms would do well to ponder. In any case, it is clear from the grave language recently used by Sir Edward Grey in the House of Commons, that this life-or-death struggle is the alternative the Powers have to face if the new effort to put reality into the Macedonian Reforms is frustrated."

A second quotation will serve to show how deeply rooted were Bulgaria's designs, how bad the Macedonian situation was, and how idle it is to suppose that the Young Turks, as some writers have seriously suggested, had only themselves to blame and might easily have averted catastrophe had they been more regular in their attendance at the mosque, and refrained from wearing European collars and from similar shocking acts fraught with deep political consequence. Like the previous passage it was written when, as far as

THE ORIENT EXPRESS

Europe knew, the Young Turks were non-existent and Abdul Hamid was an unchallenged ruler. I wrote it in August 1907—

"The pride of Bulgaria and the soul of Bulgaria was her army. It was a conscript army, for she was a nation in earnest, and her aims were too high to be entrusted to starvelings. It was a national army, and it lived because it was the Army of Freedom. Ministers and Cabinets came and went; policy veered with the wind that set from St. Petersburg, Vienna, or Constantinople; but no Minister, however pacific his declarations, ever dared to propose a reduction of armaments. Money was spent like water on the manifold needs of a new State, but no economist attacked the army estimates. No peasant grudged the burden the Army of Freedom imposed upon his pocket. No father grudged his sons the months in which they left the plough to carry the Mannlicher. There were dark pages in the history of the young nation. Law reigned in the villages, but the political assassin lurked sometimes in the streets of Sofia. . . . But, whatever malign influences might vex Bulgaria's politics, one idea possessed her people. There was one word the magic of which never failed—Macedonia. And so the army grew from year to year, and battery was added to battery. Their Macedonian kinsmen had, for one brief moment, drawn the breath of liberty with them in 1878, only to be hurled back by the decree of Europe in congress at Berlin into chains that eat the flesh more cruelly, and prison darkness that seemed more deathly after sight of day. The hour would come when free Bulgaria would strike a blow for her brothers.

"To the Macedonian the hour seemed long in coming. In 1903, with the courage of despair, he

WHO CAUSED TURKISH DISASTERS?

raised the flag of revolution, and hoped that Bulgarian bayonets would save him from the awful vengeance of the Turks. The Macedonian Bulgar has the same practical matter-of-fact temperament as the free Bulgarian, but he was subject to the limits of human endurance. The Bulgarian was not under this stress, and he refused to have his hand forced. He would not risk the failure of his cherished hopes. His guns were not ready, and without guns he could not beat the Turk. A fierce wave of sympathy rolled over the country, and acting on the more eager spirits, swept it to the verge of war. But the Government stood firm, and Prince Ferdinand's ever-cautious nature allied itself to them. Macedonia was desolated with fire and sword by the Turkish soldiers and the infuriated Bashibazouks. Europe supped full of horrors, and read how in the small country which it had so lightly put back under the Turkish yoke twelve thousand houses were burnt to the ground, seventy thousand people were left homeless and starving on the eve of the cruel Balkan winter, five thousand were put to the sword, while more than three thousand women and girls suffered a worse fate. The country sank back once more, with the tears and groans of utter despair, into its crushing slavery. Bulgaria overflowed with refugees. She housed and fed them. They were a new and moving appeal to the Macedonian sympathies of her citizens, but a sad strain upon her resources. Moreover, they soon entered into economic competition with their new neighbours, and made themselves felt as a political force working for the redemption of Macedonia. The movement was redoubled. Bulgaria watched the paper reform schemes of the Powers with sceptical eyes, and gave a new order for Creuzot guns.

THE ORIENT EXPRESS

"The Concert of Europe tinkered away at the Turkish machine, but never once touched its secret springs. It sent officers to remodel the gendarmerie, and commissioners to reform finance. The officers were not allowed to issue an order; the commissioners were not allowed to spend a penny. The Concert shrank from cutting the wires that led from every village to Yildiz Kiosk, and it became a sacred principle not to impair the sovereignty of the Sultan. Ambassadors munched the unctuous formula solemnly, and only in rare moments of furtive frankness winked across the dinner-tables of Pera and Therapia. They knew well enough that one might as well try to take a return ticket to infinity at a wayside station as to reform Macedonia without impairing the sovereignty of the Sultan. But there were reasons of State why the misery should be prolonged. It was the order of the day at Berlin that Turkey must be befriended, and that the time to settle the Eastern Question was not yet ripe. Austria listened to Berlin with respect, and the makeshift diplomacy inveterate with her, which has in truth often served her passably well as a substitute for statesmanship, told her that she had much to gain by keeping the Question open. Russian autocracy, staggering under the blows of Japan and faced with a prospect of revolution at home, had no stomach for a settlement at a time when its prestige was low. England, France, and Italy urged the dangers of delay; but the Concert was hopelessly divided, and the Sultan throve on its divisions. The British Government in two successive Administrations, Conservative and Liberal, made gallant efforts to galvanize the reform scheme into life. . . . But all failed."

WHO CAUSED TURKISH DISASTERS?

Lastly, I venture to give an extract from an article written in July 1908, on the very eve of the first public appearance of the Young Turks, and published in *The Albany Review* for August 1908. I believe it to be a true and faithful picture of the pass to which the statesmanship of Abdul Hamid brought the empire.

"What, then, are the prospects in regard to the eternal Macedonian Question? Since the ill-starred insurrection of 1903 the country has been sinking deeper and deeper into a slough of savage anarchy which has no parallel in the modern world. The Powers which undertook its reformation have thought only of policy, and have let humanity go by the board. The corrupt clique at Yildiz Kiosk, which is the curse of the Ottoman Empire, incapable of government under fair conditions, has made no effort to deal with foul. Alternations of massacre, obstruction, and fraud, along with cunning appeals to the simpler fanaticism and patriotism of their dupes, have been their only weapons. It has been said that every people has the government it deserves, but those who know the virtues of the Turk must marvel that he should be delivered into the hands of the extortioners and thieves who haunt the Palace, men who care nothing for Islam or their country and sell its interests daily to the highest bidder. The fierce and foolish chauvinism of the Balkan States has prevented any adjustment of aims or policies, and has led to the development of quite the most astounding propaganda by means of murder that has ever been carried on in the name of Nationalism, and to one of the most shameless and bloody crusades that has ever been carried on in the name of Christ. Patriarchist and Exarchist convert each other by killing women and children, by burning in oil, by mutilation, and by torture. The Turkish Government looks on in glee while the Sons of Christ—for this is the style and title of some of the bands—cut the throats of villagers, lends its support and not infrequently its troops to one side, acts as an *agent provocateur*, and denies justice or redress in its courts of law. Musulman murder-bands and roving Albanian brigands join in the general pandemonium. While a European reform scheme, heralded five years ago with much trumpeting, is nominally in full swing, the death-roll swells in volume from month to month, barbaric anarchy increases, and it would seem that the very elements of a social state are dissolving. The immemorial loyalty and patience of the Turk is at last exhausted, and the spirit of revolt against the iniquities and fatalities of the Constantinople cabal, which is plunging the empire to destruction, is widespread."

It is commonly said that the Young Turks accomplished little or nothing in the way of material progress. I may be permitted to give my own testimony on this point. After the initial superficial success of the Young Turk movement, I was absent from Turkey for four years. The accounts which I read in the newspapers were at first highly optimistic, but gradually they became less and less favourable in tone. I was witnessing before my eyes the failures and futilities of the Persian reformers—though they, too, must be acquitted of having wrought their country's ruin—and I had therefore only too much reason to suppose that reform in Turkey might be making as little headway. It was clear that the marvellous tide of luck upon which they had floated into power had long ago turned against the Young Turks, and that the actual business of preserving the empire must in itself be absorbing all their

WHO CAUSED TURKISH DISASTERS?

energies, leaving little for the introduction of useful measures of reform. They had revolution on their hands in Albania and in Arabia. Then came the war with Italy and finally the Balkan thunderbolt. When I reached Salonika, therefore, on the last day of 1912, I had no expectation of finding many signs of material improvement in Macedonia. Yet to my astonishment I saw on every hand signs of progress, which even the devastation of the autumn campaign had not effaced. There were fine new roads and bridges where no roads and bridges had been before. In Drama, there were great granite piers for a magnificent bridge, upon which much money had been spent and which was approaching completion when the war broke out. And in Drama and other country towns of Macedonia, formerly plunged in darkness at nightfall, there were now powerful street-lamps. A new strategic line of railway avoided the dangers of Dedeagatch, and another connected Ainpoli and Kirk Kilisse. I motored from General Savoff's headquarters at Dimotika to Ortikoi by a new and excellent road. Nor were these isolated instances. It is part of the irony of fate that the improvements made by the Young Turks in the last few years have now passed into the keeping of their enemies.

As for the condition of the army, we have been told that the Turks, by insisting that officers should pass through the military school, had decreased efficiency. I believe that the exact reverse is the truth, and that the old "ranker" officer, whose virtues were suddenly discovered by the critics after the Turkish disasters, had done his country little service in the past, and was extremely unlikely to do it any in the future. And I humbly agree with such competent

THE ORIENT EXPRESS

critics as General Savoff and Colonel Topaljikoff, the Bulgarian military attaché at Constantinople, that the Turkish officers were superior, the men better fed, better clad and better trained, and their war stores and equipment of every kind more complete at the outbreak of the Balkan War than they had been for some years. In spite of this the army failed hopelessly. As to how that failure came about in Thrace, something will be said in the next chapter. But the causes which produced failure, alike in Thrace and in Macedonia, are at once simpler and deeper. The reorganization of the Turkish army had not gone far enough. Generalship cannot be produced at will, and in any case the Turkish soldier was no match for the irresistible *élan* of the Bulgar and his Balkan allies. To the Bulgar the supreme moment had come for which the ages had been waiting. He was ready with his plans, his men, and his guns, for the war was neither the sudden turn of fate nor the foolish passion of politicians. It had been long coming and long delayed, and the final blow was struck in the cool Bulgarian way, when preparations were complete and postponement perilous. He fought for the soil to which his fathers had been bound, on which they had ever lived in shame and died in torment. The Turk was the age-long oppressor, and the Bulgar's day of reckoning had come. The fire of national pride was alight, the desire to win for his race glory in the field, renown amongst the nations, and a tribute of respect from Europe and from those mysterious Great Powers which must now recognize Bulgaria's independence.

Neither Old nor Young Turk could withstand such a spirit of vengeance fortified by the science of war,

CHAPTER XXVIII

SIC VOS NON VOBIS

It was Bulgaria that broke the power of the Turks in Europe. She has since been defeated by her own allies, and in the hour of her humiliation she has even been forced to give back to the Turks the battlefields of Kirk Kilisse, Lule Burgas, and Bunar Hissar—the scenes of those most brilliant victories which at the time all men thought decisive—and the long-beleaguered city of Adrianople, the fall of which was her crowning triumph. But in spite of this appearance of partial revival the Turks' day in Europe is for ever done. From Bulgaria's swift, sledge-hammer blows in October 1912 there can be no recovery. The Greeks, the Servians, and the Montenegrins fought manfully. The sieges of Yanina and Scutari, the battle of Kumanova, and the capture of Monastir, were fine feats of arms, but the Bulgarian blood, which ran like water in Thrace in those early, all-important hours of the war, was the tide upon which Greek and Serb have floated to a new heritage.

To write the full and true story of the campaign in Thrace it would be necessary not only to have access to the archives of the Bulgarian General Staff, but also to have a connected Turkish account of the struggle. We may suppose that some day the story will be written. But it may be of interest to give here a very short sketch of those critical early days of the

THE ORIENT EXPRESS

war. My sources of information are purely Bulgarian. General Savoff placed an officer at my disposal who, like the staff with which I lived for some three weeks, was very willing to answer all questions. Neither have I, nor, as far as I know, any one else, been allowed access to documents, as General Savoff told me that it was the staff's intention to publish its own official history of the campaign.

Before the war the Turkish main army was at Ainpoli, where the Kirk Kilisse railway joins the main line. A second large force was at Kuleli Burgas. Abdullah Pasha, the Turkish commander-in-chief, expected the main Bulgarian advance west of Adrianople, and hoped to send the Kuleli Burgas army to check this, while developing his own offensive in an alignment north-west of Kirk Kilisse. The disposition was, indeed, excellent for any eventuality, as the main army was massed at the two railway junctions. The plan of campaign, whether German or not, was in itself a good one. But its inadequately concealed motive underlay the Turkish army manœuvres both of 1909 and 1910, and the Bulgarians seem to have had a very shrewd idea of its nature. They foiled it in two ways: in the first place by making no advance westward of Adrianople, and in the second place by sending General Radko-Dimitrieff eastwards, with Kirk Kilisse for his objective. The Bulgarian position at the outbreak of the war was as follows. The staff was at Stara Zagora. Ivanoff's and Kutinchieff's armies were massed on the frontier. Ivanoff, with Adrianople as his objective, was on the right; Kutinchieff held the centre; and on the left Bulgarian cavalry effectively screened the unexpected advance of Dimitrieff from Yamboli. Instead of advancing

SIC VOS NON VOBIS

westwards, General Ivanoff and the Second Army marched southwards against Adrianople itself; General Kutinchieff and the First Army advanced on the left; while still further to the left General Dimitrieff with the Third Army, in three columns, was making forced marches of thirty-eight kilometres a day, in a mountainous country, from Yamboli. Dimitrieff's extreme left column curved eastwards of Kirk Kilisse.

The Bulgarian plan, in brief, was to send one army to neutralize Adrianople, and another to find and defeat the enemy east of Adrianople. This latter army, unknown to the Turks, really consisted of two—the First and the Third. The appearance of the Third Army under Dimitrieff, which the Bulgarian Staff considers to have been totally unexpected by the Turks, had, as will be seen, a decisive effect. In fact, the staff regard this advance as the key to their overwhelming success in the first week of the war. This was the jealously guarded secret which successfully defied all the efforts of correspondents and attachés, the first of the two great secrets of the campaign in Thrace. Immense precautions were taken to preserve it. The Bulgarian army itself had no suspicion of it. Officers and men alike, who were entrained for the "front" and were quite certain they would be taken towards Adrianople, stared to find themselves at Yamboli. It should be said that there is some evidence that Abdullah Pasha guessed the secret, and had some knowledge of Dimitrieff's movements. If so, he made singularly bad use of his information.

On October 18 the first blow was struck. Ivanoff

THE ORIENT EXPRESS

and Kutinchieff crossed the frontier, and their advance guards met the enemy's outposts at Mustafa Pasha and Levki. Similar encounters took place on the 19th north of Adrianople, and as Kutinchieff's front moved eastwards, his cavalry came into contact with the enemy's at several points on the 20th. The Turkish army was at the same time advancing everywhere. Two divisions of the Third Army Corps were moving from Kirk Kilisse towards Petra, Eskipolis, and Eriklar. The Second Army Corps from Kavacli was making for Enidje, but probably never got into action until its return to Kavacli, where it later played the part of rearguard. From Hafsa, Eski Baba, and Ainpoli columns, chiefly of the First Army Corps, came north to complete Abdullah's centre towards Siliorlu. On the left of these there was a strong cavalry force, while a portion of the Fourth Army Corps, moving north-east from Adrianople, completed Abdullah's left front. On the 21st the first important encounter of the war took place. On that day began the three days' battle in continual rain which, owing to the absence of war correspondents, has come to be known as the battle of Kirk Kilisse. In actual fact, it took place over a front of some thirty miles in an alignment north of and roughly parallel to a line drawn between Adrianople and Kirk Kilisse. At Kirk Kilisse itself there was no fighting at all, and the Bulgarians finally entered it on the night of the 23rd without a shot being fired from its forts.

By the 21st the Bulgarian cavalry was reconnoitring all along this line. Abdullah Pasha behaved as though still unconscious of the advance of Dimitrieff, and may even then have supposed that the Bulgarian

SIC VOS NON VOBIS

Third Army was west of Adrianople. The fight of the day took place at Siliorlu, and by a strange accident, which the superstitious on both sides seem to have swiftly taken for an omen, it was the First Sofia Brigade, part of Kutinchieff's advance guard, consisting of the Battenberg regiment and the Ferdinand regiment, which met the First Constantinople Division. Both sides were advancing under cover of artillery, and fought with fierce bravery. On the left of the Constantinople division, between it and the Adrianople army, was a strong body of about fifty squadrons of Turkish cavalry, but for some reason it appears to have done nothing to turn the position of Kutinchieff's advance guard, and by the 22nd it had begun to fall back. On the night of the 21st both the Sofia brigade and the Constantinople division entrenched themselves, and the fight raged furiously again on the 22nd. It should be said that the Sofia brigade was supported not merely by its own batteries, but by the artillery of a whole division. So magnificent was the service rendered that when the infantry conquered new positions, and above all when they reached, as they finally did, the enemy's guns, they cheered the artillery. The Bulgarian General Staff attaches immense importance to the exploit of the First Brigade at Siliorlu, and places it and the piercing of the Turkish centre at Karagatch in the battle of Lule Burgas as the most gallant feats of arms in the war. It is clear that the *élan* of the infantry in this the first grapple with the Turk surpassed even the sanguine expectations of the staff. The peasant army burned with a hate that would not brook defeat, and I heard many well-authenticated instances to prove the spirit in which the fight was waged; such as the fall of an officer who received a bullet in his forehead as he stood upright, with sword in air, upon the breech of a Turkish gun at the end of a charge. Early in the day a Bulgarian column came up on the west of the Sofiotes. The artillery duel demonstrated the superior skill of the Bulgarian gunners, and under their effective protection the infantry pressed on and on, making repeated bayonet charges. The Turkish artillery was practically silent a great part of the day, yet the Turkish infantry gave ground very slowly. Everywhere the opposing armies were getting into closer touch, and fighting was general all along the line. The surprise came when the great Bulgarian cavalry screen on the east fell back and Dimitrieff's weary, but eager, columns of hard-marched men disclosed themselves swinging up to the positions left for them by the cavalry. Dimitrieff got into action at Petra, and that night the Turks broke.

On the 23rd more Turkish columns from Hafsa and Kavacli were still pressing forward, but the columns of the front were in retreat, and all along the line there was a general Bulgarian advance. At sunset the Bulgarian cavalry deployed in pursuit towards Enidje, and late at night some of Dimitrieff's troops entered Kirk Kilisse without opposition. On the 24th Dimitrieff himself made his entry. But there was no rest for his army. In mud and over roads and tracks that cannot be described the pursuit continued. The Turkish retreat, unlike the later panic after the battle of Lule Burgas, was not an undisciplined flight, and there were instances of scattered bodies of infantry standing to their ground in desperation, and receiving cavalry with their bayonets. Abdullah Pasha left two

SIC VOS NON VOBIS

divisions of the Second Army Corps as a rearguard, which checked the pursuit on the evening of the 24th at Kavacli, and held their trenches till the 25th, when they broke. The Bulgarian cavalry, which had in vain sought an encounter with the Turkish cavalry, pursued it to a point south-west of Hafsa, but it succeeded in making good its escape eastwards.

This ended the first phase of the campaign, the centre of which was the miscalled battle of Kirk Kilisse. Of this period it remains to be said that by October 23 Ivanoff's army had completely surrounded Adrianople, and the cavalry was already southwards along the railway. By the time the Bulgarians reached Kuleli Burgas the Turkish army centred there had been moved to the north-east, and the Bulgarians met with little resistance. They seized the bridges at Uzenkupru and elsewhere and captured Dimotika.

For the second phase the absence of correspondents again served the Bulgarians well. We have seen that in the first phase Kutinchieff, with the First Army, led the main advance, Dimitrieff coming up later on his left flank. The position was now reversed. Dimitrieff wheeled to the left and took the front in a new alignment, while the First Army came slowly up on his right into the new position, facing the Turkish front which extended from Bunar Hissar to Lule Burgas. Further Turkish troops had come up from Rodosto, Midia, and Constantinople, and it is said that there was a total of eight Turkish army corps entrenched in several lines. Dimitrieff made his first reconnaissance on the evening of October 27, and on the 28th began the battle now known as the Battle of Lule Burgas. On the 29th it raged furiously. The

THE ORIENT EXPRESS

Turks, under Mahmud Mukhtar Pasha, concentrated in great strength on the right at Bunar Hissar, and endeavoured to deliver a knock-down blow. On the 30th Mahmud Mukhtar made his final effort, and it is clear that he very nearly succeeded. Positions were lost and retaken many times, and Dimitrieff was in serious danger. But while the Turks were concentrating all their efforts on the right, the Fourth Bulgarian Division pierced their centre near Karagatch, the infantry pressing home under a murderous fire, and at the same time Kutinchieff and the First Army, which had been wheeling up on the Bulgarian right, suddenly presented itself at Lule Burgas. Further south the cavalry made their appearance behind the Turkish left. On the 30th the Turks, seeing that their blow at Bunar Hissar had failed to make a rout, their centre pierced, Kutinchieff on their left, and cavalry already behind them, broke and fled. The panic grew to madness, and that tragic retreat, which many witnesses have already described, began. The pursuit was slow.

It was in this wise that the Bulgarian army achieved the task for which it had been preparing from the hour of Bulgaria's birth. Others have entered into its labours. But the end is not yet.

CHAPTER XXIX

A LITTLE MAGIC

> "Up from Earth's Centre through the Seventh Gate
> I rose, and on the Throne of Saturn sate,
> And many Knots unravel'd by the Road;
> But not the Knot of Human Death and Fate."
> *Omar Khayyam* (Fitzgerald).

IN July 1909 I stayed in a country house in Hampshire. There I had my fortune told, in an amateur way, clearly and well, but not being given to ponder much on such things, I chose to adopt a semi-sceptical attitude towards all mystery and "occult" science. I was, therefore, straightly challenged to go and see a good professional palmist and clairvoyant, with the statement that such a visit would convert me to belief. In the comfortable and compliant frame of mind that ought to go with after-dinner hours, I promised to do so, whereat the subject dropped, and I forgot to ask where the "good professional" was to be found.

A week later, strolling down Bond Street to my rooms, the sign of a purveyor of these mysteries caught my eye, and liking to think myself a man of honour, I paid him a visit and gave him two hands wherewith to diagnose anything he liked as to my past, present, and future. The result astonished me, as my seer, unaided by any comment from myself, who maintained a passive and uninterested exterior, displayed an amazing knowledge of my travels and my way of life, and committed himself without hesitation or hedging to most precise details about my future fortunes. This he did, or so he said, by a combination of palmistry and clairvoyance. I paid him his half-guinea cheerfully, reflecting that, were he a true prophet, my luck was cheap at the price, and took the street, momentarily impressed with the fleeting feeling that there were more things in heaven and earth than we had time to bother about, or could be expected always to remember.

The wretched summer rolled away, and autumn found me back in town. Late in the afternoon of Friday, October 9, my eye lit upon the board of a sandwich man in Regent Street and read that Miss —— was a clairvoyante. I remembered that I had undertaken to test for myself both palmistry and clairvoyance, and though my palmist had combined the two I had a notion of some purer art of second sight. I imagined to myself a female figure gazing into the mysterious depths of a crystal ball, staring at a pool of ink, or otherwise fulfilling the ancient profitable rôle of the priestesses of hanky-panky. So, the sandwich man being conveniently placed near her temple, I ascended to it on the third storey. Miss —— looked very British, and was indisputably very honest. She could not use the crystal, she told me, or achieve clairvoyance apart from palmistry. But, seeing me wear the look of one who is sent empty away, she volunteered the statement that she thought Madame K—— could do what I wanted, and gave me Madame's address. It was on my homeward way, so there I called and was introduced, not to Madame, but to her husband, K—— himself. He told me that

A LITTLE MAGIC

he was clairvoyant, and he proceeded to read my hands, grasping at the same time a crystal ball in one of his own, and occasionally glancing into it. The reading was interesting, but the crystal did not seem to affect the issue very much; so, at the end, I invited him to abandon palmistry for me and give me an exhibition of pure clairvoyance. He confessed his inability to do this, but said that his wife would do it. She did not use, or need, a crystal, but she was a natural clairvoyante, and might, or might not, be able to see things of interest to myself. Some unkind suspicion crossed my mind that this was a convenient arrangement for tempting clients into paying a second fee, but, not having the slightest objection to being cheated with my eyes open, I expressed a desire to see Madame K——. But I had heard that clairvoyance was exhausting for its possessor, and as it was now six o'clock, I volunteered the suggestion that Madame K—— might be tired and that it would be better to come another day. K—— said he was quite certain that his wife could see me now, but that the mornings were undeniably better. So it was agreed that I should come next morning.

I recite these preliminaries because it is fair to say that I had been to see K—— before the morning of Saturday, October 9. But he knew nothing whatever about me. Neither to K—— nor to the Bond Street palmist had I given either my name or address, or any information about myself. I was simply a man out of the street. In reading my hand, K—— had obtained from me only two pieces of information, and of these, one, as the sequel will show, though not meant to be false, was eminently calculated to mis-

THE ORIENT EXPRESS

lead him, had there been fraud afoot. I confessed in plain, unvarnished affirmatives to the interest in politics of which he accused me, but when he asked me directly whether I was a soldier, I replied, in good faith, that I was not. Whereupon he had to content himself with the statement that I had a turn that way, and that he thought there was every appearance of a soldier's life, along with "visits to the East, frequent dangers and frequent preservations." The theory that between six on Friday evening and eleven on Saturday morning K—— had me traced by some agent, and gleaned some particulars about me for his wife's use, would in any case be highly improbable. For what is an unknown man in London's millions, and is it to be supposed that Regent Street professors of mystery find it worth their while to keep going a vast detective service, when their rooms are open to all comers? He had had his guinea for his own service; and his wife's fee was only the half of it, which, moreover, I should presumably pay whether I considered myself cheated or not. Why, then, should he attempt an elaborate and dangerous fraud? As I have said, such a supposition is in any case highly improbable. But it is ruled out altogether in this case by the fact that Madame K—— proved to be the vehicle of information which no inquiry could have obtained for her, and of facts which were known to no one in the United Kingdom but myself.

On the Saturday, then, I saw Madame K—— for the first time. In a small room we sat on opposite sides of a small table, and save that once or twice she touched with her fingers my hands, which rested on the table, Madame performed no ceremony of any

A LITTLE MAGIC

kind. She simply appeared to "see" things, closing her eyes to "see," and opening them again when speaking to me. She began by telling me my Christian name and my age correctly, then described accurately various friends, gave me my mother's name, and described various recent events in my life. She next described a fair man of more than medium height, with a short, stubbly moustache; "a good man, a friend of yours and a good influence." The following is a correct outline, written down immediately afterwards, of the conversation that followed, during which I had, I believe, a quite uninterested and unemotional appearance.

"Do you recognize this man?"

"I may have such a friend, but I cannot say. The description is too vague. No one suggests himself."

"He seems to be a soldier."

"Then I don't know who it is." The description corresponded to no intimate friend.

"But you are a soldier."

"No, I am not."

"Then I cannot understand. This man seems certainly to be a soldier, at any rate a volunteer of some kind, and that is his connection with you."

I shook my head.

"You do not understand," said Madame K—— "This man is on the other side. He is dead, but his influence is with you. I see him as a soldier fighting. You are there too, and he is killed. If you say you are not a soldier, I do not understand it at all. I cannot be mistaken, it is too plain."

I had replied in good faith that I was no soldier,

since I never conceive myself in that light. But as the description corresponded exactly with the circumstances of Baskerville's death in Tabriz, and she had also described his appearance quite accurately, I answered—

"Yes, I think I understand you now. I am not a soldier, but I have fought. What do you see?"

"I see you riding with this man. And then, again, I see a battle. It is in an Eastern country. You are with Asiatics, not negroes; it might be India; they are wild-looking men, with black eyes and thick black hair, untidy and irregular. They seem to be all natives; I do not see any European officers except you two; I do not know whether the officers are native or not. The ground is flat, and very bare and trampled. The heat is terrible. You are forcing yourself to keep on, in spite of the heat and thirst, which are the things you are feeling most. There is great danger all the time. You are in great fatigue. The other man is killed. He seems to be killed doing something very brave, and to suffer great pain. It is not long ago; not more than five years at most. And now his influence is with you. He guards you, and he wishes to communicate with you."

"What do you mean?"

"Well, you'll probably smile at such a statement, but the spirits of the dead do sometimes watch over people. Good people exercise helpful influence. This man is with you, and whenever you are in danger he averts it. You have several times nearly lost your life since, and each time he has intervened, and he always will. You think nothing of it. You are a person who does not realize or reflect on your escapes;

A LITTLE MAGIC

you may perhaps say to yourself, 'That was a close shave,' and you think no more of it. But the danger is there just the same, and you are particularly subject to them. But you are always preserved, and he is now your protector. You may smile at all this, but it is so."

"But why?" I asked, so puzzled by her description of the last sortie at Tabriz, that I only smiled a little at her purely fanciful picture of myself as a sort of cat of nine lives.

"Well, this, perhaps, you didn't know—this man was greatly attached to you. That is the only explanation I can give. And he wants to tell you something; there is something he wants you to do."

"What?"

"I don't know; I cannot make out, but probably you will know what it is?"

I shook my head.

"Is there not something you have left undone? What did he wish you to do?"

"I know nothing."

"Was there nothing you discussed with him?"

Remembering an abstract discussion on a day when we had ridden round Tabriz, I replied, "Yes."

"Well, as the result of that, was there nothing you were asked to do?"

"Nothing at all."

Madame K—— seemed at a loss.

"Had he a sister?" she asked.

"I believe he had both sisters and brothers."

"I get the initial 'J.'"

"It may have a meaning, but I do not know it."

"And 'C.'"

THE ORIENT EXPRESS

Again I shook my head.

"Does he wish me to write to his mother?" I asked.

"I think he would like that, but whether that is what he is trying to make known I do not know. I can get no more. How long ago did he die?"

To which I replied, "About six months ago."

I admit that I was somewhat impressed, and in the evening an idea of the nature of the communication, which appears to have been erroneous, occurred to me, and accordingly on Monday morning I visited Madame K—— again. When she entered the room, she said, "I have seen you before, haven't I?" This in any case her husband had probably told her, as it was he who ushered me in, and went to tell her of my arrival. But that appeared to be the extent of her knowledge. She professed, and I was entirely convinced of her good faith in the matter, to remember nothing she had told me on the previous occasion. "It all goes from me," she said.

It is well to state here that she was still, as far as I was concerned, and is at the date of writing this, in complete ignorance of my name and address, my occupation and my tastes; also that the scenes she described took place in Persia. On both occasions she made the same error of date, stating that the events happened "not long ago," but appearing to mean by that a period of nearly five years, although on this point I corrected her at the conclusion of my first visit.

Finding that she did not remember what she had told me, I reminded her that on a previous visit she had told me that a friend who was killed in battle wished to give me a message. "You said one or two

A LITTLE MAGIC

things," I added, "which at the time I could not connect. I now think I may possibly know the subject of the communication, though I do not know what he wishes me to say on it. I think, therefore, that if you can get any indication to-day, I may more easily know what is meant."

Madame said she would do her best, but warned me she was quite at the mercy of what she "saw," and could not control it. Thereupon began a new *séance*, as long as the previous one, for Madame did not, till the end, come to the purpose of my visit. She again described my mother and others, saying nothing in contradiction of what she had said before and nothing incorrect, but giving some different details, and describing some quite different scenes and people. At last she came to Baskerville, and again she described the last sortie.

"There are two sets of men with him," she said, "both Asiatic. But one set are quite small men, almost boys, like Japs; the other are very big men, bearded, unkempt-looking. Some of them are on the other side now, like himself; some are not—they are alive."

Now Baskerville's command consisted of two distinct companies. One consisted chiefly of former pupils of the American school, mere youths of sixteen and seventeen, sons of rich merchants and notables of the town. They wore a grey uniform. The other company were Nasmiya, or police; very tall men for the most part, and answering exactly to her description.

"He was hit here; I feel the sharp pain of it," continued Madame K——, and she brought the tip of her forefinger sharply down high up on the left side of her body. This was the exact spot where the bullet passed through Baskerville's body. I saw his coat after his death, and the American Mission doctor who examined the body explained to me that the hole was just above his heart.

"He suffered great pain," she continued.

This also is true, as there is evidence that he lived for some ten minutes in agony. Madame K—— appeared to feel the pain herself intensely.

"Has he anything to tell me?" I asked.

"Yes, there is something," she said, and paused.

"Do you get any name?"

"I hear the name Cyril. What is that?"

"I don't know," I answered.

"I hear him talking in a foreign language to these men," she said. "It is not French, or any language that I know. It might be Russian."

After some time she said, "He wants to write."

"What?"

"You are a writer. There is some writing you have not finished. He seems to point to an incompleted MS. He wants you to go on."

"What am I to write?"

"I think it is about what happened. He wants you to write all about it."

"Is that all?"

"That is all I can get. But perhaps, if you ask some questions, something more will come."

"Where is he?"

"He is working. He was a great worker, and he goes on working."

"At what work?"

"The same work. You perhaps did not know it,

A LITTLE MAGIC

but this man was an unusually good man. I don't mean that he was merely all right. He was more than that. He was always working for these men that I see with him, these Eastern, wild-looking men. They are very lost and ignorant, and he was always trying to raise them a little higher and to teach them. He goes on doing that just the same. He is influencing them now, though they are not conscious of it."

She then referred also to his interest in myself and his protecting power, in much the same terms as on the previous visit, and asked me to ask another question.

"Is he happy?"

"Yes," very emphatically. "There is no doubt at all of that. He is very happy."

This was all that Madame could say. I made a further suggestion, as she had said nothing which touched the idea which had brought me there. But it prove quite unfruitful, and Madame K—— could get no light on it. She explained the difficulty by saying that he was not long dead, she supposed "not more than five years." When I corrected her again on this point, she expressed great surprise that she should be able to see him at all. I asked why this was, and she said it was very difficult to explain, but certainly a fact that time usually had to elapse before the spirits of the dead could be seen. She complained of the pain above her heart, pressing her hands to her breast, and said that she would continue to feel it for quite half an hour after my departure. This seemed a gentle and legitimate hint, so I took it and my departure immediately.

As to the meaning of it all, there are two alternatives. It is open to me to accept Madame K——'s statement as a fact, and believe that through her Baskerville's spirit has communicated with me. Or I may accept what I confess seems to me the very pseudo-scientific explanation, which it is the current fashion to give for such phenomenon. According to this theory, quite unconsciously, "quite without your knowing it," the incidents at Tabriz made a deep impression on my mind and memory. By some process of telepathy Madame K—— delved the facts from the depths of my sub-consciousness, and then proceeded, with the knowledge thus "simply" attained, to "fake" a spirit communication. Or perhaps, if the scientist is charitable, he may suppose that Madame, being highly strung and a believer in her own powers as a medium, imagined the spirit communication; or that I was "unconsciously" expecting such a communication, and so, again by telepathy, the result was obtained.

In criticism of this, I can only say that the mental processes attributed to me must have been very "subconscious" indeed. The whole of the Tabriz incident produced singularly little impression on my mind at that time. I went to Persia, prepared to take a great interest in the country, but the corruption, cowardice, vice, and lying which I found on all hands broke the back of my enthusiasm. Consequently, I had no sooner left Persia behind than Turkey, with its real men risking all for their country, and the various Balkan races, reasserted their claims on my affections. I never thought of Persia, or of my fights. The chapter was closed. My friends sometimes asked me to give an account of my experiences, but I much

A LITTLE MAGIC

preferred to discuss Turkish politics. I always felt inclined to refer them to a long article which appeared in *The Times*, and to say, in the manner of a Minister replying to a questioner, "To that statement I have nothing to add." One or two other articles I wrote, but the whole story remained untold, partly because I was no longer in the least interested in it, and partly because of the inherent difficulty and doubtful wisdom of telling the whole truth. To reveal in its entirety the rottenness of the state of Persia would, I knew, give great pain to some of my good Persian friends, and to some of Persia's good friends in England. It might help to discredit a cause which, for all the folly of its exponents, had my sincere sympathy. I believed that I had said good-bye to Persia for ever, and never supposed that within a year I should find myself in Tehran. So, gradually, I let the whole subject drop. Certainly nothing was further from my thoughts on that Saturday morning, and it came to me as a surprise to hear some one insisting on the fact that I was a "soldier." Other facts noted by Madame K——, such as the composition of Baskerville's force, had quite slipped my memory, and I had never stated them in print. I was, in fact, conscious of following after Madame K——, not of leading her; of being gradually reminded of details, such as the fact that Baskerville, who for any serious explanation had always to employ an interpreter, used frequently to speak to his men in broken Azurbaijan Turkish, the local dialect, which is plentifully spiced with Russian words.

The "sub-conscious" theory may, of course, be true. But in order to believe it true one has to surmount so many difficulties, and in the end to credit

THE ORIENT EXPRESS

Madame K—— with such marvellous telepathic powers, that it seems to me almost simpler, and less wonderful, to take her statement as it stands. The "sub-conscious telepathy" explanation seems to me to be in this case much the more difficult of the two. To speak more plainly, it seems the straining of the pseudo-rationalist, who will swallow anything which enables him to avoid admitting what he wrongly supposes to be something supernatural or a violation of a natural law.

Personally, I do not believe there was anything supernatural, nor do I believe in violations of natural law. My chief objection to what I have heard of spiritualistic *séances* has always been the apparent folly of supposed spirit manifestations. To me it has always seemed deplorable to believe that after life's fitful fever, when presumably one would wish to sleep well, one might be rung up on the universal telephone and summoned to attend evening parties held by "inquiring" mortals. The spectacle of the shades of pious old gentlemen being asked what would win the Cambridgeshire has never thrilled me with the hope of immortality. Table-rappings do not seem to add much to the sum of human knowledge, and spirit messages are frequently of a very dull character, or concerned with very trivial subjects. That seems to me a very good reason for taking no interest in them, but not at all a good reason for rejecting all such messages as entire hallucinations or frauds. To say that a thing is false because it seems unreasonable to us appears to me the argument not of a scientist, but of one who is a babe in the world. Has such a one ever seriously considered in the light of human

A LITTLE MAGIC

reason the life of a man or of a woman, whether of a high type or a low type, of a rich class or of a poor class? Could anything be more amazing, more laughable, more "unreasonable"? Consider the machinery by which he is brought into the world; the sexual relation, with its keyboard that runs to the depth of degradation and to the height of blissful, selfless union. Consider the pains that attend his birth; his physical characteristics; his physical necessities. Consider how his life is spent; the worthless and petty motives that often govern him; the vain fancies that sway him; the thoughts that torment him; the follies that seize him; the freaks that delight him; the chances that touch him; the fun, the frolic, the madness, the hates, the loves of the world.

Consider all this, and then reflect on the odd fact that man possesses all the time this lamp of reason, in whose clear, cold light he can stand outside and judge critically the whole mad medley. Truly, sometimes reason seems the most unreasonable quality of all. Feeling tells him that on the whole the world is good and man is made for love; but reason tells him that the arrangements of the world and the doings of man are a joke, a thing at which to roar, a dear indignity, a maze of crossed purposes, a perpetual parody; a farce in which a man may fly the channel with the ease of a bird, but gets up in the middle of the night to be the first to do it, while his unsuspecting rival sleeps; for both these supermen must sleep like the rest of us. There is applause and brandy for the tired winner; floods of tears and smelling-salts for the loser; twenty-four hours in the day and the natural functions and appetites of man for both.

THE ORIENT EXPRESS

And yet it is seriously put forward as disproving the authenticity of spirit messages that they are often not very serious in subject, or that they contain no revelation of new truth. This seems to be the greatest madness of all. As this world is certainly absurd in some of its aspects, it seems reasonable to suppose that absurdities persist in other states. When the only world which we know is absurd, why should we expect a spirit world to be free from absurdity? There is a great deal of common sense, of high thinking, and of unselfishness, which is greater than either common sense or high thinking, in this world. Yet it seems to me not improbable that if some one of our fellow-citizens of this empire were by accident to stumble on a means of communicating with Mars, the first words from this world of sense and high purpose which would greet the ears of the astonished inhabitants might be "What ho!" or "Here we are again!" or some other excrescence of pantomime.

"What an absurd world!" we can imagine the Martians saying, when the profound import of this greeting had been grasped. And perhaps the knowing ones would say, "Too absurd. Obviously it can't exist. This is a clear case of fraud." And think of our universal chorus of laughter, in which all but the insane would join, when the newspapers gave us the text of our first message to Mars!

But it may be argued that it is just because we feel the limitations and absurdities of this world that we cannot bear to think of them as persisting in another world. We feel that what is absurd here will disappear there. That is our only conception of a future life, if there is a future life. To which I reply that it seems to me a conception maintained in general

A LITTLE MAGIC

because it is void of content. We can conceive this world as governed entirely by reason, but the facts of life destroy the conception. We know little of the facts of another life, and when any alleged facts conflict with our conception we reject them in order to cling to the conception. To me it seems more reasonable to suppose that a man who up to the hour of his death was trite or brutal, entirely immersed in the material affairs of a selfish life, should find himself after death very much what he was before. Why should he become a totally different person? It is a possible theory that for a time, at any rate, as his whole heart had been in selfish interests here, his whole concern might still be with this life, and the loss of his body, the vehicle of his pleasures, might be a torture to him, till gradually a higher spirit life dominated him and lifted him in the scale. It takes all sorts to make a world—even, presumably, the next world—and on such a theory there would be all sorts of spirits. The suicide who hopes to end all his troubles would find that he had gained nothing but the loss of his body, and that he himself was much the same. The average kindly man would find his good, or unselfish, qualities immensely intensified by the loss of the flesh, which had warred against the spirit, and would consequently rise in the scale of being and of happiness; while the man whose life was knit with his friends, the man who did not exist apart from his loves, friendships, and sympathies, would attain powers and knowledge beyond anything possible in this life, though his surviving friends would for long keep him specially concerned with life "on this side."

A supposition of this kind is based on the assumption that Love is the only rational explanation of the ultimate meaning of the Universe, and is the only true meaning of the term "good," by which we test everything. It abolishes death altogether, and makes life a continuous progression. Hell and Heaven are our future states, and the transition is more marked and important at "Death," but that is all. We are always making our own future, according as we live well or ill, for our friends or for ourselves, and this future stretches from the present moment beyond the river of death, to cross which we leave behind our mortal bodies.

This is, of course, pure theory. I have told you what happened at the palmist's—rather unwillingly, for you may think it almost too queer for credence, but with a sense that it were better told. You must make what you can of it, and perhaps the Society for Psychical Research can make a lot. I have never got very far, and have given it up.

THE END

Richard Clay & Sons, Limited, London and Bungay.